WILDCATS TO TOMCATS

THE TAILHOOK NAVY

Captain Richard L. "Zeke" Cormier, USN (Retired)

Captain Walter M. "Wally" Schirra, USN (Retired)

Captain Phillip R. "Rat" Wood, USN (Retired)

With Barrett Tillman

PHALANX

ISBN: 1-883809-07-X
Library of Congress: 94-069497

Text by:
        Richard L. Cormier
        Walter M. Schirra
        Phillip R. Wood
        Barrett Tillman

Cover design by: John Valo

Published by:

Phalanx Publishing Co., Ltd.
1051 Marie Avenue West
St. Paul, MN 55118-4131 USA

European Distribution by: Air Research Publications
                        P.O. Box 223, Walton on Thames,
                        Surrey KT12 3YQ Great Britain

Printed in the United States of America

TABLE OF CONTENTS

INTRODUCTION

Retired Navy captains are practically a byproduct of San Diego, California. You can hardly swing a cat between Chula Vista and Solana Beach without scratching a former four-striper, and according to the statistics, one in four of those was a Naval Aviator.

Aviators are different. Everybody agrees with that sentiment, though perhaps not with exactly the same things in mind. Consider the conventional wisdom about aviators. Tie their hands and they lose fifty percent of their communication skills. If their lips are moving, they're lying. And as for who's the greatest aviator of all—forget it. Claimants to the title are legion.

Against this background, it might seem pointless to pick out a trio that regularly meets for breakfast at The Inn at Rancho Santa Fe. But these three really are different. Aside from their obvious professional interests, they share an outlook—a camaraderie, a rivalry of aim—that marks them as interesting individuals. Mix them together, stir vigorously and sit back. They take over and provide extremely pleasant company.

Collectively, these three represent forty-five years of naval aviation history. Richard L. Cormier—better known as Zeke—was designated an aviator in 1941. Walter M. Schirra graduated from Annapolis in 1945 and won his Wings of Gold three years later. And Phillip R. Wood, an aviator since 1960, retired in 1986. Among them, Zeke, Wally and Phil have held every job description worth having in Naval Aviation: fighter ace, MiG killers, squadron and air wing commanders, landing signal officers, Blue Angel skipper, test pilot, astronaut and carrier captain.

While some similarities might be expected of three carrier aviators and combat fighter pilots, the career overlaps are more than coincidental. It began in Korea in 1950-51 when Zeke was on the allied staff, Wally was flying an exchange tour with the Air Force and Phil was a teenage destroyer sailor fishing unlucky aviators out of Wonsan Harbor.

But there were other common mileposts along the career path. As fighter pilots, all three men flew from Miramar Naval Air Station at San Diego. And they shot down enemy aircraft in World War Two, Korea and Vietnam. Zeke, with eight confirmed and a probable, holds the coveted title of fighter ace—the most glamorous of all military occupations.

Zeke and Phil both learned to fly from former navy pilots in Piper Cubs and both commanded Air Wing 11, twenty years apart. Zeke was executive officer of USS *Wasp* (CVS-18) and Phil wrapped up his career as skipper of *Kitty Hawk* (CV-63), a San Diego landmark for thirty-three years. Wally got diverted from "boats" and literally took the high road of naval aviation, becoming the only astronaut with flights in each of the space programs: Mercury, Gemini and Apollo.

But those are merely the basics, the framework on which to hang the story. More to the point is the over-riding attitude the men share. Wally, a legendary punster and innovative prankster, speaks for the group when he addresses the importance of humor in his trade. "Humor is the lubricant of adversity," he says. For naval aviation especially is rich with diversity; the thrill and satisfaction of flying high-performance aircraft off carriers day and night, and the sorrow of losing friends and shipmates on an all-too-regular basis. Even in peacetime, it is rare for an aircraft carrier to complete a six-month deployment without a few fatalities among ship's company or air wing.

This book, then, is composed of lubricant. It is the distillation of a half-century of humor, including the gallows variety, which has sustained naval aviators through peace and war. The ability to find humor in adversity can be a saving grace long after hanging up the hardhat, whether in battling politicians or cancer. If a collection of "sea stories" needs a moral, no better one can be found.

Barrett Tillman

BOOK I
ZEKE

1939
LEARNING TO FLY

The City of San Diego in the 1920s and 1930s provided a delightful way of life for young folks—especially adolescents. It was bounded by the broad expanse of the blue Pacific on the west, the burgeoning sleeping giant of Los Angeles to the north, the mountains of the Lagunas and the seemingly endless wastes to the east, and to the south was the sleepy little Mexican village of Tijuana. A tranquil island set off in the southwestern corner of the United States, seemingly just waiting to decide what kind of city it wanted to become. But what it did know was that it was a Navy town, and it was happy in that knowledge. The Pacific Fleet made its home there, and had for decades.

As part of the scene of those early days in and around the city, the airplane played a major role. All aspects of the flying profession were present: the fledgling units of the military, the pioneering airplane builders, experimental activities and all the other cats and dogs of aviation. Even the Navy's great dirigibles, the *Akron* and *Macon*, made appearances in San Diego.

One could not look at those blue skies and their fascinating aerial activity and not recognize flying as something absolutely absorbing. Therefore, what could be more natural than for the young men of the area—those with an inquisitive, adventuresome nature—to consider flying as part of what life offered in that unsullied corner of the nation?

The federal government recognized that there would one day—perhaps soon—be a need for young men with preliminary flying skills. Who the far-sighted planners were has long been forgotten, but wise they were. The Civilian Pilot Training (CPT) Program was established in the late Thirties, and flying schools of every size, shape and description sprang up across the country. San Diego was especially well represented.

The Tyson Flying Service of Chula Vista was one of the suddenly active, suddenly important flight training schools that previously had been hard-pressed to keep beans on the table. The low-tide mud flats of San Diego's south bay was the runway, but was quite suitable for the school's two aircraft. Both were tried and true Piper Cubs—the early, early model which would barely sustain powered flight!

The CPT program could afford to be picky because of the abundance of would-be aviators. But I completed ground school with a superior grade, largely by dint of being lucky since I surely was not one of the more studious applicants. As aviators have always said, I'd rather be lucky than good any day. But whatever the reason, I was ready for the great adventure.

My instructor was, rightly enough, a former Naval Aviator who had been released from active duty because of budgetary restraints—a common occurrence in the 1930s. But he wanted to pursue a flying career, so there he was. Needless to say, early on I was introduced to the well-established concept of "the right way, the wrong way and the Navy way," but I managed to adapt and the preliminary dual instruction advanced without major incident.

Then came time for my first solo! It was an event fraught with no less potential trauma for the stalwarat instructor than for his student, as this struggling young entrepreneur had a limited number of flying machines. So, to say the least, Tyson Flying Service was very protective of its assets. With a visible tear in the corner of his eye, he announced that I was ready to solo. And off I went in search of high adventure.

I advanced the throttle with my left hand, felt lift reluctantly overcome gravity, and nursed the little Cub off the ground. Takeoff and climb were just as advertised. The airwork—turns, climbs and glides—were, well, not bad. With my spirits and my courage up, why not try a power-off stall just for drill? It went so well, in fact, that with power off the engine declined to answer the throttle, as if it had a mind of its own. It stopped cold, the prop frozen in space about three feet before my nose.

No panic here—just look for the field, set up a glide and head on in. I wish I could say that it happened with that much ease, but I did get the airplane on the ground in one piece, at the right airport.

As I was rolling to a stop in the middle of the field, still aware of my pounding heart, I spotted my very anxious instructor racing toward me in his Model A Ford. I envisioned all manner of congratulatory kudos—maybe even an "attaboy"—but it was airplane inspection time first. Was it bent or bruised? (Never mind whether I was bent or bruised!) What happened to the engine? But eventually I was happy with a "You did good," and the knowledge that after this "routine" solo hop the rest of the course should be a piece of cake. Not that it was, but it seems so now, with benefit of fifty years hindsight.

Needless to say, once you have tasted the excitement and the exhilaration of flying, such an experience introduced an entirely new spectrum of fantasies. How about space travel with Flash Gordon or Buck Rogers, or flying one of those speedy pursuit airplanes? It was a youthful time of alluring reveries. But in the real world Uncle Sam was being very persistent in fulfilling his needs in the draft, so it was decision time for me.

The choice was clear. Uncle Sam and the carrier navy needed me!

1942-43

SUB HUNTER

For my Flight Class, the final days of training at Pensacola, Florida that spring of 1942 only could be described with glowing, overworked adjectives, ranging from thrilling and rapturous to seductive and alluring. The sheer thrill of flying engendered all these feelings, and the attitude remained despite the fact that we were training for combat. To more than a few of us, I know, that knowledge only added to our sense of anticipation and excitement.

We had everything going for us. The brand-new base at Opa Locka on the edge of the Everglades, with the allure of glamorous Miami, made the locale the most sought-after of all training bases. And we had become—at long last—the tritons among the minnows of the cadet ranks. Our few perks included open liberty, though a cash shortage imposed some rigorous restraints; and we could even converse with the senior instructors on something approaching human terms. But best of all, our flight had the good fortune to be assigned the sports car of biplanes: Grumman's agile little F3F-3. It didn't have the feline nickname of subsequent Grumman products, but it probably should have been called the "Pussycat," perhaps better yet (if a little more reverently), the "Catamount." Whatever you called it, the F3F was the epitome of scarf and goggles aviating.

However, though only three years out of fleet squadrons, the F3F belonged in the technological attic with its hand-cranked landing gear and meager two-gun armament. I would describe it as a very busy, athletic cockpit. With all that cranking, our formation takeoffs were something to behold—the planes bobbing up and down like kangaroos in heat. But the airplane was ideal for introduction to fighter tactics, and a genuine confidence-builder with the sheer joy of "on-your-own" familiarization flights or tailchasing in and out of the towering white clouds over Southern Florida.

The icing on our cake was the fleet-wise, irrepressable pillar of the Navy fighter community, Lieutenant Joseph C. Clifton as our flight instructor. He rose to rear admiral in the postwar Navy, but he was "Jumping Joe" to those who knew him—occasionally "Whispering Joe" among the sardonic, for it was widely reported he could communicate plane-to-plane without resorting to a radio. In either case, Joe Clifton made an indelible impression on us. His enthusiasm was of olympian scale, perhaps matched only by his capacity for ice cream, and we basked in the company of the Navy's fighter elitists.

So, with Joe's strident philosophy still ringing in my ears, I gathered my prized new Wings of Gold with my Pacific Fleet orders, and bade farewell to my training class comrades who were spread to the four winds. I jumped into my classy 1936 Ford convertible, put the top down, conned the local dealer out of two new "war-rationed" tires, put that little beauty in gear and headed westward, destination California.

My orders read: "Report to the Aircraft Carrier Training Group (ACTG), North Island, San Diego, for further training and subsequent assignment." It was the final step in transitioning from student pilot to operational fleet aviator. That long-sought glimmer on the horizon was getting brighter.

San Diego at that time was literally bursting with Navy activity. Ships and men encompassing every facet of the Pacific campaign were assembling or repairing, training or just gathering their breath. Our final polishing amidst this seemingly desperate flurry of activity gave new meaning to the all-out effort of national resolve. Abruptly, more of the reality of our new lives faced us head-on. However, I think most of us recognized that the singular elation of flight, which had thus far so consumed us, was about to turn serious: kill or be killed.

ACTG's aircraft included first-line fighters, Grumman F4F-4 Wildcats straight from the fleet. For the most part, the equipment was in remarkably good shape despite some obvious hard use. Some planes bore visible battle damage, others sported combat squadron markings and even a few of the coveted "meatball" victory flags. It was heady stuff for nugget aviators.

Our instructors, most of whom had just returned from combat in the

Pacific, held warm feelings for the tough little Wildcats and expected us to display due regard for these valuable assets. We made every effort to abide by the edict, but after some hair-raising takeoffs and landings, most of us found the Wildcat well named; neither easy to fly nor very forgiving. The accident rate reflected that sad fact.

The training was rigorous, brief and intense; it was total commitment time. But what the hell. We were all young, eager and perhaps patriotic to a fault. We accepted the hard work, risk and responsibility without question or hesitation.

Our division's instructor was Lieutenant Ed Pawka, a consummate fighter pilot; tall, lean and Gary Cooperish with the demeanor to match. He gave full attention to his assignment as our mentor and demanded the same from us. He wanted excellence, and on occasion we performed to his standards. But usually one caught a frown or a head shake that spoke quietly of his concern for our questionable progress—to say nothing of our future. Ed inevitably guided his class through the perils of aerial combat tactics, imparting some personal do's and don'ts based on his own experience. A very brief ceremony consisting of hand shakes all-round concluded Lieutenant Pawka's burnishing. As time proved, he did his job well.

With ACTG graduation papers in hand, we considered ourselves fully-qualified, ready-for-general-quarters fighter pilots. However, there's an old saying in Navy Air that timing is the grist of luck, and I still think that being lucky is the number-one big medicine in the flying business. As luck would have it, several members of my class were a bit too late in the pipeline to make the rosters of air groups departing for Pacific combat. We were, however, ready and available for the Atlantic-bound escort carrier squadrons about to do business with German submarine wolfpacks which at that moment were raising holy hell with Allied shipping. Thus I entered the antisubmarine warfare (ASW) business; a hell of a note for a would-be fighter ace.

In the fall of 1942 I joined my first fleet unit, Composite Squadron One (VC-1), an ASW outfit based on the escort carrier USS *Card* (CVE-11). She was one of several merchant cargo ships converted to "baby flat-tops" destined for the newly-formed Tenth Fleet, whose responsibility was escorting transatlantic convoys while hunting and killing U-boats. Certainly there was plenty of work for everybody, as the Germans were very effective; in late 1942 and early '43, a half-million tons of Allied shipping went to the bottom almost every month.

Our ASW training involved ground school, the dreaded and little-used Morse Code, ship recognition which included friendly and enemy submarines, navigation and other naval stuff—all orchestrated by VC-1's commanding officer, Commander Lexington R. Black, USN. He was my introduction to a skipper of The Old School, a hard-core fleet-experienced survivor of the gentleman's club of naval aviators. A stern disciplinarian of grave demeanor, he was distinguished by one green eye and one blue. This genetic hiccup cloaked Commander Black with a pretentious presence, for he would berate us with his green eye and praise us with the blue. It was a truly unique experience, made more vivid by the fact that in those days three-stripe commanders were second only to captains among those on speaking terms with the Almighty. (Admirals conducted their arcane affairs somewhere in a loftier and even more rarified atmosphere.) Until joining VC-1 I'd never even stood in the presence of a full commander, much less conversed with one.

While Commander Black and I had our differences (they were numerous and varied), I owe him one lasting legacy: my nickname. For some reason the squadron had a plethora of Richards and Dicks, so many in fact that the CO took to alphabetizing us. I reckon that I stood right at the bottom of the ensigns' pecking order, because when he got around to handing out monikers, mine was Zeke.

Commander Black did mellow somewhat, and eventually we became accustomed to focusing on his blue eye while communicating. However, he had considerable misgivings about Reservists—especially we junior-junior officers—who aspired to partake of all the privileges of Naval Tradition, Custom and Usage. His attitude was especially evident when he greeted his officers at the daily all-pilots meeting with, "Good morning, gentlemen and ensigns." Fortunately, I had the good sense to keep all of this in perspective but continued to address my section leader, Lieutenant (junior grade) Robert Hass, as "Mister Hass" for the entire tour. Commander Black approved.

Unfortunately, I had the misfortune to forget that our CO and his leading chief petty officer were long-time shipmates and therefore shared strong bonds of loyalty. Chief Wiley was in charge of the flight line where the squadron's temporarily-assigned aircraft—Curtiss SOC-3s—were arrayed. They were flying machines of times past: biplanes with fabric-covered wings; bracing wires and open cockpits; even an "observer" aircrewman—the works. Top speed was about 80 mph straight down, but they were all we had until our combat aircraft arrived.

There was one benefit of familiarization flights in those antiquities. They stilled forever the haunting reveries of classic aviation films of the 1930s; great movies like **Dive Bomber** with Errol Flynn or **Eyes of the Fleet** with Wallace Beery. We began to place less emphasis on glamor and more on pragmatism, even though the SOCs were all we had at the time.

I fell afoul of the Wiley-Black team while taxiing to the parking area in what the good chief deemed excessive speed and wound up in the CO's austere presence with the baleful green eye affixed upon my countenance. Result: I was allowed to contemplate the indiscretion in my room for three days, otherwise known as being "in hack."

With the disciplinary interlude behind me, I gleefully took to the new equipment now at hand. With some familiarization and tactics hops under our belts, and carrier-qualified in the F4F-4, we gathered up our gear and boarded *Card* that fall and steamed past Point Loma—on our way to war at last.

The transit from PacFleet to LantFleet was executed without major incident, but there were some sad faces and perhaps even a tear or two when the blue waters of the Pacific were left in our wake. Arrival at Norfolk, Virginia—our new homeport—was routine, though since we were among the first of our kind to join Tenth Fleet, everyone on board thought that at least a welcoming brass band might be in order. But no such luck.

So we were to be hunter-killers, flying TBF-1 Avenger bombers and F4F-4 fighters, stalking Admiral Doenitz's U-boats in the middle of the Atlantic Ocean. Needless to say, in my reveries I always pictured myself in the cockpit of a swift "pursuit" aircraft; cockpit canopy slid back, white scarf flowing in the slipstream, goggles firmly in place over eyes that constantly searched the skies for the enemy.

Reality proved decidedly less satisfying and certainly less glamorous. We learned that VC squadron composition was being changed to include additional TBFs and fewer F4Fs. More bombers meant some of us fighter pilots had to transition to Avengers, including Yours Truly. Such are the breaks of Navy Air.

Taking on a new role, especially one as specialized as aerial ASW, required concentrated training and a firm resolve. The Navy recognized that ordinary flight training was insufficient to qualify aviators for hunting and killing submarines; special training was required in tactics, radar, sonar, depth charges and a variety of super-duper weapons most of us hadn't even heard of. And, of course, there always was the final consideration of getting back aboard that little carrier in a big bomber with a heavy load.

Card sailed from Norfolk, with VC-1 embarked, to engage Hitler's naval elite in early 1943, full of confidence, anticipation—and just a touch of anxiety. But the squadron could not have been more talented in any category, from flying airplanes to keeping the books. A change of command also furnished us the inspired leadership of a new skipper, Lieutenant Commander Carl E. Jones. He possessed all the right tickets to take the lead: a superb flier and tactician plus an appreciation for the strategic nature of our new charter. Commander Black was reassigned as Card's operations officer, where he continued to keep his "eye" on us. He was very pleased. So were we.

The squadron's proficiency was well matched by the ship's company, especially by the young but extremely accomplished commanding officer, Captain Arnold J. "Buster" Isbell. He had been accelerated in promotion, not only because of the war and the resulting influx of freshly-commissioned officers, but also because of his professional acumen. Isbell also surrounded himself with talented people, knowing that our concepts and tactics were new and largely untried. But the skipper and his team were absolutely determined to make them work. The Germans were building U-boats faster than the British and Americans could sink them, so Card and CompRonOne were out to make a difference! In a word, we were motivated.

Our first cruise on the transatlantic run came under Category B for boredom. We learned that the nature of ASW was tedium; long, unproductive patrols. The searchers quartered the wide expanses of ocean day after day for nearly a month without sighting a wisp of the enemy. We knew the subs were there, apparently zigging whenever we zagged.

One thing about carrier aviation, though. Regardless of how dull the mission was, you always got an adrenalin boost at the end of the flight. Landing aboard that proverbial postage stamp of a flight deck, some 400 feet in length, was a real pick-me-up. It was especially delicate during bad weather and heavy sea state, and therefore potentially hazardous to one's well-being.

I have to admit to one episode that, even in retrospect, still produces a white-knuckle syndrome. The weather was dismal, and daylight was running out when my F4F escort and I returned to the ship after about a three-hour "no contact" search. Ensign Jack Stewart in the Wildcat landed on the first pass, displaying some first-class airmanship. My first pass was a little high so I was waved off by the landing signal officer (LSO) for another try. Passes two through four garnered the same result. On the next go-rounds I really concentrated, but witnessed a series of flight deck undulations which presented, first, a plan view of the entire deck, followed by an alarming view of the "spud locker" at the stern—including the exposed ship's propeller. Poor little CVE-11 was pitching to the extent she took green water over the bow.

Passes five and six were okay but I got no "cut" signal from the LSO because of the fouled deck.

By now it definitely was getting dark, which seemed to produce a deleterious effect on my throttle-control technique. Thus, passes seven and eight were merely fly-bys. Now it was not only for-real night time, but the folks on board were growing tired of Ensign Cormier's one-man airshow. Rumor had it that the gunnery department was alerted to uncover the five-inchers in case they had to bring me down the hard way. Embarrassed beyond all hope, I sulked in my Avenger's cockpit, imagining some German submariners out there, laughing their asses off.

Extreme situations require extreme measures, so in spite of the electronic silence normally imposed on us, our super-talented landing signal officer opened up on the radio. Lieutenant Commander Ed Deacon informed me that "we" were going to land on the next pass; wind, water or night be damned! He sweet-talked me into the best trap I made during the entire cruise and has been my hero ever since.

I decided that I wanted to be just like my savior-hero, and under Mr. Deacon's tutelage I became qualified and served as one of the squadron's LSO team—but never quite reached the expertise of my mentor. Deacon was simply one of the best paddle wavers in the business. If it had occurred to me, I might have tried passing along some of those skills to young Phil Wood—but what can you tell a smartalec kid of ten?

Back in Norfolk with our initial trip behind us—without contacting the enemy—VC-1 turned to refining techniques of searching for and attacking the opposition. The U-boats were pulling off one of the most devastating series of merchant-ship sinkings in history. The situation was eloquently described by Winston Churchill as "a war of groping and drowning, of ambuscade and stratagem, of science and seamanship." But in the Battle of the Atlantic, the anti-submarine escort and attack groups only had uncorroborated evaluations of their efforts. Sightings and attacks usually were a black-or-white assessment: sunk or not sunk.

I, too, had little appreciation of the damage inflicted during my one personal encounter with a U-boat. But one thing evident in retrospect was that the German submarine dominance of the Atlantic lifeline between the Old World and the New was about to end.

Card's next line period was proof of the change. The ship took on fuel oil at Bermuda and joined a giant convoy called UGS-13, then peeled off to hunt. Captain Isbell's plan was to charge right into the reported U-boat concentration. His tactic worked, and during three weeks in August we all became experienced subchasers.

I got my shot at a German submarine on 3 August 1943. Ensign Arnie Paulson was my fighter escort in his trusty little Wildcat; it was his first experience with the enemy as well. Late in the afternoon we had searched the ocean for nearly two hours without a glimmer of a moving object. Just another ho-hum sortie. Then a tiny dark bump appeared on the horizon, and as we closed I could clearly discern a surfaced submarine. My heart just about jumped out of my flight suit. We had caught a U-boat cruising slowly eastward, the crew basking in the late-afternoon sun during a schnapps break. I called for Arnie Paulson to join up, saying we were going to General Quarters. I pointed out the target, placed all weapons on "armed and hot," tightened my straps, remembered to say a little prayer, and maneuvered to put the sun at our backs. By this time it was low on the horizon. We attacked toward the stern, Paulson leading the way with all guns blazing.

Some forty years later I received a detailed written account of this engagement from a former German petty officer, Herr V. Nosch, who was aboard the submarine at the time. Even in retrospect, it touched the quick:

"I came to the U-66 after I had served aboard U-68, based in Lorient, France. Our operations took us from a mission on the west coast of Africa to the Caribbean up to Cape Hatteras. The boat attacked two large tankers, sinking one, but the other got away even though we hit it with two torpedoes. After operating for twelve weeks in the Caribbean, the boat started following a large convoy sailing east of Bermuda, but couldn't attack because of surface and air activity.

"On 3 August, around eight o'clock in the evening, we were proceeding east above-water. I was the aft watchman in the tower. Suddenly, out of the sun, aircraft from the auxiliary aircraft carrier attacked our boat with machine guns."

Following the fighter, I fired my single .50 caliber on the approach, then set up to drop depth bombs. The initial strafing wounded several men in the conning tower and kept the crew from manning the gun mounts. True to the script, my depth bombs failed to release on the first pass! As I passed over the boat I could clearly see the duty crews rushing around the tower hatch, and my guess was that they were about to dive. The classic attack had some variables!

"The second watch officer, Schütz, gave the warning, 'Plane attack!' but then was killed by a shot. The hatch to the tower was still open and Schütz was lying dead across it. Engineer Olschewski had to stop the diving of the boat. Kapitain-Leutnant Markworth and the gun crews then immediately came on the bridge and engaged the airplanes with artillery."

It didn't take the Germans long to man their guns and start filling the air with steel, but Ensign Paulson brought his .50s to bear again and discouraged further action from the German batteries long enough for me to make another run. This time I successfully released two bombs, which landed alongside the conning tower. (I was very happy with my cool.)

"The airplanes attacked again and Private Lorenz was hit and killed by machine gun strafing. Kapitain-Leutnant Markworth was seriously wounded. Eight other of our crew were hit and injured. As our machine proceeded in a big curve, the injured were pulled into the boat and we were able to dive.

"I should mention that a bomb fell right on top of the front antenna and tore it apart, then fell into the water. Then, during the explosion, it damaged some of our batteries and a torpedo in the first tube, which had to be quickly released. The second bomb, which landed next to the conning tower, heavily damaged the room in which the diesel was located with the cooling pumps. There was water in the boat as a result."

As I pulled off, I could see the crew gathering the wounded in the tower and buttoning up to dive. The damage was not readily discernable, but I knew we had hit them a rough blow. The boat continued in a wide arc, then suddenly submerged. I dropped my acoustic torpedo on the third pass, but obviously it missed the scent. And so U-66 escaped to attend its wounded and dying, and to repair the damage.

That was my introduction to the shooting war, and I cannot over-state the morale boost it provided. Antisubmarine work, above all types of hunting, requires patience. Finally to see your prey after hours, days and months of fruitless patrolling—well, that's how ASW folks spell relief!

The epilogue to this drama was remarkable. Still licking her wounds, U-66 again came under determined attack by VC-1 aircraft, this time in company with a supply submarine.

"Since our commander, Markworth, and First Watch Officer Herbig were incapable of continuing their duties, a replenishment submarine with a doctor on board was promised us. On 7 August, west of the Azores, we met the submarine milch cow U-117. Just as we were getting provisions and needed medicine on board by rubber boat, we were attacked again by airplanes. The milch cow stayed on the surface to give us protective fire, but as we proceeded at periscope depth we were able to see that U-117 had been sunk."

The saga of U-66 continued. Returning home 1 September 1943 for major refit, it sailed again in January 1944 for more adventure. In May the U-boat was sunk by a destroyer, USS *Buckley* (DE-51), in a night hand-to-hand battle in mid-Atlantic. Petty Officer Nosch was still aboard and, happily, survived to tell his tale.

Most other U-boat crews were not so fortunate—three-quarters of them went down with their subs. That applied to U-664, another member of the wolfpack that fell victim to *Card*'s experienced hunter-killers on 9 August 1943. But talk about the vagaries of war—the Navy's preeminent historian, Samuel Eliot Morison, discovered in his postwar research that on the night of the 8th U-664 sighted a "large tanker" in the twilight and fired three torpedoes. Fortunately, they missed, because the "tanker" was USS *Card*! We sailed off into the dusk—fat, dumb and happy.

However, the next day the boat was sighted sixty-five miles from the carrier and was taken under determined attack with depth bombs and strafing which rendered her dead in the water, sinking. The skipper, being a pragmatic sort, decided that discretion comprised the lion's share of valor. He ordered his crew to abandon the boat, which only moments later upended and plunged into the depths. An orbiting Avenger dropped rafts and lifejackets, then destroyer *Borie* (DD-704) was sent to pick up survivors, recovering forty-four men, and might have picked up more had not another sub launched five torpedoes while our destroyer was saving their comrades. At such moments war is decidedly unglamorous.

The survivors were transferred to *Card* for safe keeping, and we charged off to continue our quest, which would take us to North Africa to rendezvous with a homeward-bound convoy.

En route to Casablanca Captain Isbell, clever fellow that he was, decided to "eavesdrop" on his newfound source of intelligence and devised a plan to listen in on his captives. The carrier was canvassed for German-speaking crewmen, who turned up in a surprising number. The eavesdroppers were stationed at intervals along the preplanned circuitous route the Germans took to their confinement quarters. The results were highly revealing, some even humorous.

The U-boat crew knew surprising details of our ship and task force, our capabilities and even something of our shortcomings. Many smiled when they saw the size of the TBF Avengers which, even with wings folded, looked immense on that little deck. Our listeners told us that the Germans figured only the Americans would be crazy enough to fly such giant planes from such a tiny ship. Those krauts were no dummies—some of us TBF pilots agreed with them! However, our guests were not too pleased to be turned over to the French in Morocco.

So we acquitted ourselves well on that cruise and the next. In fact, VC-1 sank a total of five submarines. The Battle of the Atlantic was won in the spring and summer of 1943.

Day and night CVE operations, plus a damaging attack on a U-boat, attested to the fact that I had paid my professional dues. With this experience safely behind me, it was time to consider my "apprenticeship" accomplished in preparation for my not-so-secret desire to strap into a fighter cockpit again. The Pacific air war beckoned.

Some urging and, ultimately, unabashed begging, did the trick. My new skipper, Lieutenant Commander Dick Beverage, finally relented and launched me on my way to join a fighter squadron. My orders were to join a newly-formed unit in Atlantic City as the "plankowner" air group of the newest *Essex*-class carrier, USS *Ticonderoga* (CV-14). I was deliriously happy: Pacific Fleet, here I come!

1944-46

FIGHTER ACE OF THE "BIG T"

Saying goodby to my VC-1 comrades and shipmates in Norfolk was done with some difficulty. These were friends pledged to a brotherhood of mutual respect and admiration; it was a tough move. But new friends and friendships awaited me in that much sought-after billet in a Pacific-bound fighter squadron in the big-carrier Navy. Destiny beckoned just over the horizon in nearby New Jersey.

The squadron was forming at NAS Atlantic City to merge with one of the new fleet carriers just coming off the ways. Air Group 80 (CVG-80) would join "The Big T," the 27,100-ton USS *Ticonderoga* (CV-14), and I reported to the fighter squadron, VF-80. I was impressed with everything and everyone, but especially my new skipper: Lieutenant Commander Albert O. Vorse, Jr., better known as "Scoop." He was a Naval Academy graduate, Class of '37, and had received his wings about two years later so he was one of the old hands in the fighter business. His early-war record in VF-2 and -3 aboard the old *Lexington* (CV-2) and VF-6 in *Enterprise* (CV-6) immediately qualified him as one of my all-time heroes. Fighter piloting was his business, and he did it very well.

Scoop was a genuine up-front type of leader. It was "Follow me," and we did—willingly. Prior to our combat debut he became commander of the air group (CAG) and imparted his brand of esprit de corps to all of CVG-80.

By late summer of 1944 we were deep into the workup schedule and back in good ole Norfolk, based at newly-commissioned NAAS Oceana before the base was entirely finished. Because of that happy situation, the bachelors were entitled to a few appropriate perks, one being living "ashore" in fashionable Virginia Beach resort hotels with some nice amenities: hot and cold running maid service and other stuff. However, at length base quarters became available and our resort living, spiffy as it was, ended.

Soon VF-80 was joined by Lieutenant E. L. Anderson with his full complement of 36 SB2C-3 Helldivers, and Lieutenant Commander C. W. Shattuck's big TBM-3 Avengers, with which I was quite familiar, thank you very much. With the fighter, bomber and torpedo squadrons present, the air group was fully assembled and it was time to indulge in some serious cohabitation with *Ticonderoga*. It proved to be a great marriage.

"Tico" departed Norfolk with CVG-80 embarked at the end of August, bound for the blue waters of the Pacific. All hands seemed anxious but pleased to be on the way. I was not sorry to see Norfolk fall astern again—the Pacific had always been my goal.

CV-14's transit of the Panama Canal was without notable occurrence, and she moored at the duty pier of NAS North Island, San Diego, for a two-day pit stop, briefings and orders. However, things did not go entirely smoothly for our magnificent carrier skipper, Captain Dixie Kiefer.

The day before our scheduled departure for Hawaii, the wives, friends, lovers and city fathers held a giant aloha party for the ship's crew in the Navy recreation park across the bay. Captain Kiefer used his gig for transportation to the "must appear" affair, and found many old friends in attendance, toasting his health and keeping his cup topped off.

Time passed. Upon return to the ship, with the gig secured alongside, our skipper hopped onto the landing and began a brisk ascent to the quarter deck. So far so good. The junior officer of the deck was an Ensign Benson who was enjoying the prestige if not the responsibilities of that nautical duty for the first time. Preparing to render the captain suitable greeting, the JOOD was astonished when Captain Kiefer, now huffing and puffing at deck level, tripped over the guard-rail chain and went ass-over-teakettle into San Diego Bay, forty feet below.

Ensign Benson went to General Quarters. Every available siren, bell and alarm was sounded, along with the nonstandard announcement, "Man overboard—this is no shit!" Nothing in the ensign's naval education had prepared him for a contingency not covered in the Watch Officer's Guide. Meanwhile, Dixie Kiefer was swimming around, looking for his hat, and generally enjoying himself.

Fetched back and approximately dried off, our skipper greeted the gathered watch-standers crowding the quarter deck and announced, "If I was scoring that dive, I'd probably rate it a five." Thus concluding his performance, he sloshed off to his quarters humming *Anchors Aweigh*.

Early next morning (0600, to be exact), "Himself" still humming "Anchors Aweigh" guided his ship out of San Diego harbor and headed West. However, his big boss, Commander Naval Air Forces Pacific had the last word: "This command is pleased that CO *Ticonderoga* is still seaworthy but next time hold swim call during daylight hours. Incidentally, happy hunting." Next stop Hawaii.

The first sight of Diamond Head on the horizon was a thrill that still is difficult to describe. All those boyhood dreams soon to become reality; the realization that Ford Island was just around the corner, where much of 7 December '41's tragedy remained in stark evidence; the doorway to our future, destruction of the Japanese Empire.

The air group moved ashore for further training at NAS Kaneohe while Tico make preparations for combat operations. CVG-80 practiced constantly, flying day and night in coordinated operations best described as "group gropes" but essential for smooth functioning of the three squadrons as a cohesive unit.

During this fine-tuning period final assignments were made for our tactical organization, and I was extremely happy to be flying section leader in Lieutenant Pat Fleming's division. His wingman was Ensign Paul Beaudry and mine was Ensign John Fraifogl. We had a ourselves a machine!

Unfortunately, the air group experienced some seemingly needless operational losses, but the intensified combat training also identified those individuals who would become their squadrons' top aviators. One standard was performance "around the boat"—those who consistently performed well in landing aboard. It has little to do with actual combat skill, but it's a great yardstick to measure a pilot's knowledge of his aircraft and his ability to make it perform to his will.

Several VF-80 pilots soon identified themselves as the squadron top guns. Among them was Pat Fleming, essentially a latecomer to fighters but who excelled in every facet of aerial warfare. He completed the cruise with a string of nineteen aerial victories as the Navy's fourth-ranking ace. Of us all, Pat really had the Right Stuff.

Another accomplished aviator was Ensign James "Shorty" Ewing, who would be airborne when everyone else was lazing on the beach. Day or night, mail runs—whatever—he would be aviating. Shorty became the squadron photo-reconnaissance pilot who did his shooting with a camera. His superior airmanship accounted for his remarkable survivability, for which he received few accolades though his shipmates recognized his superlative talent and considered him one of the best in the business.

I must mention Lieutenant (junior grade) Bob "Skinny" Innes, considered one of the most accomplished pilots in VF-80. He continually outscored the rest of us with guns, rockets and bombs. Needless to say, when the time came he did his work well and accounted for much of the damage and detriment inflicted in air-to-ground missions. But never during our entire tour did he have the opportunity to display his air-to-air skills. Such are the breaks.

Just prior to our departure from Hawaii, Scoop Vorse "fleeted up" to command the air group. His place at the head of VF-80 was taken by Lieutenant Commander Leroy "Pete" Keith, another experienced, skillful fighter pilot who imparted the same brand of leadership, though we remained known far and wide as "Vorse's Vipers."

Almost immediately we learned that the standard big-deck fighter squadron complement was being raised from thirty-six to fifty-four aircraft. Greater demands for fleet air defense and strike escort were behind the increase, which meant fewer SB2Cs and TBMs. But we cheerfully accepted our new F6F-5 Hellcats and, with them, an influx of new pilots with every degree of fighter experience—or lack of same. Some dive bomber and torpedo pilots were drawn into the process, and I'm certain none of them complained!

When *Ticonderoga* arrived at Ulithi, the huge fleet anchorage, we found the lagoon arrayed with warships and auxiliaries. Admiral William F. Halsey's Third Fleet was directed from the battleship *New Jersey* (BB-62), but the striking arm was Task Force 38's fast carriers. Tico joined Task Group 38.3 under Rear Admiral F. C. Sherman, with veterans *Essex* (CV-9), *Langley* (CVL-27) and *San Jacinto* (CVL-30). *Essex*'s Air Group 15 had sunk a lot of Japanese shipping and shot down some 287 aircraft in the previous five months, thirty-two by the CAG himself—Commander David McCampbell. In October CVG-15 was nearing the end of its tour—a long road paved with nearly half the pilots and aircrew who started the deployment in May. Our briefings with these combat-experienced gents were succinct and very sobering. But we tucked that knowledge away for future use and declared all hands ready to do battle.

Air Group 80 launched its first strikes on 5 November, targeted against airfields near Manila. The major effort was directed against Zublon Airfield, reportedly a primary fighter base for protection of the Philippine capitol. The raid was composed of a dozen SB2Cs and nine TBMs escorted by eight F6Fs, with a top cover of a twelve more Hellcats. Pat Fleming's division was the second portion of the escort, responsible for protecting the bombers from interception.

We sighted just two enemy aircraft, who were reluctant to tangle with forty-two U.S. Navy types, thus allowing the coordinated attack to make some impressive direct hits on the hangars and fuel dumps. The escorting Hellcats rolled in first, strafing to keep the anti-aircraft guns quiet, but we encountered a wild barrage of flak that scared the hell out of everyone. However, it did only minimal damage since we got in and out with everybody intact.

The fighter sweep was a different story. Eight of our Hellcats tangled with fifteen enemy fighters which attacked from a high perch. The ensuing dogfight became an unheeding melee, which immediately revealed the Vipers' total lack of combat experience and disregard of flight discipline. The squadron action report best describes this initial encounter:

"CAG Vorse and CO Keith and their wingmen, when observing the enemy high above the sweep, quickly deployed to gain altitude and to present a more advantageous position for mutual protection and counter attack. The other VF pilots who, with one exception, were in combat for the first time, ignored squadron doctrine and attempted to attack the enemy without altitude parity and without maintaining mutual support. During the ensuing battle the more maneuverable enemy VF had considerable advantage in dominating the course of action..."

We lost two of our squadronmates in this engagement, plus three other aircraft sporting an alarming array of bullet holes. In spite of this incontinent performance, Lieutenant Johnny Fair scored VF-80's first aerial victory. His conquest, with three other enemy fighters, brought the score to four confirmed kills, which was not ecstatic odds. The debrief was a glum affair: reviewing our shortcomings which, considering the four-two score, made for an extremely disquieting tally.

The last fighter strike of "Day One" was an attack against Japanese warships in Manila Bay, teaming Pat Fleming's division with Gail Anderson's as the assault force. There was an overcast all the way in, with a few breaks in the cloud base at about 3,000 feet, but good visibility was reported beneath the overcast.

As we approached Manila Bay, several large openings in the clouds revealed two Japanese destroyers underway with a full head of steam, sailing in tandem. We attacked with five-inch High Velocity Aerial Rockets and 500-pound armor-piercing bombs, scoring several HVAR hits on the bridge and forward turret of the lead ship but no bomb hits.

The second destroyer took a pounding from three 500-pounders and two near-misses, bringing the ship to a dead stop but still afloat. The entire flight was now milling around under the cloud base and experiencing an acute case of "discrete heroism" in staying clear of a skyfull of flak.

Then, lo and behold, Fleming's division was treated to a hit-and-run attack by a lone Zero. But he abruptly decided he had erred in assessing the odds and headed off toward friendlier climes at full throttle. We followed.

The pursuit turned into an on-the-deck chase toward the island of Corregidor, the single Zero in the lead with Fleming, Beaudry, Cormier and Fraifogle fanned out behind. Anderson's division meanwhile considered four to one a sufficient mix and continued to observe (at a prudent distance) the outcome of the two damaged destroyers. The heavily-damaged number two DD ultimately beached itself near Cavite.

Pat Fleming discerned that the Zero was luring us into an area of dense anti-aircraft guns, hoping the shorebased firepower would shake the four eager Grummans off his tail. In desperation, Pat took a long-range shot which providentially hit the Zeke's port wing, causing the Japanese pilot to veer left, away from the mainland. This allowed me to cut to the inside of his turn, closing to respectable shooting distance as I began calculating the mil lead in my gunsight for a narrow deflection shot.

However, our leader was having none of that. He moved over to take another shot. The Japanese pilot saw the developing play, knew he was in serious trouble, and broke right, continuing toward the shore opposite Corregidor. But suddenly he veered hard left again and struck the water—perhaps fatally damaged by Pat's initial burst. Anyway, that was number one on Fleming's hit parade, with eighteen to follow.

The AA batteries now opened up in earnest and we were just plain lucky not to end up in the water. It was definitely time to return to Tico.

Over the next two days, we launched more attacks against shipping in Manila Bay, including the abandoned DD on the beach. It made a great ordnance-dumping target. No airborne hostiles were engaged, though several were destroyed on the ground. Then, our initial combat operation concluded, we steamed away eastward.

Our withdrawal from the Philippines was welcomed by all hands; we'd lost four pilots killed or missing and several aircraft needed to be replaced.

Task Group 38.3 retired to Ulithi Atoll, a newly-acquired fleet base with an extraordinary harbor and anchorage. Upon dropping anchor, *Ticonderoga* appeared almost lilliputian in that vast array of warships. But nobody complained. The sight was inspiring, and we took pride in knowing we were a part of the greatest instrument of sea power ever assembled. While time allowed, we enjoyed the amenities of Mog Mog Island, whose chief attraction was stale beer. But the respite was short-lived. Our services were required again.

The task group arrived off Luzon Island, the Philippines again on 11 November, 1944. Though the carriers launched a predawn fighter sweep against enemy airfields, our main concern was a large Japanese troop convoy headed for Ormoc Bay on Leyte. We pummeled the transports, losing a VB-80 crew in the process, but aerial opposition was negligible.

The next morning's second mission was on deck, ready for launch, while I was strapped into my Hellcat. "Spotted" in the second row just opposite the island, I was idling my engine when everyone on deck suddenly departed for any convenient cover. Being smarter than the average aviator, I deduced that something untoward was pending. Just then every ship in the task force opened fire, with anti-aircraft guns trained vertically.

The kamikaze corps had arrived overhead.

I looked up to see a flaming enemy fighter descending in wide spirals, a victim of the AA fire from our screen's battleships and cruisers. Then abruptly the entire task group commenced a sweeping series of highspeed turns, hoping to present those suicidal souls with the most elusive possible targets.

Fascinated with the symmetry of those great warships' maneuvering, I was startled when the bridge of our sister ship, *Lexington* (CV-16), blossomed into a red ball of flame and smoke. One of the suiciders had found its mark, and it was apparent that the Lex had taken a serious hit.

Several of our deck hands scurried out to take a quick look but, after a fleeting glance and some agitated finger-pointing skyward, scrambled back for cover. Looking straight overhead, I saw a lone Japanese pilot had entered his death dive, his nose pointed directly at *Ticonderoga*'s bridge.

The shield of flak sent up from our AA batteries had no effect. As I sat strapped into my cockpit, it occurred to me that I was going to buy the farm without the satisfaction of ever displaying my talent at some Zero's six o'clock. It was extremely disheartening.

While I may have been resigned to my fate, Captain Dixie Kiefer was not. His superior maneuvering caused the kamikaze to crash alongside, drenching the Big T with salt water. Of course, the ship's laundry was inundated with new business after this affair.

The next two line periods were repeats of our first visits to the Philippines, though the emphasis shifted to anti-shipping strikes. Though we saw a few enemy singles and pairs airborne, there was no determined aerial opposition, and I had yet to lock my gunsight on an airplane "made in Japan." We did a thorough enough job on troop transports, and enemy personnel losses on those ships must have been appalling. But still I hankered for more of the air-to-air war.

My wish came true in mid-December during a fighter sweep over Vigan, north of Lingayen Gulf. Again I was Pat Fleming's section leader with Johnny Fraifogl on my wing and Ensign Paul Beaudry protecting Pat's tail. We were in company with our old friend R. H. Anderson's band of dead-eyes, Ensigns Hamblin, Smith and Rush. The eight Hellcats were fully loaded with belly tanks, five-inch rockets and .50 caliber ammo for all six guns. The weather was clear with the usual billowing cumulus buildups, cruising en route to our target at 9,000 feet.

Fleming came up on the radio, calling the "tallyho" on two large groups of aircraft ahead and slightly to our left. They were in a loose, flat formation, weaving slowly back and forth, plainly unaware of us. It was unbelievable at first; after such poor hunting previously now there were too many bandits to count. But eventually we pegged them at twenty-eight Nakajima Oscars and Mitsubishi Zekes. On Pat's command we dropped our belly tanks—some of us jettisoned our rockets as well—rechecked our guns and prepared to apply our skills.

Anderson's division was instructed to take the group "in trail" and we four would tackle the leaders. I was truly surprised at how calmly I received this preparatory order. I had gone over this moment so often in my mind that the events seemed to be occurring in a dream. Then the adrenaline kicked in with a rush.

Fleming and I each took our wingmen in separate attacks, boring in at full throttle. I picked the closest pair of Oscars, firing far out of range, but got a lucky hit on the port wing of the leader. He veered sharply left, leaving his wingman as dead meat. John Fraifogl and I chopped him up, and he went down under our guns.

Suddenly the sky was filled with aircraft, some attempting to flee, others attacking, some still wondering what the Shinto Shrine was going on. Our F6Fs sliced through the middle of this group, systematically adjusting the odds. I quickly picked off a Zero with a long shot nearly head-on, which was a tad disquieting. There was no way to practice nose-to-nose gunnery—strictly on-the-job training!

John was forced to leave me to avoid being clobbered by one of our own, who had mistaken him for "Brand X." (This lapse resulted in some very unkind remarks in the debrief.) Meanwhile, the dogfight continued. Fraifogl joined Anderson and Johnny Rush, flamed another Oscar, then evaded by diving into the clouds.

Looking around, I again spotted Fleming and Beaudry scissoring with two Oscars in tight formation, each pair seeking the advantage. My abrupt appearance from astern, with six M-2 Brownings locked on, changed the situation instantaneously. However, my high closure speed put me in serious trouble. I continued firing, saw my tracers hitting both Oscars, then flashed under the enemy leader. I expected to overrun them, staking myself right out in front of God and everybody. But the Japanese leader had no way of knowing I was close. He broke hard right, leaving his partner slightly in trail, which offered me a textbook shooting position from dead astern. The leader got away but his wingman became number three on my hit parade.

I joined with Fleming, taking a position wide abeam for mutual support and maneuvering room. Glancing down, I spotted another single Oscar several thousand feet below, paralleling our course. So I rolled in from my perch, but the Nakajima countered with a turn to meet me nose to nose. Several highspeed turns ensued, taking us down to the treetops in the mountains. But the Japanese pilot had selected a blind canyon and piled into the side of a hill. That was my "cost-effective" kill.

Climbing back up to join the action, I could not spot a single air-craft—providing me a slight twinge. Where was everyone? Even the radio, which previously had been a jumble of reports and exclamations, was quiet. Time to head home.

As I turned eastward I saw the shadow of another plane on the ground, and for a moment I thought the opposition had found me again. But to my great relief, it was Fleming with Beaudry. On the way home we collected John Fraifogl and we trooped back to the ship like the Four Mus-keteers. The score: Fleming, five; Beaudry, two; Cormier, four; Friafogl, one. Anderson's team bagged eight more for a total nineteen Japanese fighters destroyed without a single friendly loss. Vorse's Vipers were making them-selves felt.

Christmas 1944 was spent in Ulithi, following a nearly disastrous brush with "Halsey's Hurricane." Actually it was a typhoon, but just as nasty as a hurricane; the first of two the fleet commander drove his ships through.

Formosa, now Taiwan, was the area of operations for our next line period, and we became instant all-weather pilots since the weather was posi-tively rotten. Low overcasts with reduced visibility kept most targets well hidden. As if that weren't enough, we encountered a new wrinkle in the enemy's bag of tricks when barrage balloons lurked in the overcast, held by their wire tethers. Our intrepid leader, Commander Vorse, engaged one of these devices while attacking shipping in Takao Harbor. The cable cleanly clipped off three feet of his port wing. We immediately withdrew to orbit the fleet in the wildest traffic jam this side of LA at 5:00 PM.

Scoop had to put his Hellcat into the water alongside a destroyer. Skipping along the waves at about 150 mph, shedding parts with every bounce, he finally splashed to a stop with only the cockpit remaining intact. Thank you, Mr. Grumman! With a jaunty wave to all observers, Scoop Vorse calmly inflated his raft, stepped aboard and paddled to his awaiting helpmate. Incredible survivor, our CAG.

Formosa also is well remembered by *Ticonderoga* sailors as the scene of a devastating kamikaze attack. In forty minutes two suiciders killed 143 of our shipmates, with 202 wounded. We also lost thirty-six airplanes, as that 21st of January was Tico's last day operating Air Group 80. She re-turned to Bremerton, Washington for repairs while CVG-80 was transferred to *Hancock* (CV-19) as the replacement for the departing Air Group Seven.

Once embarked in "Hanna," we joined Task Group 58.2, destined to make Naval Aviation history in February 1945. For two days we trolled over the Japanese home islands, and the VF-80 history noted, "The objective of the strikes was to cut down the Japanese air power by tackling everything found in the sky and burning or destroying aircraft and installations on the ground. The assigned area was the east Kanto plain region on the Chiba Peninsula, east of Tokyo Bay with its five major airfields and ten minor fields..."

During the operation, the Hellcats of VF-80 and VBF-80 received credit for downing seventy-one Japanese planes over the Tokyo area on 16 February—a major share of the total 270 claims by the whole of Task Force 58. And next day the *Hancock* squadrons added another dozen kills to the growing list.

I contributed just three confirmed and a Tojo as a "sure probable" to that list, though I was pleased with the results, considering that my engine nearly provided me a swim in the frigid Sea of Japan. Fortunately, the R-2800 kept running long enough to get me back aboard feet dry. The maintenance officer and I had some very harsh words as a result.

Air Group 80 completed its tour with support of the Iwo Jima landings later that month, with preliminary strikes against Okinawa as well. Our last day of combat, 1 March, ended with three Japanese bombers splashed, raising the squadron total to 160. The Vipers had acquitted themselves with valor, and I was mighty proud to have been a part of that marvelous team.

1950

THE KOREAN CAPER

Following Line School in delightful Monterey, California in 1949, I had the great misfortune to be assigned to the Technical Training Center in Millington, Tennessee, about fifty miles north of Memphis. It put me in the middle of the country, many miles from both oceans and the operational navy. My previous experience as an aide obviously influenced this assignment as administrative assistant to the base commander. It was not what I had expected after being away from the fleet flying business for three years. Needless to say, I was sorely disappointed.

After spending a mighty chilly winter and tons of paper-pushing, my savior turned up in the form of the leader of the Blue Angels, Lieutenant Commander Johnny Magda. We met following their show at NAS Memphis in the spring of 1950, and he informed me he was looking for a new public affairs officer since his current PAO, Ed Mahood, was a Reservist who had elected to be released to inactive duty. So if I was interested, John would clear it with his boss, Rear Admiral John Dale Price, Chief of Naval Air Training. I told Johnny my bags were packed, the family in the car and all pointing south! I could have kissed him.

Orders were issued, the trip to Pensacola proved uneventful, the family settled into the warmer clime and I joined the Blues at NAAS Whiting Field. Not that Whiting is heaven on earth, but my job was. It was also my first experience with jet aircraft but I knew that I had found that certain extraordinary something in aviation. Checkout in the F9F-2 Panther harkened back to the informal older days with a quick cockpit briefing by Lieutenant Jake Robcke, the left wingman in the diamond. Then the details of getting the machine fired up and away you went. Today, the folks in charge would have a stroke at the casualness of it all. However, as PAO my flights and travel between show sites was done in a trusty old SNJ-5 known as "Beetle Bomb," and I got to know its cockpit very well!

Unfortunately, this idyllic life suddenly came to an end with outbreak of the Korean War, and the Blue Angels were temporarily disbanded in July 1950. John Magda and his team, minus Ralph Hanks and myself as the latest assignees, were shipped off to the west coast to join Fighter Squadron 191 and were WestPac-bound very shortly thereafter.

Ralph went to a training squadron as an instructor and I opted to enroll in the fighter-photo reconnaissance school at NAS, Pensacola, Florida thus plotting to get back to the fleet one way or another. Planning is everything, so they say—at least in this case the plan worked and I was back in a fleet squadron at NAS Miramar near San Diego, ready to do my thing for the lads in the front lines. My assignment, Composite Squadron 61, was the Pacific Fleet fighter-photo unit. It was loaded with talented and ranking Naval Aviators; old warriors with an itch to join in the action. In VC-61 they were assured of reporting "Feet dry" over North Korea during their assignment to the Pacific Fleet.

With these senior troops around, I was junior enough to be in line for laundry officer or perhaps insurance and morale officer—something really dramatic. No matter, though. I was happy to be on the west coast in an interesting, exciting assignment, and back in the flying business. Fortunately, I was senior enough to be selected for temporary additional duty as a member of the Seventh Fleet ashore team, thus posted to the Joint Operations Center (JOC) then operating at Seoul, South Korea.

The JOC naval representatives were responsible for daily situation reports and summaries of fleet activities—particularly those of the fast carriers (Task Force 77), and the evening presentation to the major unit commanders supporting the South Koreans. It was fascinating to be current on what was happening, and who was doing what to whom amid the colorful participants: General Douglas MacArthur, Supreme Commander of Allied Powers in Tokyo, and later General Matthew Ridgway, hand grenades and all; General Van Fleet, in-country ground commander; Vice Admiral J.J. "Jocko" Clark, commanding the naval forces; General "Mount" Everest leading the Air Force guys; and from all the services a host of beribboned warhorses assiduously doing their thing.

So there I was in the center of action ashore, in an outfit equipped with—guess what—an ancient, much-used but serviceable SNJ-5. With a tailhook no less! Very few JOC Navy types were interested in launching our antique "J-bird", and it was an opportunity I couldn't resist. An aircraft—not quite sporty but enjoyable to fly—possessing good range and even armed with a machine gun, albeit a small one. It was practically my very own private airplane, ready to explore the Korean countryside. I conducted some wide reconnaissance, at least in those portions of the country where we exerted some control, and generally I was most welcomed.

On one occasion, flying out to the carrier *Valley Forge* (CV-45), my SNJ was not the most popular visitor on the flight deck—a curiosity, yes, but more like the bastard at a family reunion. Then too, little did I suspect that my carrier approach could have been critiqued by a young would-be Naval Aviator named Phil Wood aboard the destroyer-escort *O'Bannon*.

I saw a lot of territory, friendly and otherwise, touched down at most of the bases and even watched Wally Schirra trundle down the runway in his trusty F-84 while flying with the Air Force. It was the first time that Phil, Wally and I were all in approximately the same place at the same time, and though we didn't realize it until years later, the continuing cycle continues to amaze me.

I was never challenged or shot at by either side. However, one stop which was not on my visit list was to see my old highschool classmate, Marine Corps fighter pilot Ted Williams. He was doing his duty for the cause at K-9, Pusan, flying Panthers on loan from the Boston Redsox.

Meanwhile, the briefings and operational planning at JOC went on every night. Periodically the Washington hierarchy attended to assure everyone back home that they were in touch and in charge. On one such evening, Vice President Alban Barkley was present at the in-country "howgozit" briefing. He added a little touch of class to the proceedings with a series of very pithy questions, like, "How does the Air Force evaluate and catalog the reported railroad bomb cuts? What about the numbers of locomotives destroyed or damaged? And how about the same for boxcars, ox-drawn wagons and pushcarts?"

The numbers were trotted out by some poor contrite soul, admitting that the numbers might indicate some zealous overclaiming and/or wild-eyed estimates of damage inflicted by USAF units. The Navy was just sitting there, snug (and probably smug) in the realization that CTF-77 played the claims game very carefully. Our boss, Admiral Clark, pursed his lips, smiled at the Veep, winked at his briefing team, blew his nose and resumed nodding. Talk about nonverbal communication—Jocko was a master at it before anybody knew what to call it! Thereafter the briefing claims from all parties were somewhat closer to reality.

It was a great finale to the temporary duty in-country and a real eye-opener on the intricacies of grand strategy. Then it was back to Miramar, preparing to take a more personal role in the Korean air war.

Actually, the war already had turned personal. My friend Johnny Magda was killed in action leading a strike against Chinese and North Korean positions 8 March 1951.

1954-56

FLIGHTS OF FANCY: THE BLUE ANGELS

"So, now that you're a Blue Angel, what is your professional military life really like in the fast lane?"

A good question, often asked, and not only by the curious. To provide an answer without seeming philosophical or heroic, I must say that assignment to the team is sheer flattery. It is to become a shareholder in a flying performance like no other in the Navy. In fact, I'm not too modest to include the entire military establishment. But to keep things in perspective, there is assuredly more to the team than just zooming around the country in shiny blue airplanes.

Belonging to the U.S. Navy Flight Demonstration Team means just that—being a "team" player. It also means a singular bond of mutual respect, exercised not only in the air but also on the ground, coupled with mutual trust and dependency. The Blues' camaraderie creates a remarkable alliance—a spirit of professional unanimity seldom found in any other endeavor. And nowhere can that relationship be more visible than in the continuing standard of excellence displayed nearly every weekend throughout the year somewhere around the world.

All the foregoing may sound like guileless bragging, but as some sage fellow once said, "When you catch a big fish, you don't take it home through the back door."

To trace my affiliation with the team, let me return to 1950 for a moment. The Blues had been in existence just four years and had transitioned from the propeller-driven F6F-5 Hellcat—the famous WW II fighter—and the sensational F8F-2 Bearcat, into a front-line fleet jet—Grumman's F9F-2 Panther.

I had a brief opportunity to witness the team's masterworks in action during the spring and early summer of that year, when I was assigned as the public affairs officer. Home base was NAS Whiting Field, Florida. It was also the home of the jet transition squadron, equipped with the redoubtable Air Force P-80 Shooting Star (later, on Wally's recommendation, redesignated the Navy TV-1.)

I wanted to share the jet-propelled adventure and, when offered a checkout ride in the Blues' F9F-2s, I jumped on the opportunity with both feet. The preflight and rides were very informal affairs. Lieutenant Jake Robcke, who flew right wing in the diamond formation, was one of the most talented fighter pilots around, and he kept preliminaries to a minimum. Still, it was a thrill for me. In the days before NATOPS (Naval Aviation Training and Operating Procedures Standardization), it was pretty much kick the tires and light the fire; guaranteed to upset the safety-conscious aviators of today. But if flying was less safe back then, I'm bound to admit it also was more fun.

Unfortunately, my creme-de-la-creme job was terminated with disestablishment of the Blues in July 1950, in deference to the nastiness in Korea. So, my full appreciation of the team's intrinsic brotherhood was yet to come.

In late 1951 the Chief of Naval Operations called for re-establishment of the Blue Angels. So it was only appropriate for Lieutenant Commander Roy "Butch" Voris, the original team leader, to saddle up again and reactivate the team at its new home in Corpus Christi, Texas.

That was the good news. The bad news: some hard-charging folks of the Navy fighter community—especially the visionary types (or, perhaps more correctly, the Walter Mitty types)—indulged in some surreptitious "no-nos." They committed these violations of regulations and good sense, secure in the knowledge that their aircraft side numbers were too small to be readily discernable from most observers' viewpoints. While this was a safe assumption in most instances, it did not apply to an eagle-eyed mountaineer who espied my photo-recce bird's unauthorized indulgences. The hiker was responsible for my visit to the CO's office for an eloquently-expressed progression of irreverent words and phrases. I hadn't realized that he possessed such an extensive vocabulary. But I recovered from the abasement without visible scars, not dreaming that one day soon I would become a legalized "buzzer," perhaps to the astonishment of my previous "buzzees." Meanwhile, however, my extemporaneous exhibitions ceased.

In the fall of 1953 I was at sea aboard USS *Oriskany* (CVA-34) in the Western Pacific, when I received dispatch orders to report to the Chief of Naval Air Advanced training, NAS Corpus Christi, on or before 20 December. My duties—officer in charge of the Navy Flight Demonstration Team! It was a total surprise. I had no forewarning that my name was being considered as the Blues' Leader, although there was much suspicion that my air group commander, Jig Dog Ramage, played a hand in the recommendation. Genuflection is not a military posture, but I could have kissed Jig Dog's Academy ring—if he wore it.

I was painfully aware that highly-desirable orders of this sort don't just happen. Somebody makes them happen, and that someone was my very good friend and erstwhile Air Group 80 shipmate, Commander Lou Bangs. He had flown with Jig Dog in Bombing Ten from *Enterprise* (CV-6) during 1944, and now was in the right place at the right time: Chief of Naval Air Training staff, where the candidates are evaluated and final selections made. Lou was there to approve my nomination and, owing to his persuasiveness, got my orders issued. I have forever been in his debt.

Atypically for a fighter pilot, the realization that I was about to lead the Blue Angels caused me to exercise more than a few moments of introspection. All manner of questions surfaced: was I qualified, was I capable, was the family willing to accept the lengthy separations, did I need new uniforms? The answer to all these and more was a resounding "Yes." As Wally would later say, all systems were go!

However, I must admit to a host of preconceived notions as to just how those breath-taking formation aerobatics were executed. My formation flying up to then had not been timid, but the prospect of performing those maneuvers before thousands of spectators did have a slightly chilling effect; let alone at ground-level with five other folks. But that was only part of the job. What about the personal appearances and myriad PR activities? In retrospect, I had a case of stage fright. But it soon passed.

And small wonder, for I anticipated an unparalleled flying experience. It might be dangerous (perhaps); death-defying (no way!); low-level (sometimes); exciting (definitely); desirous (absolutely). I'd have to think further about new uniforms.

So, in December 1953, thanks to a former shipmate and fellow believer in fate, I bundled up the family in our Ford convertible and, through rain and shine, headed for Texas.

The nucleus of the 1954 team was without exception a collection of very talented aviators, all veterans of the previous season. Lieutenant Commander Ray Hawkins, the gent whom I would relieve, not only surrounded himself with exceptionally skillful pilot and support folks, but he had the sagacity to pass along his treasure-trove of personnel to me. The ground-force roster included a complete complement of hand-picked maintenance and support people, each a specialist in his field, and they were ready to tackle the training schedule head-on. It was obvious that Ray intended the good name of the Blue Angels to last. I had numerous occasions to thank him for his foresight.

The change of command occurred just before Christmas 1953. It was conducted with quiet, dignified pomp and ceremony with my big boss in attendance—Rear Admiral Cato Glover, Commander of Naval Air Advanced Training. He was one senior officer for whom I had great admiration and respect. It was a good start.

Three of the second-year pilots made up the diamond formation, which to this day is the team's trademark. That meant that the only "new start" to be trained was the leader—me! Thus, Lieutenant (JG)s Dayl Crow, Roland Ausland and Kenny Wallace were sorely tasked. The lead solo pilot was Lieutenant Frank Jones, without question the consummate acrobatic flying magician.

Our second solo demonstration pilot was the first Marine Corps aviator to join the team. I might add that in those days the Blue Angels had no say in the Leatherneck selectee—that was determined solely by Headquarters Marine Corps. Of which more later.

A better choice could not be imagined for team public affairs officer than the irrepressible, free-spirited Lieutenant Commander Dick "The Old Newf" Newhafer. Another LCDR, Harry Sonner, was the maintenance boss, and not to be forgotten was Grumman tech rep David Scheuer.

Training started immediately after the Christmas holidays, with familiarization flights in the straight-wing F9F-5. The new-model Panther was neither the speediest nor most responsive jet fighter around, but surely it was the sturdiest. It was a living, breathing product of the famous "Grumman Iron Works," whose aircraft I had flown in both the Atlantic and Pacific combat theaters. Dayl Crow, the right-hand wingman in the diamond, conspired with me to prove just how sturdy the F9F really was when we tried to exchange wingtip fuel tanks during a practice session. Fortunately, the tip tanks didn't fit that way, and we only succeeded in frightening some fisherman and littering the Padre Island practice area with aviation fuel and bits of aluminum. We were all very happy in the knowledge that Grumman's craftsmen built mighty strong flying machines—and still do.

As training progressed, it was revelation time for me. I learned just what formation flying was all about. I found early on, for instance, that when I called for a diamond loop, that sure as there's little green apples, Kenny Wallace in the slot position would move forward and raise the nose of his Panther slightly, causing an increase in air pressure between us. Consequently, my nose was raised, thus initiating the maneuver—and up we'd go, whether I was ready or not.

The same was true of echelon maneuvers—just a little anticipatory nudge by the wingman and we'd be on the move, four of us locked together. Based on these initial experiences, I became very sensitive and conscious of the timing of my command radio calls.

Although the weather was not very cooperative, we kept busy with hangar-flying and hours of chalk talk. By the middle of January, except for some rough spots, we felt the 1954 team was ready to take the show on the road. That month the open house at NAS Saufley Field near Pensacola, Florida became our debut. And it wasn't pretty.

Obviously, our curtain-raiser was somewhat premature so we zipped back to Corpus and whipped up a practice schedule to iron out the biggest wrinkles. Again the weather intervened, so I appealed to Admiral Glover, asking if we could transfer to the sunny clime of Southern California. He agreed that we needed help so phone calls were made, papers were shuffled, and shortly we established the Blues' first winter training quarters at Naval Air Auxiliary Air Station El Centro. With unlimited flying weather, we kept the tires hot with takeoffs and landings, and the daily drills showed some promise of good things to come.

We added new maneuvers and deleted others, one of which I was very pleased to see dropped: the reverse Cuban eight, since I had a problem executing the damn thing the same way each time. Upon departing El Centro, waving goodby to our newfound desert friends, we returned to Corpus and felt ready for our "second debut" at good old Whiting Field. I wouldn't say our show was sensational, but it definitely was colorful.

First of all, the wind was blowing like hell, right down the flight line. Our first maneuver, the traditional diamond roll, went extremely well, which is always a nice way to start. The second evolution was a diamond formation loop, which I elected to do in spite of the adverse wind. Without much elaboration, the outcome lacked the quality of precision. As a matter of fact, we ended up so far from the field that the folks on the ground wondered if we were performing for somebody else.

Dick Newhafer, whom we had by now left in our jetwash to announce the show, and without benefit of radio contact, was more than somewhat chagrined by our unseemly departure. But, I thought, what the hell are practice sessions for? So I called for another loop, this time into the wind. It proved much better, and though the loop still wasn't perfectly round, we ended up over our intended show site. The Old Newf, however, had by then abandoned the script and, between ad-libs, was muttering obscenities about our heritage over the loudspeaker. No doubt the spectators endorsed Dick's sentiments.

Considering the value of our practice show, I figured why not try yet another loop, going downwind this time just for experience. The troops agreed. So there we went again, up and over, while Newf could not believe we were going to do another goddam loop, and said as much to his diminishing audience. But the third loop went just fine, and we continued on to land at Pensacola. Newhafer, now left to his own ingenuity, merely announced that since those noisy goddam airplanes finally had gone home, he would tell some things about himself. The crowd cheered in response—some being driven before the blustery wind—and Dick proceeded with *spargere voces in vulgum ambiguous*, or spreading doubtful words among the people.

The diamond foursome finally was ready, as the LTJGs had smoothed out their leader's technique, and the solos also were hot to trot. It was time to hit the road, and our first official stop was NAS New Orleans on 20 February 1954. Despite a small stirring in my gizzard before climbing into the cockpit, the show went like clockwork and we were a genuine hit. From then on it was standing room only. We performed more shows than in any previous season, talked to more people, flew more miles, kissed more babies, had more nice things said about us, and generally behaved ourselves—except for Newhafer.

NAS Moffett Field, just south of San Francisco, was The Old Newf's undoing. He had stayed two extra days to tend to "public affairs matters" and got far too public with numerous affairs in an immoderately racy crowd. He might have got away with it had he not piqued the curiosity of the Moffett tower upon departure. Sitting in his shiny blue airplane at the end of the active runway, Newf requested takeoff clearance on a "local" flight plan direct to NAS Dallas—that's in Texas, son.

Details of subsequent actions are somewhat obscure, but the matter came to the personal attention of Moffett's commanding officer, who ordered Newf to be admitted to the station sickbay for an acute hangover. The good captain also communicated these details to my boss, the long-suffering Rear Admiral Glover. It all flowed downhill from there, and I was summoned to appear at the flag office pronto for an important communique. The admiral was very calm, expressed himself with elegance, and stated that if I could not engender some gentlemanly conduct in my officers, I was first in line to become the new windsock tender on a sod field in Adak, Alaska. It was a very brief exchange, start to finish. He talked and I listened.

Admiral Glover then solicitously inquired whether I had any questions. I responded in the negative and he bade me good afternoon.

The Old Newf decided he had enough of the Navy, considering the circumstances, and since he was still a Reserve officer he would revert to inactive status. His decision saved me from further embarrassment, but I would miss a good friend, and the team would miss considerable color. Newf did bequeath us his legacy, a marvelous poem about the Blues. It said in part:

> The crowd stood dazed in the morning air,
> In an icy death-grip held;
> And from the bowels of the milling throng,
> An awesome murmur swelled.
> It rose and strained in the blowing wind,
> And hammered against the sky;
> And shouted its word to the firmament,
> That the Blues were going to fly.

> And who were these skyborn eagles then,
> Who fancied that man-made wings,
> Could lift them in loops and Cuban eights,
> And changeover rolls and things?
> Could hold those thousands spellbound there,
> Dead still in the morning sun;
> As the Arch Fear wondered himself at length
> At the things that were being done...

The rest continues with considerable irreverence and some bawdiness, but it was Dick's way of avowing his affection for all of us. He put his considerable writing skill to good use, with a series of novels and screenplays which provided an outlet for his pent-up energy. Several years later The Old Newf called me from the east coast, saying he would be in California for a couple of weeks and asking if he could stop by. I said sure—there were guest quarters where he could write.

He left two years later.

So Richard Newhafer was the only "casualty" of the 1954 season. We were due for some other new faces to replace the departing Frank Jones, Dayl Crow and Roland Ausland. The Marine also was a no-return since his hat size swelled to such an extent that his flight helmet no longer fit and we couldn't find one big enough for him.

Those of us left now welcomed the "New Blues" with warm regards. Most of our arrivals were former squadronmates or known through their reputations, so there were no surprises. The one slight uncertainty was the new Marine representative, Captain Pete Olson. He was a little short on recent jet experience, but long on personality with a clear understanding of the team concept. He looked like the right choice. Unfortunately, Pete wanted to be accepted as a full-fledged member of the team without preliminaries. He hurried his practice, tried some delicate maneuvers at ground level, got too low and tied the world record for low-level flight at Padre Island.

It was with some long faces that we welcomed the third Marine, Captain Ed Rutty, who became the Number Six man, the opposing solo pilot. He, too, had the right attitude so he fit in well.

Our new team was like Santa's grab-bag of goodies. Lieutenant Nello Pierozzi, one of the earliest Navy jet pilots with a wealth of fighter experience, had a personality to match. Lieutenant (Junior Grade) Bill Gurreck was one of the best young airplane drivers around—and one of the straightest. Bill was our designated "Mr. Clean" and would fly with Nello and Ken Wallace in the diamond.

Then there was Lieutenant (Junior Grade) Edwin "Pink" McKellar, straight from a WestPac deployment, who must have taken lessons from "Phantom" Jones in flying airplanes—any airplanes. Ed adjusted perfectly as the lead solo. We did have a problem keeping him high enough off the ground so as not to scrape the radio antenna off the bottom of his F9F. I merely passed along some of the more descriptive phrases from my former skippers, and McKellar demonstrated instant comprehension!

After a couple of false starts we got the right PAO in Lieutenant Bruce "Baggy" Bagwell. He had all the right tickets, fit in without any fuss, and became one of the best PAOs the Blues ever had. I guess that includes me, since I had a shot at that job, but Baggy was tops.

With the 1954 season behind us, it was new airplane time. Next step up was Grumman's swept-wing F9F-8 Cougar. We sped as fast as 140 knots would take us in our R4D transport to Peconic, Long Island, to accept six spanking-new honeys just in time for our post-holiday return to El Centro. We checked into base ops and found that the Farmhouse Cafe still served the best tacos in town, then rolled up our sleeves to put the 1955 team together. We were blessed with the continuing services of Kenny Wallace, not only in the slot position, but as mentor, counselor, sometime chaplain and in-house guru. In short, we began assembling one hell of a show.

Of the new maneuvers contemplated, most impressive was the Fleur de Lis, which I concocted (with some variations) after watching the Air Force Thunderbirds at the Oklahoma City National Air Races. We were impressed with their "Bomb Burst" maneuver, and though we didn't admit it at the time, it became the basis for the Fleur de Lis, which we considered sufficiently different and more dramatic so nobody suspected.

Another addition to the new show was the "Tuck-Under Break," which we unashamedly stole from Duke Windsor's VF-23. We figured, "What the hell, it's all in the family," and for the most part Duke's squadron was pleased that we thought enough of their stuff to copy in toto. Today's team still uses it, slightly modified.

The diamond pilots worked for a month, perfecting a series of flight patterns we called the "Oiler," since it was a combination of three maneuvers rolled into one. It was a continuous evolution directly over the field, right in front of the crowd, close and low. We combined a steep Cuban Eight with a very tight loop, followed by a 360-degree turn on the deck, recovering directly before the audience. We thought it was sensational, as did the aviators in the crowd. Not so the airshow spectators. They gave our wonderwork a high ho-hum, which was echoed by our maintenance guys—our biggest fans but also our severest critics. The Oiler took too long to perform, and much to our chagrin, the diamond pilots learned that the crowds wanted to see more of the solos—especially the guy who flew so low that he would surely bust his ass. So we threw out the Oiler.

We did retain one maneuver the fliers appreciated more than the common folks—the Left Echelon Roll. It begins with the wingmen on the leader's left, slightly stepped down and back at a 45-degree angle, maintaining five-feet separation. The hitch is, the flying brotherhood believes the maneuver shouldn't be done because you never turn into your wingman unless it's a dire situation—every man for himself. Otherwise the prospects for a midair collision are very high indeed.

The run-in is level, about 300 feet above the ground, with the preparatory radio call, "This will be the left echelon roll." Each of the diamond pilots acknowledges with his first name. Then the leader announces, "Up we go," raising his nose to establish the altitude before starting the roll, followed by the call, "Coming left," starting a smooth transition left-wing down. Bill Gureck, the Number Two man, waited until my wingtip was about three feet over the top of his canopy before starting his roll, then keeping my wingtip in that exact position throughout the roll. Each man in sequence followed the same technique except Number Four, Kenny Wallace, on the outside of the roll and the end of the whip. He had the farthest distance to travel so the power-management equation was complicated. The leader's flight path on the inside of the roll is tighter and smaller than each succeeding plane, so Number One doesn't change his throttle setting. However, each wingman must add more power to maintain that three-foot separation. Then there's the recovery. That same amount of power which was added must be taken off as we emerge from the roll—five-foot separation, stepped down and back. Whew! If it sounds complicated, that's only because it is.

So we continued the '55 season with eight basic maneuvers, most of which became stock in trade, though all were intricate and eyeball-to-eyeball. Our schedule included several first-appearance show sites, which subsequently became regular stops on the team's agenda: Seattle Sea Fair; NAS Spokane, following a request from a longtime fighter pilot buddy of mine; Minneapolis only because it's there; Toronto, over Lake Ontario, which proved a very sporty course; NAS Olathe, Kansas; and the Naval Academy, up and down the Severn River amongst the radio towers—wires and all. So we broadened our sphere of influence. We were pleased and so were the recruiters.

This was also the year we gave serious consideration to standardizing our radio procedure. Assignment of a discrete frequency for the team's private use was a giant step in the refining process. On one hand, it eliminated spurious intrusions into our little world, but on the other it often encouraged spontaneous color commentary, especially in event of a hiccup in the routine.

One such event occurred during a hot summer day at NAS Glenview, near Chicago. The airshow committee decided it might enhance the entertainment value of the demonstration if the spectators could be privy to our radio transmissions during the show. One little snafu: the committee neglected to inform us.

We started in the normal fashion all very professional and business-like while thousands listening to the public address system were favored with our deliberations. All went well until we completed a rather lumpy loop in the bumpy air and I asked Kenny Wallace, "Ken, how did it go back there in the turbulence?" He answered, "OK, but on top I got bounced out of formation and you left me sitting out there all by myself, like a bottle of piss on the doctor's table."

"Well," I began, "we'll make up for it..." when I was interrupted by a frantic voice calling, "Navy One, Navy One! This is Glenview Tower, Glenview Tower!" By the tone in the voice and the obvious agitation, I thought, Christ, they've had an earthquake or something.

We finally established meaningful contact and the controller informed me that our radio transmissions were being broadcast via loudspeaker to the crowd. What could I say but, "Holy shit, maybe we'll just go land somewhere's else!" The audience heard that, too.

Somebody finally was smart enough to turn the radio switch to "off," we finished the show with very few comments just in case, landed at Glenview and taxied in to loud applause from the male spectators, and mostly snickers and shame-on-you looks from the ladies. Our radio procedure didn't get much better, but neither was it exposed publicly again.

We finished the season with a show and giant party at Pensacola. It was time for a breather, some toes-up or toes-down leisure, and especially some time at home. So we put the birds to rest and enjoyed the Thanksgiving-to-Christmas holidays at home in Pensy.

Reality again was forced upon us, though, and it seemed incredible that I was beginning my third year as Navy One. The El Centro workup seemed easier than usual because we had only one new face among us as Lieutenant (Junior Grade) Sheldon "Lefty" Schwartz joined Ed McKellar on the solo team. We moved the diamond around, giving Nello Pierozzi the job of filling the big shoes of Ken Wallace, now assigned to bigger but hardly better things. But Ken would return to the Blues again and again, once more as slot pilot, then as Number One. Little old ladies were always thrilled to see Kenny's silver hair!

Bill Gureck stayed on the wing and Captain Ed Rutty, after a year as solo, joined the diamond as left wing. The practice sessions went reasonably well with a bobble here or there, but nothing serious. Rutty had a tendency to get behind during some of the maneuvers but we all felt that a little time would solve things.

We thought we had the world by the tail when we wrapped up the training and headed for our first 1956 show—Miami Beach along hotel row. We did a couple of warmup maneuvers over the water before making our run-in to start the demonstration, more to loosen everyone up than anything, and it went OK. I cautioned everyone to take it slow and easy, not to rush since it was a lovely day with nice, smooth air so first-show-itis be damned. I checked all the nodding heads, which meant "Of course. We gotcha, Boss!" We headed in.

I called, "This will be the Diamond Roll." All acknowledged; "Ed," "Bill," "Nello," "Mac" and "Lefty." My next transmission was merely for execution, "Smoke on now," followed by "Up we go," and started the roll which went left, into my wingman, Ed Rutty.

Before we had completed half the roll, Ed and I were eyeball to eyeball, staring at one another canopy to canopy, three of us on our backs at 2,000 feet over the water and all of us wondering which way Rutty would choose to go. Ed departed the formation, miraculously missing everybody. So we gathered our sorely-tested nerves and finished the show with a three-plane diamond of the old musketeers. No one seemed to mind.

Captain Ed Rutty, Gold bless him, admitted he just wasn't cut out for that type of formation flying and requested reassignment, which was granted. He was replaced by Captain Chuck Holloway, who came highly recommended and who immediately proved he was a very talented aviator. We wasted no time with niceties but stuffed him into the diamond on my left wing and flew his socks off. He fit like he'd been doing it forever. So it was Semper Fi and Anchors Aweigh for the rest of the season.

I received advanced orders to be detached in October to assume command of Attack Squadron 113 at NAS Miramar. Needless to say, I was pleased with the prospect to finally have a squadron of my own, but there was completion of the Blues' remaining schedule to be considered. That concern soon was dispelled with appearance of Commander Ed Holley, a combat fighter pilot and test pilot with a logbook full of experience. He would relieve me following on-the-job training for the rest of the summer.

It was time to turn over the lead to a new Navy One. But as the saying goes, all good things must end, and it was with great reluctance that I finally had to say, "Zeke off—and clear."

1956-57

THE STINGER STORY

It is difficult to adequately express, in retrospect, the emotional perturbations I experienced upon receipt of the news that a command assignment awaited me. Suffice it to say, it was a proud moment. Still I felt a touch of disquietude knowing that an appointment of this distinction was a singular privilege. So it was that time to respond and exercise those tenets of leadership which had been so carefully yet on occasion forcefully, nurtured by some of the inspirational role models along the way.

Thus, in the fall of 1956, newly designated Light Attack Squadron VA-113, was to pipe aboard a new command officer. This also meant a return to the Fleet, the Pacific Fleet – it was a mighty nice feeling.

Lest the reader fret over the "defection" of this consummate fighter pilot to the Attack Community, a word of explanation is in order. The answer is not a simple, "Well, it just happened." I admit to some industrial-grade soul searching but my Officer Detailer in Bureau of Personnel did not exactly open a floodgate of options. However, the final choice was a tough one, but the contributing factor was unquestionably the prospect of flying the hot, spanking new tailhook A4D "Skyhawk". It was touted as the mighty midget with an abundance of muscle. Besides the aircraft platform, the light attack community's mission had plenty of sex appeal - delivery of nuclear weapons! There was also the promise of an entirely new array of attack hardware plus the new imaginative delivery techniques to match. It meant that the attack guys would definitely be in the midst of the action. Besides, I figure that if one were going to exit with a bang, where else could one do so in such flamboyant style.

I must admit too that the final clincher was the beckoning sunny climes of San Diego with the first-class facilities and the familiar, friendly environs of NAS Miramar - the picture was complete, it would be a joy to be back under the wing of AirPac again.

Fortunately, my detachment date coincided with the conclusion of the Blue Angels demonstration schedule, making the change of leadership with the new skipper, Ed Holley, a piece of cake. Ed took the reins with ease.

Without delay the trusty Buick station wagon was jammed with essentials: the family, the dog, a stalk of bananas and we hit the road for the Golden State. The way across the Southern states was a familiar route, uninspiring and long but we arrived at our designated destination safely, a little weary, but well.

In my anxiousness to reach my new duty station, I accelerated the schedule somewhat and learned that AirPac wasn't quite ready for me yet. What to do?!

It was determined, with my full concurrence, that I would be stashed for a couple of weeks in the Fleet Air Gunnery Training Unit, better known as the FAGU in good ol' El Centro. It meant flying with the elite of the fleet - essentially the fore runner of "Top Gun". It was a fortunate happenstance. And the fanciful good fortune continues. VA-113's new incoming Executive Officer, Pat Cunningham, an old and treasured friend, plus, the new operations officer, Mitch Simmons, unfamiliar but with an impressive reputation were all to share this singular respite in the same FAGU Flight Class. With the top three soon-to-be Stingers on board, we flew up a storm, practiced our new tactics, shot up caseloads of ammo, and established a comradeship that gave new meaning to Corps d'elite. It was one of those flying experiences that was pure joy and remains as one of my fondest memories of this naval aviation business. It was time to join the squadron and put all these perks to work.

At NAS Miramar, I relieved an old friend, Commander Doc Davis, a popular and skillful skipper who had molded VA-113 into a finely tuned combat-ready group of attack professionals. With the new titles in place, we were geared to accept the splendidly new equipment and continue the process of being ready for deployment.

Despite all the good words and promises from high command, one delay after another prevented delivery of the much awaited A4Ds. Therefore, we Stingers consoled ourselves with the old tried and true Grumman F9F-8s, in which I had already logged many happy hours. Flying Cougars again was like the Lone Ranger finding Tonto on the Arizona desert after a long separation - we knew one another intimately and held no secrets.

The Great Day finally dawned, however, and before long we had a row of shiny new Skyhawks on the Stinger flight line. Our morale - already disgustingly high-accelerated like a catapult shot. One-Thirteen's plane captains applied the bumble bee motif with the oversize stingers to each aircraft, and we were in business. With a good thrust-to-weight ratio in light configuration, the A4D was a nimble little hotrod, and some of Miramar's hot F9F pilots had their hands full trying to shake a Skyhawk from their six o'clocks. We may have been obnoxious, but were we motivated!

Things came into focus with our first deployment to the N AS El Centro complex. So again the home of FAGU provided the venue for some happy aviating, even if it included the potentially grim business of nuclear weapons training. In fact, the evolution proceeded superbly - everybody got along well, and the squadron genuinely melded into a unit during that stint in the desert. It recalled the sentiment I'd known in the Blues.

Our practice bombing targets took a hell of a pounding from our entire repertoire of lethal instruments, and individual scores showed we possessed some outstanding "shooters". Regrettably, the CO's name was not always found at the top of the bombing ladder - a fact that my Exec, Pat Cunningham, did his best to disguise. But inevitably the truth was discovered: the skipper did not, in fact, walk on water.

Among other things, we discovered that our bantam bomber was a wonderful formation airplane (a fact to which the Blues tumbled a decade or so later) so we put together a VA-113 flight demonstration team. I thought it was a good way to show what the Skyhawk could do. Of which you will read more late. It was to be the Stinger Demo-Diamond no less.

It was clear we had a winning team; not only among the pilots, but up and down the line. Our maintenance troops were thoroughly professional, and we had fine support from our factory tech rep, the redoubtable "Hook" Royer. Even now I can't recall his given name - to Douglas Aircraft and the U.S. Navy, he was simply "Hook." But the A4D itself deserved the kudos. It was extraordinarily well designed, with built in "maintainability" - a Douglas Aircraft/Heinemann trademark.

Upon our return to Miramar we were surprised to find ourselves listed on the schedule of events for the upcoming Miramar open house and air show - a yearly event of some import in San Diego. The events coordinator was a longtime friend and often time ship mate who felt that the VA-113 "friendly" squadron should show off the newest fleet-gray painted addition to the operational forces. He suggested a flyby, followed by a carrier-type approach and landing, plus a nuclear weapon delivery demonstration, perhaps the new 'over-the-shoulder" bombing technique. We readily agreed, knowing we could aptly comply.

It was planned that the fly-by would consist of a couple of high speed passes in the "Demo-Diamond", plus a formation roll at an altitude where the spectators could have a laudatory view of our birds, then, a formation landing, taxi to the parking ramp in pairs, open the canopies upon signal and wave hellos to the crowd - just like the Blues - well, maybe close. We would be billed as the "Albino Angels" - not the greatest title, nor what we had in mind, but what the hell, we'd be lucky not to end up in hack anyway. Little did I know.

The bomb drop was something else - that posed a two-fold problem. First, we had to release a practice bomb close enough to the spectators for them to appreciate the complexity of the maneuver and to observe our accuracy. Secondly, we had to achieve our goal with enough leeway to guarantee spectator safety, yet plant the bomb right on target.

After brainstorming the situation, we decided that the two goals were totally incompatible. In the real world of nuclear combat, we could literally afford to miss by a mile. Such parameters simply would not do with an airfield full of tax payers. The answer was really quite simple - use guile.

In pursuit of our subtlety, the troops fabricated a small building resembling nothing much more than an outhouse and placed it in an open area on the field about 200 yards in front of the spectator stands. My ordnance guys then implanted a hefty explosive charge in the "ground zero" structure rigged with a trigger device to be remotely activated from the announcer's stand.

Our delivery pilot would merely demonstrate the maneuver while the man on the mike delivered a blow-by-blow description of the action. We held a mini-audition in our ready room to determine the Stinger who could most enthusiastically (not to mention dramatically) describe the phantom bomb drop. The mission called for an exquisitely detailed narrative: from the moment the plane was sighted on its run-in, through the pull-up and weapon "release," then following the imaginary trajectory to "impact" with superb accuracy resulting in a "direct hit" on the target and resultant fiery explosion - it would be sensational.

The most junior ensign, Sam Jones, won the competition with a truly Shakespearean presentation. Pat Cunningham, the delivery driver, was equally superb, and VA-113 received rave reviews. The folks of San Diego still talk about "that air show" with the fleet fly-bys and the marvelous little gray airplanes flying tighter formation than the Blue Angels. And how about that bullseye bombing that demolished the outhouse? But there may be some from that audience who insist they never saw no goddamn bomb.

We were still basking in the glory of the moment a few days later when I was invited into the presence of Commander Naval Air Forces Pacific. "Hmmm. More kudos for the Stinger," I shrewdly assessed.

Presenting myself as requested at Vice Admiral A.M. Pride's office, I was ushered into the inner sanctum and there sat the legendary commander - I was impressed. However, the look on his face did not bode good things. He smiled slightly, the kind of smile that Big Fish use on Little Fish just before lunch. I stood at attention the prescribed distance from his desk, head up, remembering that it seemed that I had done this before, trying to appear self assured, without a glimmer of what awaited me. He didn't ask me to sit or stand at ease - it was very quiet - it would not take a rocket scientist to know this was not to be a lengthy meeting. Then, without preamble, ComAirPac inquired as to my recommendation for selection of a commanding officer for VA-113, then without pause, asked as to my "thoughts" regarding immediate assignment as windsock officer on the remote South Pacific island of Kapingamarangi. While I tried to formulate an appropriate response to either question, wondering too if there really was a place called Kapingamarangi, Admiral Pride interrupted my deliberations - the one sided conversation that followed made it plain that there was but one flight demonstration team in the US Navy and its name was the Blue Angels. Further that no time - that is, never, would there be another, especially with Mel Pride's assets. Now, if I did not understand the message, I should be fitted for a grass skirt, as that reportedly was the uniform of the day where I would be sent.

The message came through - loud and clear. I said something that sounded like, "Thank you, sir," then about-faced and marched toward the door. On the way out, however, I did hear him remark offhandedly something like, "The fake bomb wasn't bad."

With my course of action clearly defined, and with my priorities properly aligned, I turned VA-113's attention to FCLP: field carrier landing practice. It was one of the many blocks we had to fill before "hitting the boat" in preparation for a Pacific Ocean deployment.

Fortunately, I was blessed with Lieutenant George Boaz, the premier landing signal officer of the Pacific Fleet. Experienced, solid, extraordinarily talented, George sharpened us to a fine edge. Almost before we realized it, we were ready for the real thing: USS *Shangri-La* (CVA-38), a late World War II carrier of the *Essex* configuration. Not only VA-113, but all of Air Group Eleven did uncommonly well in an impressive display of professional ability. I know that as Stinger One, I was proud to be affiliated with the "Shang" team.

Sailing in Fall 1957 for WestPac, we hunkered down for the rigors of the Operation Readiness Inspection (ORI) in Hawaiian waters. There the Shang and her escorting ships passed their proficiency tests, and were duly certified as combat-qualified. Now all we needed was an adversary.

During calls to familiar ports - Subic Bay in the Philippines, Atsugi in Japan, etc., etc., we were blessed with super flying weather. It was a near idyllic interlude featuring some quality liberty, interspersed between planned fleet exercises.

Since I had decided I wanted nothing more to do with the airshow business following my tete-a-tete with Admiral Pride, the parade formation flying was done during lulls in our operational exercises - and then only somewhere remote for the gratification of my own pilots and any passing pelican. But only the most hard-core Stingers persisted in such endeavors; not everyone enjoyed the nifty sensation of going straight up or straight down or even upside down. Even so, the Albino Angels prospered quietly.

One unexpected opportunity did arise to perform publicly however. During a three-day orientation conference aboard *Shangri-La* , senior naval officers of the Southeast Asia Treaty Organization (SEATO) paid us a visit. The task group commander, Rear Admiral Paul Ramsey, wanted to provide the dignitaries a glimpse of his air group's prowess and laid on a live fire power exercise. He also hinted broadly that a flight demo of the Skyhawks would be in order if VA-113 cared to do the honors.

It was like turning a blind dog loose in a meat locker. My operations department went ballistic. "We can fly a series of nuke profiles, high and low angle bombing, maybe shoot a missile, maybe a high altitude training bomb drop. And, oh year, let's crank up the Albino Angels with colored smoke." Et cetera, et cetera.

I was on the spot, caught between a legitimate request from on high and my own troops' enthusiasm from below. But what's leadership, anyway? I threw caution to the wind, shook the dice and let 'em roll. How bad could it be at Kapingamarangi anyway?

A request to confer with Admiral Ramsey went through the CAG, who understood what was afoot, and bucked it up to Shang's skipper. He in turn sniffed around the problem and a conference was approved. As it turned out, my worries were ill founded since Paul Ramsey was well aware of my admonition from AirPac. He told me to rest easy, that the whole show including the demo flight had been cleared all the way back to D.C. Talk about relief. I was thankful to join the flock of "Ramsey's Little Lambsies."

We did the thing up right, complete with smoke, and red, white and flue fuel dumped from our belly tanks. Very colorful, though we left some ugly red and blue fuel stains on the flight deck as a result of the catapult shots. But the entire air wing show was spectacular. The SEATO folks went ashore totally mesmerized, except one British officer who had insisted on watching the cat-shots from up close. His dress whites still must look like Uncle Sam's uniform.

Then the Quemoy crisis popped.

At first we didn't know very much - situation normal for such events. Our big bosses in Pearl Harbor directed us to make haste toward the east coast of Taiwan. Scuttlebutt had it that the Chinese Communists were rattling their rice bowls. Something to do with the channel islands between the Taiwan island and the Asian mainland.

It shaped up as some rinky-dink rhubarb at the twilight end of our WestPac deployment, forcing our task group to stand by for possible intervention on behalf of Nationalist Chinese. The mainland ChiComs announced out of the blue that the islands, Quemoy and Matsu, belonged to them. The ChiNats, in effect, said, "To Hell with you guys. They're ours." Intel had it that an invasion fleet was assembling on the Communist Chinese coast, and all of a sudden our rinky dink back yard dispute assumed proportions of the real thing.

Three days of solid briefings covered everything from the global geopolitical picture to the hard realities of the hardware we might have to deliver. This was serious stuff. It got even more so with issue to all air crew of little bars of "Honest-to-God" bullion - bartering material in case we made an unscheduled visit to "the real China".

Aboard Shang, CVG-11's operations plan designated VA-113 as the major offensive unit to neutralize ChiCom airfields with "X" miles of the course - the details of which I have long since forgotten. But it shaped up as one A tough chore: low-level lay-down bomb runs on the runways and major installations. At this late date I'm not sure what the planners thought the MiGs would be doing during all this time, but nobody above squadron level seemed overly concerned. Outwardly, neither were we.

However, I pondered the irony. The glamorous nuclear weapons capability of the skyhawk had been a major selling point in switching to light attack from fighters. But here I was, preparing for an old fashioned iron bomb mission by reference to chewing-gum on the windscreen and the mark-one eyeball. So much for over-the-shoulder nuke delivery that had so impressed the good folks of San Diego.

Enemy landing craft and shipping would be the responsibility of the tried and tested AD-6 Spads of VA-115 while the whole operation was to be covered by the fighter outfits, VF-111 and -114, in addition to ChiNat F-86s from ashore. Just like the days of yore. Well, to a degree.

Despite any misgivings, picking my first team for the initial launch, a 0400 go in the dark - was the hardest part of the operation. We all felt it would be a very short war, one way or another, and the Stinger ready room was filled with a bunch of glory hounds, and frankly I can't exclude myself from that characterization. As the saying went, "It might not become much of a war but it was the only one we had."

As the Stinger' intrepid leader, I was expected not only to lead the pack, but to make some heroic remarks about duty, honor and other glorified incentives to call my men to arms. But, on reflection, the latter appeared wholly unnecessary. My young warriors were stoked and ready for action. I merely quoted some of General Patton's pointed statements. I still think what he said about the folly of dying for one's country makes a lot of sense. I'd rather make the other guy die for his.

As was only right, I would take the first launch with my regular division, plus Mitch Simmons and his three pilots: eight Skyhawks in all. The section leaders and wingmen were all greener than grass but all had good heads and hands, and there always has to be a first time to fly in harm's way. We received the latest situation report that, yes, the Chinese were loading troops into the landing craft, and the big guns on Quemoy were banging away at the Reds. Our airfield targets were strangely quiet. The briefing continued with a review of flight plans and attack procedures, right down to viewing day-old reconnaissance photos. Then it was suit-up time and we shrugged into our flight gear.

Girding for battle - whether the steed be a valiant charger or a sporty Skyhawk - seemed to draw a line for a warrior. By pulling on a suit of armor or a flight suit, he tells himself that he is preparing to conduct his business. Thus, when "Pilots, man your planes." Flashed across the teletype screen at 0330, we hit the flight deck running. But the night was blacker than inside your hard hat so we proceeded at a more leisurely pace to preclude self-inflicted casualties.

Manning up was uneventful, and we went about our business preparing for the 0400 launch. Strapped into our cockpits, there we waited - and waited. Mentally pacing, pondering all the imponderables, we slipped from anticipation, to concern, to unease. Hours ticked by and the sun rose behind us. Everybody who's ever been in the Navy knows about "standing by to stand by" but this was ridiculous. Finally, after my entire body had gone bye-bye, the flight deck PA system came through with The Word. Over the IMC we learned that the war was over. This seemed to be the only sensible conclusion to this squabble.

Throughout the *Shangri-La* , which had been off Japan on 15 August '45, it was like V-J Day all over again. The Chinese Communists came to their senses, possibly wondering what was so important about tiny barren islands. My sentiment exactly - I'm not so sure about the hawks.

Still, I couldn't have been more proud of my troops, or of the entire Air Group and Ship, for that matter. The curtain had fluttered, ready to rise on another conflict and the front line would-be combatants strapped on the battle gear and began passing the ammunition.

So with that done we went about making preparation for our last visit to Hong Kong and then home. It had been a very eventful exercise and the cruise was only eight months away.

I would fly home since I had a rendezvous to keep with my detailer, Commander Air Wing Eleven was on the horizon.

1958

LUCKY ELEVEN

Only with great reluctance did I relinquish the driver's seat of VA-113 to the new CO, Commander Spence Matthews. My lamentations were twofold: because my idyllic interlude with the Stingers was so short, and because the skipper's job was not passed on to my talented and deserving executive officer, Pat Cunningham. He was unquestionably the mainspring of 113's leadership team, and his personal contribution provided the Stingers with a touch of class.

Despite my recommendation on Pat's behalf, the mysterious manipulators of the personnel management in D.C. had their way. However, Pat shortly got his own squadron, proving a dynamite front horse. I was pleased, because the situation allowed me to "fleet up" to the "top gun" spot of Air Group 11—in name if not in fact! Command of a carrier air group (now called an air wing) was the goal to which most naval aviators aspired. But leadership skills were at a premium. It's one thing to be a tiger—entirely something else to become a tiger tamer!

But this was, after all, still the United States Navy, and the niceties had to be observed. That meant Catching Up On Paperwork. At this time NavAir had promulgated a directive which more or less permanently assigned each air group to a specific aircraft carrier. Actually, it wasn't a new idea—merely an old one reinvented but nonetheless perceived as Something New. In short, Air Wing 11 (CVG-11) was "permanently" mated with USS

Shangri-La from our previous cruise.

That was the good news. The bad news: we were to deploy on an extended WestPac in ninety days. The worse news: it wouldn't be a standard six-month deployment, but an eight-month cruise to meet U.S. interests in the Western Pacific. Reactions to this highly-interesting bit of intelligence were both predictable and varied: pissing and moaning among the married folk; something approximating enthusiasm among the bachelors for "getting out of town."

At this point, I might note that the term "cruise" always seemed incongruous for a combat-ready ship-air group team ready to meet any National Emergency. To me, a cruise is something you take on a love boat. But the term originated sometime in the 1930s, when carriers spent far less time at sea, and it's now part of naval aviation jargon.

Regardless of sentiment or syntax behind our mission, as CAG my directive had to be, "OK, gang, let's make this thing work." And damn if we didn't. I leaned heavily on my second- and third-cruise people who had the experience and ability to get the myriad of things done on time. Besides carrier qualification landings for all pilots, there were just oodles of Other Things To Do: fitness reports, periodic howgozit reports, maintenance and materiel inspections—almost everything for poor ol' CAG—except flying!

However, at length "Shang" sailed westward and my accumulation of baleful trivia was consigned to the deep somewhere off Hawaii. My CAG staff was aghast. The ship's secretary was appalled. And the task force admiral's flag secretary was positively apoplectic. I just figured, "Screw it. I'm gonna fly."

As we neared Hawaii we prepared for the dreaded Operational Readiness Inspection (ORI). This evolution always carries an air of emotional expectation about it, though the old WestPac hands considered it an inevitability akin to the virgin bride's realization that "abedding time" is neigh. The attitude—in both instances—is approximately the same: "We know it's inevitable, but how long and how hard is it going to be?"

ORIs are better described as simulated combat—an exercise conducted during a short stay in Hawaiian waters to measure the ship and air wing's preparedness for war. Every aspect of carrier ops, from fire-fighting to putting ordnance on target, is scrutinized by an on-board investigating team usually composed of hard-nosed, war-wise observers who seemingly relish every minor flaw they uncover. Some CAGs and carrier skippers have admitted to preferring root-canal work—or a genuine war. ORIs have probably never made anybody's career, but they've certainly curtailed a few.

Well, we got on it. And the old "Shang" with her air group and escorts, while displaying some raggedy patches requiring rehab, generally performed with excellence. The inspectors admitted surprise, but the admiral's staff was astonished, the captain was overjoyed, his department heads demonstrated elation, and the ship's company was positively ecstatic. As for CVG-11, we were not surprised. We figured we already knew about "outstanding" ratings!

For instance: during the air-attack phase, the designated targets on Kahului island practice bombing range took a tremendous drubbing, resulting in several exceptionally high bombing scores. The "Spad" drivers of VA-115 turned into aerial deadeyes. In their propeller-driven Douglas Skyraiders, they flew attack profiles of eight hours from launch to landing. Some pilots had to be lifted from their cockpits after recovery. Sitting on an unrelenting, rock-hard parachute pack after a standard four-hour cycle was bad enough. Believe it, the aviator's rear ends were transformed into hocks of dead meat, so just imagine the literal pain-in-the-ass after twice that time.

But my Spad drivers, God love 'em, ignored the extreme discomfort, delivered their ordnance with deadly accuracy in a bold display of skill and daring. Despite being a confirmed fighter pilot, I had to admire the piston-slappers. Their attitude seemed to shout, "Jets are for kids!"

My only personal glitch of the ORI was trying to get aboard one night—it wasn't even particularly dark. After two bolters resulting in low fuel state, I was "bingoed" to the beach. The carrier controller gave me a vector to NAS Barbers Point, pointedly adding that I could try my luck landing there! I thought it a mite snide, then recalled my sweaty-palm evolution as an escort-carrier aviator flying that big old TBF in the stormy North Atlantic. Pride can be such a burden.

Saying aloha to the islands, the task group continued westward with flight ops en route, affording the aviators sight-seeing privileges to many WW II battlegrounds. I couldn't help contrasting the situation with the first time I'd seen those same places from a Hellcat cockpit. The natives had turned downright friendly!

The first glimpse of Mt. Fuji rising majestically on the far horizon announced our arrival in Japanese waters. For a little while we would enjoy flying from shore at our old stomping grounds of Atsugi. There our aircraft would receive much-needed maintenance, as the marvelous Japanese crafts-men employed at "Atsugi Base" could turn a salt-and sun-faded old bird into a like-new spring chicken.

Not the least consideration was the Sagami-Osaka tea houses which anticipated a brisk trade for a couple of weeks. While some of the local samurai perhaps were not overjoyed at the prospect, they nursed a well-honed appreciation of the Yankee Dollar. Our unofficial headquarters was an establishment called the Green Garden on the outskirts of Yokosuka (pro-nounced Yo-kus-ka, for some damn reason.) My attack squadrons seemed to settle in for the duration, making it easy to keep tabs on the VA guys. The others scattered to the four winds. In those bygone days of yesteryear, al-most any American could afford an evening in Tokyo. No more!

Returning to sea for our appointed rounds of the Pacific Rim, "Shang" linked up with her sister ship, USS *Oriskany* (CVA-34), commanded by Cap-tain Tom Connolly, who had many stars in his future. Three of 'em, to be exact, to say nothing of undying fame as inspiration for the name of the F-14 Tomcat. We knew even in those days that he was a force to be reckoned with, especially when teamed with CAG Lee Johns and his merry men—a talented bunch of carrier aviators.

The at-sea rendezvous and joint operations were a stirring sight, and brought back memories of similar compositions from the not-too-distant past. Shang's entire crew reacted to the stimuli; there was a visible increase in zeal as CVA-38/CVG-11 paraded our superior modus operandi. But *Oriskany* responded in kind. It was probably a standoff as to the superior team, but naturally we claimed dominance. Naturally, Tom and Lee thought other-wise.

Therefore, we sought to settle the affair with a joint social affair, gath-ering the two air groups ashore at Cubi Point in the Philippines. It was one humongous assembly, resulting in the air group superiority matter being laid to rest, if not solved. The method: two very carefully-selected reps, one from each air group, engaged in toe-to-toe combat. Well, that may be an exaggeration. Actually, we decided upon a leg-wrestling contest, two out of three falls to determine the winner.

The Cubi officer's club had all the trapping of the professional arena: wild cheering, raucous taunting, with the "Hunk" and the "Hulk" indulg-ing in much flexing, grunting and sneering—right there on the O'Club floor. The roar that went up when our very own Hulk prevailed was probably heard in the Bagio highlands, where the natives probably thought, "Christ, the Spaniards are back with an new Inquisition." Not to worry. The crazy (and no doubt ugly) Americanos were merely celebrating another glorious victory. We had some shrewd engineering types who calculated that Hulk's low center of gravity did the trick for "Lucky Eleven." But victory never comes cheap. As victors, we were required to become the hosts for the rest of the evening—a very wet evening, too!

With the critical issues settled, there was time for one more quick R&R period before our final time on the line. Hong Kong's lovely harbor beckoned, and that meant one thing: Shopping Time. If you've ever criticized your female relations for an inbred "shop til they drop" complex, you should have beheld CAG-11 and company. The Colonial Island and environs was the premier liberty port in those days—sailors actually re-enlisted just to return to the fabled city. To me, Hong Kong always will be the Pearl of the Far East, and if that sounds like a hackneyed travel brochure, so be it. Anybody who Joined the Navy to See the World got his money's worth at the fabulous Crown Colony.

The final weeks of our cruise were conducted with relative ease amid the relaxed assurance that we had done our job, and done it damn well. However, I soon recognized this operating period as the concluding chapter in the carrier flying days of my life. The top slot in an air group was merely a fleeting privilege. To me, it was a stunning realization! The flying assignments after a CAG billet were considerably fewer and therefore much more difficult to acquire. And even then, they could never replace the everyday adventure and challenge of flying off a bird barge.

With this pitiable awareness firmly in mind, the flight schedules were filled with CAG's name in every type of mission the air group performed. The flying included rides in the A3D-1 Skywarrior, better known as the "Whale" for its great size. Ed Heinemann's masterpiece proved a survivor—four decades later it's still flying in the Navy, though not from carriers anymore. Nevertheless, I admit that I didn't try to repeat my night hop. Those Whale drivers deserved double flight pay if for no other reason than merely keeping up with their laundry bills! My brief fling with the heavy attack detachment reaffirmed my professional admiration for those folks, whether they dropped bombs, pumped gas or blasted electrons.

The pure joy of flying was achieved with VF-111, led by Jack Godfrey. He was a fighter skipper of the old school—kick the tires, light the fire and have at it! The refresher in the Grumman F11F-1 Tiger was more than just a convivial use of time. It's the only way of knowing where one's capabilities lie. For a fighter ace, it was like being back in the saddle again, and I felt that the seat fit me as if molded to my form. True, there were some snide comments from the Sundowners—mostly concerning CAG's prospects of hitting a bull in the behind with a bass fiddle. But fighter aviating was sheer pleasure, and I did hit the bulls at least a couple of times.

I filled my logbook with all manner of wonderworks, and let the paperwork be damned. If I had it to do again, I'd try to double that flight time!

Yet inevitably I turned over the leadership of CVG-11. To make matters worse, I had to atone for my good times in "Shang" by doing penance in the Puzzle Palace on the Potomac, slaving in OpNav in Washington. I went where I was ordered, but psychologically I was dragged away with a doorknob in each hand and heel marks on the floor.

I still see some of my old friends and shipmates from those happy days. But poor old Shang herself went to an inglorious end—sold to the Japanese, she was towed ignominiously across the Pacific and scientifically sliced into razor blades.

1961-1962

WINDAGE ON THE WASP

In the fall of 1961 I returned to sea in a "new" home-away-from-home: the antisubmarine carrier USS *Wasp* (CVS-18). My billet was the number-two spot as executive officer, which meant I was at least nudging closer to the skipper's chair on the bridge. It also meant that I'd be home-ported on the Atlantic coast, scene of my tailhook origins lo those many years ago. As Yogi Berra said, it was deja-vu all over again: shades of hunting U-boats from the Good Ship *Card*, vintage 1943.

I had hoped my orders would be to an area of operations that was familiar, friendly and fraternal. Some of the more cynical members of the profession might have sensed warning signals tickling the hairs on the backs of their necks at "change of ocean" orders—especially considering it had been nearly twenty years since I'd darkened AirLant's door. If nothing else, I resolved to return to the public park that bore the sign, "Sailors and dogs keep off the grass." Not surprisingly I discovered that, with a little enlightenment, attitudes do change

However, there was one bit of luck: *Wasp*'s home port was Boston, where I found the English language spiced with a touch of compelling distinctiveness, some with a hell of a dialect. Fortunately, the South Boston Naval Annex proved a hospitable retreat, but it was a far cry from the familiar, harmonious, unassailable Pacific Fleet. To this day I harbor dark suspicions about the motives of the "flesh peddlers" of BuPers...

...ne year old Richard L. Cormier, aspiring ...ator. Not yet knee-high to a 30 x 5 wheel, the ...ure fighter ace sizes up a Ryan Brougham at ...tch Flats near San Diego. (Cormier)

Closer to wings of gold, Aviation Cadet Cormier in 1941. The training aircraft in the background is a Naval Aircraft Factory N3N-3. (Cormier)

A Grumman F4F Wildcat of VC-1. (Cormier)

...e's first fleet aircraft was the Grumman TBF, which he flew on anti-submarine patrol in the Atlantic ...ing 1943. The Avenger made a fine vehicle for hunting U-boats, but left much to be desired for a ...ld-be fighter ace. (Cormier)

The aircraft carrier, *Card*, CVE-11, had a dainty 400 foot flight deck. Aircraft on deck with wings folded are Grumman Wildcats and Avengers. (USN via Lambert)

A pair of German U-Boats under aerial attack by *Card* aircraft. (USN via Lambert)

The Grumman F6F-5 Hellcat, which Zeke flew in the Pacific, produced more American aces than any other aircraft. (USN)

rils of the profession. Zeke's wingman, Ens. John Fraifogl, nearly burned up in his F6F upon landing oard *Ticonderoga* on 1 July 1944. The jar of landing dislodged his belly tank, which was thrown rward into the propeller. The resulting fire incinerated the Hellcat but Fraifogl escaped. (USN)

The war's not over 'til the paperwork's done. Lts. Pat Fleming and Zeke Cormier getting their stories straight for an after action report aboard USS *Ticonderoga* (CV-14) in 1944. Fleming ended the war with nineteen confirmed kills; Zeke with eight. (Cormier)

Zeke's friends insist, "You can clean him up a take him anywhere." Lt. Cormier in dress wh December 1947. (Cormier)

Why is this man smiling? It's de rigueur for the skipper of the Blue Angels, the Navy precision flig demonstration team, circa 1954.

The team's shiny F9F-2 Panthers in trademark diamond formation. (USN)

The 1955 season featured swept-wing F9F-6s, here trailing colored smoke in tight formation with wings overlapping. If you do it right, it looks as easy as it appears here. (USN)

Diamond four plus one, pulling up during practice at the Blue Angels' home drome, Corpus Christi. (USN)

The Stingers of VA-113 flew the A4D Skyhawk, which Zeke promptly put to service in the impromptu "Albino Angels" aerobatic team. Officialdom was not impressed. (USN)

Zeke as Exec of the *Wasp*, 1961. (Cormier)

e good deals just kept coming. In 1958 Zeke was
mmanding officer of Attack Squadron 113, here
nferring with his executive officer, Lt. Cdr. F.F.
nningham. (USN)

sp 's task group in action: airborne S2F Trackers, AD Skyraiders and helicopters with five
troyers. (USN)

Like the ads used to say: ask the man who owns one. After flying Skyhawks in the Navy, Zeke liked them so much that he began selling them for Douglas Aircraft. L-R: test pilot Nick Knickerbocker, Pres. Jack McGowan, sales reps Bob Canady and Howard Cleveland with Zeke. (Cormier)

American Fighter Aces Association meeting at San Diego, 1970. These five aces accounted for 77 Japanese aircraft in WWII. L-R: Marion Carl (Marine Corps), Robert L. Scott (Army Air Force), John Alison (Army Air Force), Zeke and fellow Navy ace Gene Valencia. (Cormier)

So, United States Ship *Wasp* received a new executive officer, better described as the officer of stewardship—even better described as the housekeeper. I would be stepping into the brown shoes of a very capable friend and fellow fighter ace, Commander Leo B. McCuddin, who was off to bigger and better things leading to flag rank. He had been an outstanding administrator, especially in exercising his considerable talent for finding just the right person to satisfy any tough assignment onboard. All those individuals were in place and "happy in their work," so my transition to XO was pleasant, with little trauma. However, looking after some 5,000 souls takes some doing—as I was soon to discover.

Despite my exalted position and authority, I was still second man on the totem pole. *Wasp* was blessed with the leadership of a South Carolina gentleman, suh—Captain William Wiley, USN, a genuine aristocratic patriarch of the patrol-plane persuasion. However, while an extremely accomplished naval officer, long on southern charm and incantations, he was short on flying experience—especially in carrier operations. With this quality of guidance, we were the social darlings of navy society when tied to the South Baaston pier, but at sea during flight quarters the captain's inverse directions made for a less-than-convivial atmosphere on the bridge.

Wasp had long enjoyed a special reputation as the carrier *grand seigneur* of the antisubmarine world, and her crew was more than anxious to keep it that way, so the captain's bridge on occasion lacked the cheerful quality it may have known in days previous. During such times of tension I tried to be elsewhere, looking after my housekeeping chores, but it was not to be. I spent many hours on the bridge, at Captain Wiley's express invitation, wringing my own hands when not holding his.

The saving grace in keeping our seagoing kingdom from anarchy, if not actual revolt, came in the person of Rear Admiral Paul Buie, the task group commander. He flew his two-starred flag in *Wasp*, as the carrier was flagship of Task Group Bravo, and therefore was ever close at hand.

Paul Buie was an old-school fighter pilot who had plied his trade aboard a variety of carriers, from the big, beautiful *Saratoga* (CV-3) and the first carrier *Wasp* (CV-7), sunk off Guadalcanal, to the second *Lexington* (CV-16). If you wanted to ask about the fundamentals of flattop strategy or employment, Admiral Buie was your man. Through his guiding presence—though primal and vigorous at times—our shipboard sovereign could not but help learn to rule with a steadier hand. Paul Buie simply would not let his Task Group Bravo tread the well-worn path of mediocrity; only trail-blazing excellence would do!

In part, I suspect that the captain kept me on the bridge to share the specter of Admiral Buie's eternal presence: if Wylie were apt to get yelled at, he wanted to share the honor with a deserving champion. There could be no doubt—our forthcoming cruise was shaping up as a real lulu.

So our at-sea training progressed colorfully. The good admiral, being the way that former fighter pilots usually are, badgered poor old Bill Wiley without letup from the moment flight quarters were underway until the last airplane was safely secured. At the conclusion of an operating period that had been reasonably-well conducted, it was not uncommon for the flag bridge to use the squawk-box to send up a message from the admiral: "Well, Bill, don't you think this is more fun than flying those old P-boats?"

To which our southern gentleman might reply, "Ah don' think this venue can be considuhed with cruise-ship jocularity, admiral, suh." The meaning of which remained open to interpretation. I always suspected that Captain Wylie wanted to say, "Screw you...suh!" Which, of course, any fighter pilot would instantly comprehend and appreciate.

Meanwhile, I didn't have anyone looking over my shoulder as most execs do, checking on the manner in which my duties should be conducted. Lacking such guidance from on high, I just pretended that I knew what the hell I was doing, and all hands pressed on.

However, I did make one solemn pledge—I would make a concerted effort to perfect those activities directly under my control: food and living quarters, liberty and recreation, discipline, etc. The opportunity to exercise that vow was soon upon me.

A serious winter-time base-transportation discrepancy surfaced, the discrepancy being that there was none! The Naval Annex essentially had been deactivated and the transport vehicle pool had been first to go, so the poor folks coming and going from the ship to the main gate slogged through all manner of New England weather. We badly needed some wheels and a bus was the logical answer, but how to acquire one?

Taking the initiative (always risky business for an exec), I declared the situation fell under the heading of "recreation." *Wasp's* recreation officer—whose ancestors just happened to be New England horse traders—

armed with an expenditure authorization chit (duly signed by ship's executive officer), removed himself to the local "pre-owned" automobile emporium. He returned with one each, sturdy, well-cared for ex-school bus ready for new duties. Our pedestrian troops were so overjoyed that they had it in and out of the paint shop in days, appropriately decked out in *Wasp*'s official colors—which, happily enough, were mostly blue.

The sole dissenting group from CVS-18 was the ship's baseball team, which realized there would be mighty slim pickings come spring when they needed new equipment. But we determined to burn that bridge when we came to it. Personally, I hoped we'd be at sea by then and the problem would solve itself.

The next phase of the campaign involved convincing the captain that our newly-acquired rolling stock should be listed as part of "essential" hangar-deck equipment for our upcoming European deployment. We couldn't very well describe our Blue Whale as plane-handling equipment, but we came close by labeling the behemoth plane handlers' gear. (We were probing the semantic envelope, but what the hell—if it works, it works.)

The justification plan was going favorably when a minor engine casualty required that we find a hard-to-get part. That glitch blew the Whale out of the water. The skipper's rationale—that it could happen in a foreign hinterland, and we'd have to strap down the Whale, taking up precious hangar-deck space—probably had merit.

If we had given the problem a tad more time and some extra-creative thought, it would have solved itself. One of the genius metal-benders in the ship's machineshop allowed as how he could mend or make any part for any piece of rolling stock—new, old, antique, foreign or domestic—you name it. And he did! With the new "Wasp Works" replacement part in place, the Blue Bomb proved a survivor—at least in Boston.

Task Group Bravo departed Boston Harbor that winter of 1961, anticipating a long and alluring list of ports of call: Bermuda, Iceland, (*Iceland*?), England, Scotland, Norway, Denmark, Germany and Holland, plus points in between. A cruise like that did wonders for our re-enlistment rate. Imagine that, join the Navy and See The World!

First stop, Bermuda. Marvelous. Nothing could be better to shake off the dreary mindset of a Massachusetts winter. We sailed into shirtsleeve weather, the ASW aviators stowed their foul-weather "poopy suits" and flew to their hearts' content. Even I was happy—it felt like being back in WestPac.

It was also a good time to pay attention to the waning opportunity of maintaining my neglected flight proficiency. To this point, those hard-earned skills were showing signs of rust so I hit upon a novel solution: learn to fly the ship's helicopter.

The chopper detachment's officer-in-charge, a nice young and impressionable lieutenant (JG), had been a Blue Angels fan since flight training. Furthermore, he and I determined that we had met during a Pensacola social engagement when he was just a pup. (I reminded myself that it always pays to be nice to people—you never know when they can do you a favor!)

Consequently, my young friend allowed as he'd be pleased to fly with a former Blue Angel, no matter that the not-so-current driver always had problems patting his head while rubbing his tummy at the same time—a procedure widely rumored to indicate latent rotor-wing talent.

If this young heloperson hadn't been blessed with a double-dose of patience, I suspect the task would have been impossible. However, through diligent persuasion and much blind faith, I did qualify in the ship's Piaseki HUP-2 and spent some unfettered time looking at wavetops and, occasionally, a foreign countryside. However, I'm bound to admit that the deckhands and planehandlers usually appeared as though they were searching for a nice, deep foxhole in the flight deck each time I came aboard. It was never publicly stated, but there was always that trace of disbelief in their eyes, betraying their thoughts: "Good Christ, here comes the exec again! Get that crash gear out so we'll be ready when he busts his ass!"

Despite the full slate of activities and responsibilities that occupy an executive officer, there are some amenities and perquisites which brighten his day. One such is the eternal presence of a United States Marine lance-corporal orderly. This crewcut, earnest, deadly-serious young man watches over the well-being of the XO, including the comings and goings of persons to the exec's office and quarters. Without exception, the orderly epitomizes the recruiting-poster Marine: uniform immaculate or better, hat in place just so, brim at eye-level, leather and web gear spotless and then some. Hell, I got so I felt inferior in the kid's presence—I never looked so good!

When the XO moves about the ship, his orderly is always a close companion. It's a naval tradition, the reason for which is somewhat obscure but undoubtedly was required during the Captain Bligh era of seafaring. But to this day, the exec and his orderly are a familiar sight throughout the ship. With the right chemistry, the bond between these two grows very strong.

My constant escort was a bright, personable young man of Irish extraction from the Great State of Oregon. Mike O'Donahoe seemed the personification of the best in Gaelic culture. He was proud of being a Marine and particularly pleased in his assignment as my safeguard. One day, as we were making a look around the myriad spaces in the ship, we passed through the berthing quarters of the Marine detachment—the "MarDet." About fifty leathernecks were performing routine maintenance on their weapons, which even to my untutored eye looked spotless. Mike's comments indicated that his CO was very particular about the traditional spit-and-polish of his troops, and their adherence was obvious.

Upon completion of our tour, Mike asked if he might make a request and I said, "Sure, request away." He said that it was his fond desire that I personally inspect the Marine guard during the forthcoming personnel inspection. Normally such duty is the prerogative of the ship's captain, and on most occasions it was a perfunctory review, not the direct examination of each Marine's equipment and weapon. What Mike O'Donahoe wanted touched a nerve.

On the spot I was hooked with the thought—a naval officer conducting an inspection in the Corps' time-honored close-order drill, including handling and examining the rifle. The troops would be so stunned that they would drop their socks! I heard myself say, "We'll do it."

First I cleared the deal with the skipper, who was initially reluctant but truthfully relieved to be free of the chore. Then the strategy session with Mike. He would bring his rifle, in absolute secrecy, by whatever means required ("Don't ask, Cormier," I told myself) to my quarters every night for two weeks. There we would practice the formal procedure. "But," I added, "if you are discovered during the commission of this arrangement I will disavow any knowledge of said plot and you will probably be keel-hauled—or at least dealt an appropriate stint in rustication for divulging the Secrets of the Corps." O'Donahoe wasn't sure about either of those potential perils but he calmly replied, "If Mr. Phelps can get away with a 'mission impossible,' what am I—dog meat? Sir!" My silent sentiment was *That's my boy!*

The lance-corporal's M-1 rifle suffered several tense moments over the next few days, but nothing occurred of major or calamitous consequence, and eventually I could twirl, whirl and otherwise flourish the Garand without dropping it or sighting down the wrong end. I admit, however, that even under Mike's expert tutelage, I still fell short of "the Few, the Proud, the Marines."

Inspection day arrived, and I made my appointed rounds with more than a little anticipation about the impending MarDet encounter. Then the moment arrived! The Marine captain saluted smartly, as only Marine captains can do, and assured me that his command was "ready for inspection, sir!"

I said something impressive, like "Very well," and started down the front rank. Eyeing each Marine carefully, noting the excellence of their appearance, I stopped and faced the fifth man in line—a tall, nordic-featured youngster with a barrel chest, a waist any lady would die for, and arms about twice the diameter of mine. This was the moment of truth. Why, I wondered, why the hell did I pick such a formidable-looking specimen for my initial attempt at this? But it was now or never, do or die, there's no tomorrow. (At that point I ran out of cliche's.)

At the last moment another thought flashed through my mind: If this big Swede doesn't let go of his rifle as he's supposed to, I'll really be in deep shit. I envisioned a tug-of-war between one surprised, possibly frightened Marine and a desperately earnest naval officer.

Shoving the image aside, I grasped the rifle, flipped it out of his hands, spun the piece around and peered down the barrel. Then I turned it upright, peered into the open breech and handed it back to the Swede in one fluid movement, just like I knew what I was doing.

The Swede didn't blink an eye, but did allow a sly smile—we were instant friends. The Marine captain was absolutely dumbfounded and stood transfixed as I continued trooping the line. He caught up in time to witness my next test case, just to prove to all hands—myself included—that the previous exhibition was not an aberration. The second bit of business went equally well! Though the remainder of the assemblage was given a thorough looking-over, I knew better than to press my luck with the weapon inspection. The Marines were pleased and remained proud; I was happy and proud; Mike was ecstatic. He still talks about that event today.

British liberty ports were especially pleasant, including Glasgow and the Firth of Clyde in Scotland. But the crew's favorite was the old seafarers' town of Portsmouth, whose enduring association with those who sail the seas instilled an alluring sense of charity toward spirited young sailors of any navy. The townsfolk took very good care of our young men, and I suspect the shore patrol was ever so grateful. I know I was!

Portsmouth also provided a wealth of naval presence and maritime history. In this regard, I was priviliged to have as tour-guide a retired Royal Navy commander whose wartime exploits as a destroyerman during the U-boat scourge would make a book in itself. Under his astute leadership as docent, there wasn't a piece or place of naval history left unexamined. My favorite was Admiral Horatio Nelson's flagship, HMS *Victory*, in fullly restored splendor, still flying the commander-in-chief's flag as she had in the Battle of Trafalgar.

For lack of a better word, the tour was inspiring. Visitors are guided through the ship by sailors dressed in 1805 uniforms, and we saw it all. After we had toured the foc's'le, the carronades, the shot garlands, the tiller head, the after-hanging magazines, the shot locker and powder room (a real powder room, not the feminine variety), we made our way onto the quarter deck. There our young attendant pointed to a brass plaque imbedded in the deck plating and explained that it marked the spot where the gallant admiral fell. From the back of the tour group, the voice of a staid-looking English woman rose, saying, "Oh, yes. Well, I'm not surprised. I almost tripped over the damn thing meself!"

Wasp's excursion in western Germany was filled with a long list of events beyond the norm for a carrier task group deployment. Kiel, with its famous shipyards, is one of the principal naval bases for the Federal German Republic, was a port of call for ten days in the spring of 1962. We were told that CVS-18 was the first aircraft carrier so honored, but I learned it wasn't quite true. Actually, *Wasp* was the first operating flattop so honored— and thereby hangs a sea story.

During the early days of WW II the Third Reich built two *flugezeuge traeger* in Kiel's shipyards, named *Hindenberg* and *Graf Zeppelin*. The former was destroyed by allied bombing but the latter—the most fascinating naval might-have-been of the war—was never outfitted, never had aircraft aboard, and fell into Soviet hands. *Graf Zeppelin* foundered under tow back to Russia and was lost. So USS *Wasp* was the first operating carrier to visit Germany's motherland of shipbuilders. Needless to say, we became an instant attraction.

However, getting to Kiel took some doing. We had to transit the channel waters of the Skagerrak between Norway and Denmark, then navigate the narrow strait of the Kattegat into the Baltic Sea. However, we had practiced our close-in seamanship two weeks prior to the German port visit with a trip up the Christiania Fjord leading from the Skagerrak to Oslo. The only anxious moment was when the old senior fighter pilot on board got a mite nervous, but Admiral Buie let Captain Wylie do his thing.

Our stay in Kiel was blessed with a succession of reciprocal social events with the extremely-hospitable citizens and with the naval personnel of neighboring Kiel-Holtenau, home of the Federal Republic's aerial ASW training base. Naturally, *Wasp*'s aviators had much in common with their German counterparts, and all hands consumed vast quantities of superb champagne with appropriate toasts to everyone but the messboys, though I suspect they too became toastees since it's poor form to repeat a toast. In European fashion, there was much crashing of glasses following each salute, and the stone fireplace took a severe pounding but I heard that such high-spirited behavior was considered natural when observing the interests of allied unity.

The capper to the Kiel visit was an open house aboard ship for anyone in the vicinity who wished to partake. We enlisted the help of Federal German Navy sailors to control the attendees on base, and to manage the comings and goings of folks along the quay. The plan was to have our guests enter by the forward gangway, go up to the flight deck on the forward elevator, down the deck to the aft elevator, thence down and through the hangar bays where aircraft were parked, and to depart via the after gangway. Coffee and doughnut stands were stationed along the route. It sounded like a good plan.

The appointed morning brought drizling rain and a chilling breeze, which prompted the disturbing thought that we'd be all dressed up with nothing to do. Worse yet, what would we do with mountains of doughnuts, not to mention a reservoir-full of coffee?

Nevertheless, the German sailors arrived on time, jumped out of their lorries, adjusted their uniforms, lined up smartly, clicked their heels and announced they were ready for inspection and instructions. I was totally impressed, and remember thinking, "Jeez, I'm glad they're on our side this time!"

The troops both ashore and aboard were no sooner in place when the main gates were opened and a flood of people, all armed with foul-weather gear of every description, swarmed over the dock and USS *Wasp*. Again I was impressed—the crowd was massive, but nothing but orderly. The planned traffic pattern worked well, with one little hiccup. Nobody was to be allowed below the hangar deck without special invitation, a strategem that worked reasonably well except for some "special" invitations extended to young German girls in short skirts, which there seemed to be in one hellacious abundance, cold or no cold. But who could fault a sailor with an eye for long, leggy frauleins? Not the XO, that's for sure!

Everything went off splendidly, and despite the inclement weather, we had plenty of coffee to ward off the chill. We even ran out of dough-nuts. But more importantly, we made a lot of friends. The mailroom was filled for weeks after our departure, bulging with thank-you notes and even some astonishing invitations (details are best left to the imagination as to Teutonic inventiveness). Captain Wylie was in his glory, the winner by far in his stack of mail, for he'd put his Carolina charm to good use.

Our return to Beantown was uneventful but welcomed. We had set no operational firsts or records, but we did bring back everyone with whom we set out, which is the first criteria of a successful deployment!

And so much for sea duty.

1986

THE CAIRO CAPER

I'm bound to admit that Wally Schirra and Phil Wood are two topnotch fighter pilots. Each of them bagged Soviet-built MiGs in aerial combat—Wally while flying F-84s on exchange duty with the Air Force in Korea and Phil as an F-8 pilot over North Vietnam. But I brought back a real live, tame MiG to San Diego, and if anything that's even harder than shooting the blasted thing full of holes.

The San Diego Aerospace Museum and the U.S. Air Force Museum both wanted MiG-17s, and we found them with the astute help of a McDonnell Douglas pal, Jack Crosthwaite – in Egypt. So late one March evening I found myself crawling off a British Airways L1011, my biological clock skewed after fourteen hours en route. Not the best way to handle the Cairo airport terminal, which, to coin a phrase, is an absolute zoo. The first impression was none too favorable. I had expected a representative from the Defense Intelligence Agency to meet me, but because the message traffic from Washington was lost or garbled, it was with firm resolve that I nailed the flag to the mast and joined the fray.

Two serious issues were immediately evident: no visa and no Egyptian pounds. Both were necessary just to get into the country. However, since the Arabs have been in the money-changing business a long, long time, the exchange of the required $150 was accomplished merely by selecting the most reputable-looking booth from a row of six or seven stalwarts of the Egyptian banking community. The exchange was made with one of the more friendly thieves. As it turned out, the visa was not difficult, either, once one had money. The same money changer admitted he would provide a visa stamp for an amount which apparently fluctuated with one's ability to pay— or the state of one's consciousness.

With visa, passport, Egyptian cash and resolution, the long line for immigration was next. Now, knowing a bit of how the system operated, I avoided the delay at immigration and customs with a twenty-pound note for a young Egyptian lady who identified herself as an expediter. And, sure enough, she was. Everything stamped and initialed and in order in a matter of minutes. It obviated about two hours of line-standing.

Next I got a cab, also with the help of a friendly opportunist, which only cost me ten pounds. But that palm-greasing also was well spent since it included a call to the hotel confirming my reservation, baggage handling and a reasurring guiding hand through the thousands (I do not exaggerate) of "well-wishers" at the terminal exit on the street. My newly-acquired, freshly-paid companion added much solace.

The cab ride into the city in the middle of the night, with the vehicular traffic maneuvering manically, was an experience in itself. I felt like I should put in a voucher for combat pay—if I returned home. But we made it to the Nile Hilton about midnight local time without dents, scrapes or even harsh words—mostly thanks to adroit driving and loud horn blowing.

Next morning was a clear, bright San Diego-type day so I decided to walk to the U.S. Embassy. The air, however, smelled a little like gym clothes that had remained too long in the locker. And the walk proved a very sporty course. I discovered that as a Cairo pedestrian I needed the same motor skills and steady nerves required of a carrier aviator. The previous night's drivers were still on the road but now joined by all the day drivers—it was a great race.

Upon arrival at the embassy I found stern security measures in evidence. After an examination of my passport and person, and a short wait at the reception desk, I was escorted to the office of Colonel Dennis Stiles, USAF—a member of the military attache' staff. He represented the DIA, which coordinated the MiG-17 acquisition for the two museums. He was surprised but happy to see me and explained the communications gap from D.C.

Colonel Stiles then presented a situation report stating that the two

MiGs had been designated by side number by the Egyptian Air Force (EAF) and that the Dayton aircraft already had been dismantled. However, he had not personally seen either plane so we were scheduled to meet with the Egyptian project officer that morning to arrange for an inspection. It was a short, concise report and I found the colonel very personable and supportive of the San Diego proposal.

We departed in a van driven by an Egyptian who obviously was geared to handle the helter-skelter street traffic. The EAF headquarters are on the eastern edge of the city, out near the international airport. The trip was blessedly unexciting and in fact even interesting thanks to Colonel Stiles' exceptional knowledge of the city and the culture.

However, our contacts in the EAF were hard to find since Stiles had no previous rapport with the people in the MiG loop. One officer who supposedly was the "main man" was totally surprised upon our appearance in his office. After an hour of conversation in Arabic with Colonel Stiles, he acknowledged vague recollection of how the exchange was to occur. The loop being closed, the EAF colonel arranged for another officer to provide the necessary papers and whatever else was needed for an on-the-spot look at the two MiGs. All this was to happen three days hence, since Friday was a religious holiday and Saturday was needed to complete the paperwork.

To say the EAF HQ building was shoddy would be a gross understatement. The building complex was of many times past, without intervening care or maintenance. An understanding of the budget funds for the military could well be a major part of the picture, but one complete sweepdown and perhaps some soap and water would have done wonders. Obviously, their emphasis was elsewhere.

Friday night I had dinner with Colonel Stiles and his wife Mary Jane in their quarters. Mrs. Stiles proved as charming and talented as her husband, serving an Egyptian dinner which was both tasty and savory, elegantly served. Even so, the Tums were a welcome relief. I was tremendously impressed with the ease in which the Stiles conversed with their two housekeepers—the language school had done a splendid job.

Also at dinner was an old friend of Dennis and Mary Jane, retired Air Commodore Moustafa Hafex, whom they had known in a joint military station previously. He was an extremely interesting gent; a longtime fighter pilot with experience in a series of MiGs and a combat veteran. He had been shot down while strafing an Israeli target and was taken prisoner. He just might be the right choice for "our man" in Cairo.

I never thought I would get so close to the birthplace of Christianity on Easter Sunday and not take pause to contemplate the origins and import of the faith in our lives, but such was the case. Dennis and I spent the entire day meeting with representatives of the EAF, each with some interest in the MiG project but many were mighty obscure. Again Dennis displayed his superlative language skills, including technical aspects. The importance of these briefings could not be over-emphasized since the entire retinue of participants were appraised of what had to be done, by whom, in what order.

Following tea and briefings at HQ, we gathered in the office of Colonel Hamde Nasar, who headed the armament section and would handle the financial details. His office provided us with the necessary papers for admittance to the air base. The field was nearby and we drove there by jeep in a matter of minutes.

"Ramshackle" is inadequate to describe the base facilities. It appeared the war was still on—I wondered if the Egyptians knew something I didn't. Dennis and I were escorted to the aircraft maintenance office where we were met by six officers, each representing a department. After more ceremonial tea drinking, and the attendant trip to the facility where apparently ancient legions had relieved themselves, we headed off to inspect the Dayton MiG first.

Everything was gathered in a war torn hangar at the edge of the field. The major components were in holding fixtures ready for shipment with all the ancillary pieces and fairings stacked nearby. The aircraft was in remarkably good condition; paint still intact, canopy clear, no major dings or holes, and tires a bit weary but inflated.

Next we drove across the field toward a remote revetted area. The evidence of recent wars was all there. Bunkers in every directiion, some undamaged, many not; a boneyard of aircraft hulks with bullet holes and rocket blasts in many of the buildings, much of the damage unrepaired. Several aircraft resembling modernized DC-3s were parked at random along the perimeter road, all with parts missing. The area had all the aura of some WW II airfield scenes I had witnessed.

But we reached a remote part of the field among large revetments where we found the San Diego MiG-17. It looked like it was ready to launch. Everything was attached: guns, bomb racks, rocket launchers, combat camera, the works. The plane captain jumped up on the wing and opened the cockpit enclosure just as if I were suited up and ready to take the jet around the patch. The cockpit looked complete, like the last day the plane flew. I was sold without reservation. We all departed assuring everyone that it was the aircraft we wanted, expressing our pleasure with the manner in the EAF had taken care of its equipment. Of course, I also stated that we wanted to receive the machine at the other end of its journey in the same condition. All nodded agreement.

The shipping aspect also involved partial payment as earnest, a potentially thorny issue. After lengthy discussions ranging from use of a U.S. Air Force C-5 to requesting an EAF C-130, Dennis recommended investigating a commercial carrier. Four Winds International Shippers were under Egyptian contract and provided costs, dates and options in transporting the MiG by Friday, 4 April.

I paid my respects to Colonel Dennis Stiles and Mrs. Stiles who had been so gracious during my brief stay and headed out again for no-man-land at the international airport, this time prepared for the fray. However, it was much of the same with a generous tip here and there for local knowledge and some creature conveniences.

Across the Atlantic again with British Airways was a mirror image of the eastbound leg – even the same menu – incredible. Eventually the MiG made its way to San Pedro and finally to San Diego – also considered incredible. But the museum presently exhibits a pristine airplane and I would wager that Wally and Phil spent more on the cost of fuel and ammo to bag their prey than we did for the entire episode. Of course, the aircraft marking makes a difference – a big difference.

For me it an experience not soon forgotten, and the museum will forever be indebted to our perspicacious coordinator, Jack Crosthwait and his State Department friends.

Now I'm back having lunch with Wally and Phil – not nearly so exciting but still provocative since we still talk about our days in the Tailhook Navy.

BOOK II
WALLY

1945

WHAT SHIP IS THIS?

Four significant events occurred in the Western Pacific during August 1945. Atomic bombs were dropped on Hiroshima and Nagasaki the sixth and ninth of that month, and the Japanese Empire agreed to unconditional surrender on the 15th. Between the latter two dates I reported for duty aboard USS *Alaska* (CB-1), the timing of which seemed to confirm that Tokyo had heard I was coming and, in a state of panic, rushed to capitulate.

That's how I saw it. Historians may differ.

Peace was about to break out—a disgusting state of affairs for an ensign two months out of Annapolis. I arrived at Buckner Bay, Okinawa, fresh from the Naval Academy Class of 1946, which was graduated a year early. But my debut in the combat theater was a good deal less than glorious. I sloshed ashore on a muddy beach that threatened to ruin the spit shine on my black shoes—common for non-aviators in those days, as fliers traditionally sported brown shoes. Ruefully I recalled my decision to apply at Annapolis instead of West Point, prompted in no small part by the knowledge that the Army lived in mud and tents while the Navy had steel decks, soft bunks and great chow. Well, what do ensigns know?

Surveying the beach, I spied a motor whaleboat with a lieutenant (junior grade) as boat officer. He had graduated from Annapolis a year before, as attested by the grandeur of one and one-half stripes on his shoulder boards, which I enviously noted bore the greenish gold of the "salty navy." This officer had seen sea duty, while my one shiny gold stripe seemed so new—and lonely.

Summoning my courage, I approached my fellow ex-midshipman, sloshed grandly to attention and announced: "Ensign Walter M. Schirra, Jr., U.S. Navy, reporting for duty, sir!" God, that sounded good. And since the jaygee didn't ignore me, I announced my intention of joining my ship.

"Sure, I can take you out to *Alaska*," he said, and off we went to the biggest ship anchored offshore.

I climbed the ladder with my seabag in my left hand, not really anticipating being piped aboard, which was fortunate because I wasn't. I popped my smartest salute to the flag, then another to the JG who was officer of the deck. "Ensign Walter M. Schirra, Jr., U.S. Navy, reporting for duty aboard USS *Alaska*, sir!" It still sounded good.

The OOD looked me up and down. "Son, this is not *Alaska*. This is *Cleveland*." He let that bit of intelligence sink in. After all, *Alaska* only had 17,500 tons and about 200 feet on a light cruiser. Anybody could make that mistake. "Call your boat back and report to the proper ship."

I slinked down the ladder, reboarded the whaleboat, and we conducted a search for the right ship. I wondered if Horatio Nelson or John Paul Jones had started their careers on a like note.

Once properly aboard *Alaska*, I assumed the exalted duties of a fresh-caught ensign. We patrolled with carrier task forces and I stood JOOD (junior officer of the deck) watches, trying to comprehend the complex maneuvers.

Then, on the 15th, World War II was over! We anchored again in Buckner Bay, enjoying peacetime movies on the after deck, interrupted only once by a reportedly last-minute Kamikaze who tried to sink the battleship *Pennsylvania* (BB-38). Two weeks later the formal surrender was signed in Tokyo Bay on battleship *Missouri*, 2 September 1945.

Without much else to do, we entertained guests of almost every stripe. Years (and years) later I was astonished to learn from fellow astronaut Deke Slayton that he had dined on board the good ship *Alaska* that same month. Deke had been an idle B-25 pilot on Okinawa and, lacking profitable employment, decided to see how the other half lived—and ate!

Suddenly all the salty greenish-gold stripers were on their way home, ending their Naval Reserve careers. As a now-experienced ensign, with all of three months active duty, I was put in charge of the number two turret. (Most likely they figured I couldn't do much harm, seeing as how the war was over.) A three-striper selected for captain was skipper for our lengthy trip back to the Boston Navy Yard.

The commander/captain announced that he would exercise the number two turret en route to Hawaii. Totally shook, I fell back upon centuries of seagoing heritage and did what ensigns have always done. I went directly to my senior chief petty officer and, in so many words, said "Help!"

Following about three days of total immersion in technical data and drills with my crew, I felt safe enough to report, "Number two turret ready, sir!" In retrospect, I suppose we really were ready—but it was the naivety of youth coupled with a healthy dose of indestructibility that allowed us to fire safely and successfully.

Four and a half decades later, I was particularly taken aback when the number two turret exploded on USS *Iowa* (BB-61) in April 1989. Among the forty-seven lives lost was that of the turret officer.

I really felt proud of my *Alaska*—for I considered her such—as we approached Pearl Harbor, returning from The War. Then suddenly, out of the sky, a four-plane formation of Grumman F8F-1s buzzed the ship. The airedales aboard *Alaska* told me the Bearcats were the Navy's newest fighters, but hadn't made it in time for combat. The emotions I felt watching those little blue bumblebees almost humbled my pride in the sleek battlecruiser, beginning my transition from black shoe to brown shoe. Eager aviators like Zeke Cormier, anxious to take a hot fighter like the F8F into combat, became my new role-models. Such are the fickle ways of ensigns.

But now I knew what I wanted.

1947-49

BROWN SHOES AND BATSMEN

By the end of Feburary 1947 I had accumulated a grand total of 12.50 hours in the Stearman N2S-5, a biplane trainer sometimes incorrectly called the "Yellow Peril." Of that, I boasted one-half hour solo flying. I was on the way to wearing the coveted brown shoes of a Naval Aviator. I had also acquired a severe critic. Jo Fraser Schirra, my wife of one year, occasionally leaned over the fence at NAAF Grand Prairie, Texas and noted, "He wobbled his wings and bounced a bit on his first solo!"

Flight training began in earnest at NAS Corpus Christi in the SNJ-5 advanced trainer, and a blur ensued: through Pensacola up to arrested landings on USS *Wright* (CVL-48), a straight-deck light carrier. Then on to PBY Catalinas—an outright insult to would-be fighter pilots—and the Beechcraft SNB utility plane with transport rating lurking over the horizon.

Zeke and Phil fought the system to get fighter assignments. In my case I was set up for a acareer in fighters or a short future as a "yoke boater", PBYs. Lieutenant (j.g.) Pinky Howard, USNA '45, and I, Ensign Schirra, USNA '46, reported to a little old lady civil service clerk, (about thirty-two years old) and were told to draw straws to see who would go on to fighters. Pinky said, "I outrank him. I'll take fighters."

"Draw," said the lady, "Rank between j.g.s and ensigns is like virginity among whores." Pinky resigned within a few years.

I lucked out and was assigned to NAS Jacksonville, Florida for advanced training with the F6F-5 Hellcat, famous for combat success in the Pacific less than two years before. Gunnery and air-to-ground rocket firing built up a "nugget" aviator's confidence. We were slowly annealed from those raw nuggets into the polished, finished product—eligible to wear

Wings of Gold.

At length, Jo pinned on my wings and we set off for NAF Quonset Point, Rhode Island. My first squadron was VF-7A, flying F8F-1s—the Bearcats that had stirred my emotions and seduced me away from my three-month love affair with surface ships in general and *Alaska* in particular.

Reporting to the duty officer, I learned that Fighting Seven-Able was "in session at the officer's club"—a not uncommon situation, I inferred. The local scuttlebutt had it that my skipper was a double ace from the Pacific, and for once the rumors proved true. I was introduced to Lieutenant Commander Armistead Burwell Smith III, as he stood on his head in the corner, drinking a martini. The impression was a lasting one. The squadron's newest pilot, with all of 300 hours in his logbook, realized there were some esoteric techniques yet to be learned.

"Chick" Smith was a role model if ever there was one: a double Ace in the Pacific, exceptional good looks, cultivated charm and a Carolina accent as smooth as the Pratt and Whitney engine in his Bearcat. One look told the story. This was an officer and a gentleman, and no Act of Congress was necessary. Yet how was Chick to know that I would cite his negative one-gravity stunt to skeptical doctors concerned about drinking at zero gravity during the beginning of America's space program? It was sort of like the bumble bee or the hummingbird—theoretically impossible but obviously practicable.

The slow, casual development of graduate aviators accelerated with first flight in the F8F-1. I loved the Bearcat; it was the closest thing to strapping on a pair of angel wings. The cockpit fit like a well-tailored glove with the canopy rails rubbing your shoulders. It had everything a fighter jock could want: speed, maneuverability and an eye-watering rate of climb. As far as I'm concerned, it was the last of the sports cars.

In less than three weeks I was a wingman in a "group grope" with all four of Air Group Seven's squadrons droning about in formation over Idlewild Airport on opening day—8 August 1948. As with so many institutions, like Cape Canaveral, Idlewild was renamed for John F. Kennedy in 1964.

Less than a month from joining the squadron, I was carrier-qualified on board USS *Leyte* (CV-32), and shortly thereafter I landed in another country when VF-7A plunked down at Roosevelt Roads, Puerto Rico. By November 1948 we had flown from "Roosey Roads" to Newfoundland, exercising our Bearcats in environmental extremes from the tropics to sub-arctic.

Our comfortable tropical flying uniform gave way to a large rubber bag with arms and legs—a "poopy suit" to protect us from possible cold-water immersion. We had a few involuntary swimmers on that cruise, and an equal few who made it back to the ship with near engine failures.

I never will forget one cold day after a long launch delay. We were finally in formation circling *Leyte* when my wingman complained of severe stomach cramps and an impending bowel movement. (Actually he said, "I've got to shit—now!")

The carrier came back into the wind as the deck frantically was being cleared for him to land. Our skipper pushed over into a dive to lead the formation into the landing pattern. But that nose-down bunt induced a short pulse of near zero-gravity weightlessness, with predictable physiological results. It induced a transmission of, "Oops, cancel my request for landing." Later, down in the ready room we determined what a poopy suit really was for!

Eventually all Atlantic Fleet squadrons deploy on a voyage to the Mediterranean Sea. The vernacular calls this evolution a "Med cruise," evoking images of sunny beaches, villas, micro bikinis, Brigitte Bardot and Maurice Chevalier types. In truth, the dream is replaced with the reality of filthy arab bazaars and cities like home. Our excursions ashore were enhanced by an edict from the Sixth Fleet commander that all officers wearing civvies on liberty must also wear a hat. No explanation (the Navy isn't big on explaining orders), just comply. Or else.

Well, hardly any of us had thought to bring a civilian hat. What to do? We tried the blue covers from our uniform hats, attempting to make them resemble something akin to berets—one time. Then in Naples we discovered Borsolino hats that could be rolled up for stowage. We all looked like the popular caricature of Russian spies with those damn hats and sports clothes. So, other than a uniform hat, I can't recall ever wearing a fedora again. What ComSixthFleet didn't know wouldn't hurt us.

Carrier landings were becoming routine, and I was honored with a plaque and the traditional wardroom cake for making the 15,000th landing on *Philippine Sea* (CV-47). Usually such events are coincidental, since it's hard to arrange yourself in the pattern to make the umpteen thousandth "trap" on any particular carrier. The evolution is further complicated by waveoffs of planes ahead of you, or a fouled deck requiring you to go around. By the time you're lined up again, somebody else has his name on the ward-room plaque and already is cutting the biggest slice of cake.

My favorite carrier landing was one I observed from the landing signal officer (LSO) platform one evening. Phil Wood became an LSO and Zeke already has explained the trauma occasionally involved in carrier land-ings. So what follows exemplifies how Naval Aviators ease the pain of oc-cupational hazards by indulging in gallows humor.

Air Group Seven had swapped ships and LSOs with a British car-rier, HMS *Ocean* near Malta. I had launched from *Ocean* and was brought aboard "Phil Sea" by the duty "batsman," as the Brits called LSOs. Later I went aft from our ready room to observe some of our aircraft on the evening recovery.

The batsman was working one of our birds, giving "low dips" slowly at first, then frantically. The message was, "Pick up your nose and add power. You're settling into the ramp!" Still no good. So the Brit waved off the plane in the groove, ordering him to go around.

But by now the approaching aircraft was boresighted on the bats-man, who threw his paddles at the offending plane. With a mixture of amaze-ment and admiration, I saw the paddles bounce off the plane's nose just as the Brit yelled so loudly that we all heard him: "Fuck me, I've had it!" And he dived over the side!

We scurried for cover, waiting for the impending rampstrike that would, at the very least, wreck a perfectly good airplane. But the pilot made a last-second recovery, bounced off the deck and resumed flying. The batsman, who had literally abandoned ship, was picked up by the planeguard destroyer and returned to Phil Sea in exchange for a suitable amount of ice cream.

Lest this episode be misinterpreted, just remember who made the major contributions to carrier aviation. Angled decks, mirror landing sys-tems, steam catapults—even the first jet landings—all courtesy of the Royal Navy.

When we were back swinging round the hook at Malta's Halfar Har-bor, some of us were invited to HMS *Ocean* for a dining-in. Remembering the time I hoped with ensign's eagerness to be piped aboard *Alaska*, only to learn the ship was *Cleveland*, I finally got my formal reception. The Brits did it up right, and this lieutenant (junior grade) was thrilled to be treated just like a naval officer, as I was piped on board

We had a great series of cocktails. The Brits drink on board if they do not anticipate flights, whereas apparently the French drink regardless—with no visible effects. Then we settled down to a splendid banquet. The smoking lamp was out until we had passed the port and toasted Her Majesty the queen. Then we toasted everyone and everything imaginable, and things got a teensy bit out of hand.

The evening degenerated into barrages of fruit and general mayhem. The dignity of our formal uniforms and manners were rapidly dispelled—it was a terrific evening.

If I may modify a biblical phrase, through a haze darkly I remember being sculled back to *Philippine Sea* lying in the bottom of a civilian bum boat—not quite ill, but with my salty LTJG stripes covered to conceal my rank. An old Navy procedure not part of the Annapolis curriculum...

Our Med cruise ended 18 May 1949, less than a year after Jo pinned on my golden wings. Now I had ninety-nine carrier landings, and was anxious to log Number 100. It was great to be among fellow fighter pilots and to be accepted as one of the team.

Then the bottom fell out.

Harry Truman's Secretary of Defense, Louis Johnson, was no friend of the Navy. For that matter, neither was Truman—a WW I artilleryman. With a severely-reduced budget, we became worried about getting enough flying time. It was a continual fear of the gung-ho professional aviator. Insufficient flying means loss of proficiency which, in turn, often leads to loss of aircraft or a pilot's life. Many expendables—fuel, lubricants, even cleaning cloths—were allocated under a tight budget. Consequently, VF-71 (redesignated from VF-7A in August 1948) pilots brought in our old skivvy shirts for cleaning our planes—to save money for fuel! It was comparable to giving up cigarettes to save on matches.

Our flight schedule was badly reduced, and we tried to mooch fuel from the multi-engine guys at Quonset Point. A P2V Neptune squadron gave us some of their allotment—how well I remember! I had pitched out for landing behind a P2V in my F8F and was about to touch down when the Neptune's wingtip vortex tossed my little Bearcat on its back. I pushed the stick forward (thus climbing inverted), simultaneously adding full throttle.

Without a sputter, that Grumman jewel climbed me out of danger. I reached a safe altitude, rolled level and continued around to an uneventful landing. Then I climbed out of the cockpit and kissed the ground.

One of the base pet peeves at Quonset was gear-up landings, especially in context of the budget restrictions. Land wheels-up and you were in big trouble. Therefore, one day a group of pilots watched the landing pattern with additional interest when an F8F gear-upped. We gasped in horror as the Bearcat skidded off the runway on its belly. A wingtip caught in the soft shoulder, slowly flipping the Grumman onto its back. It was propped on the rudder and pilot's headrest.

Several of us sprinted to the scene, anxious to rescue the pilot from his inverted embarrassment. But we needn't have worried. That was one astute aviator hanging upside-down in his seat. By increments the landing gear began unlocking, inching its way to the "down" position (straight up in the air) as the pilot frantically worked the hand-powered hydraulic pump to "lower" his wheels. If he pumped fast enough, the gear would be fully extended by the time the accident investigators arrived—avoiding the penalty for a gear-up landing!

You have to get up pretty early to outsmart a fighter pilot.

1949-51

JET PILOT AND HIRED KILLER

Jets are taken for granted today, but in 1949 they were still a source of curiosity on many Navy flight lines. Therefore, I was gratified to receive orders for temporary additional duty (TAD) to NAS Whiting Field, Florida from Quonset Point, Rhode Island. At Whiting I had my first jet flight in an F-80 borrowed from the Air Force and designated TO-1 (later TV-1) by the Navy. Officially, our blue-suit cousins rated the Lockheed Shooting Star a fighter but the Navy, entering the jet arena somewhat later, called it a trainer. Not that terminology mattered. It was a jet and that's what counted.

Three weeks later I returned to Quonset and helped VF-71 transition from the F8F Bearcat to Grumman's "hot" new F9F-2 Panther. The squadron seemed to shuck the piston-slapper overnight. We became jet jockies— talk about prestige! There was already an F2H Banshee squadron at Quonset, but we were the first kids on the block with Panthers.

In those days, Air Group Seven was assigned to USS *Philippine Sea* and I made my 100th carrier landing on her, in an F9F. But that straight deck was not hazardous enough for the planners' satisfaction, so four of us were sent to Pensacola to qualify on board *Wright*—the same floating postage stamp on which I had done SNJ and F6F CarQuals before receiving my wings. The interesting factor in the jet equation was that now we had heavier airplanes and a faster landing speed, but the higher-ups compensated by giving us a shorter, narrower deck. It all evens out, right? Right. Numbers don't lie.

Seven inspiring, knuckle-biting but mercifully uneventful arrested landings later, I was a jet-qualified Naval Aviator.

In today's Navy the term "trap" is blithely thrown about. Anybody aboard an aircraft whose tailhook snags an arresting wire can enter a trap in "his-or-her" logbook. But on today's angled decks, if the hook fails to engage a wire, the event is called a bolter (from the British term, "bloody bolter") and the pilot adds power, lifts off and goes around again.

I want to make it abundantly clear that on straight-deck carriers, there were no bolters. There were arrested landings or there were major accidents. There was nothing in between.

Our early team of jets went aboard *Midway* (CVB-41) in June 1950 and revelled in her luxurious big deck. Air Group Seven deployed to the Mediterranean in July, just as the Korean War erupted, and we all realized we were back in the weapon system business, preparing for real combat. How realistically we prepared remained to be seen.

Too often when we practiced air-to-air combat we played "I'm the Indian, you're the cowboy" game. One was "shot down," then declared himself a "new man" and returned to the game. But real bullets and genuine anti-aircraft weapons don't permit that luxury!

When we returned Stateside the scuttlebutt had it that *Midway* and Airstrip 7 would remain on the east coast rather than sailing for Korea. Immediately two things became apparent to me. I knew that (A) four Banshee pilots were earmarked for a year's exchange duty with the Air Force,but they were now on the way to Korea on *Philippine Sea*. And I realized that (B) the detailers—those bastards who give lousy change-of-command orders under the guise of career planning—did not appreciate my problem. To wit: Lieutenant Schirra, being a United States Navy weapon system, needed to get to combat.

I presented myself as a jet aviator with more than 1,000 total flight hours, available for USAF exchange duty. I was aghast to learn that I was scheduled to become a flight instructor. But not to worry. A deal was cut, not only for me but for a squadronmate, A.C. "Ace" O'Neal. How close I came to languishing two years in Naval Air Training Command was terrifying to consider. After all, I was a tiger. I was the best hired killer in the U.S. Navy. Why, in mock combat I could get on anybody's tail, ready to shoot him down. (And fighter pilots don't lie. Honest!)

Self confidence is critical to a fighter pilot, and I received a boost in that most important psychological arena. Over Boston one evening I engaged two F-86 Sabres in mock combat, poorly matched in my underpowered Panther against the Air Force's finest fighter. But we laid an overcast of contrails over the city, and when it was over I had both their asses. I mean, they belonged to me. They never had a chance. (As the proverbial sheepherder says, "Sheep lie.")

The next six months shaped up thusly:

12 January   Detached from VF-71, TAD to USAF

 9 February   Local in a T-6D (Air Force talk for SNJ)

23 February   Local in a T-33A

23 February   Local in an F-84D

 5 March   Local in an F-84E

23 June   First combat mission, F-84E

Between the first and last of those logbook entries are some stories I would like to share.

I joined the 154th Fighter-Bomber Squadron, 136th Fighter-Bomber Wing, at Langley Air Force Base, Virginia, where eight years later I would join the Space Task Group. The 136th Wing was a National Guard F-51 outfit just recalled for duty in Korea. The wing commander was the only pilot with any jet time—one hour in the back of a T-33A! So here came the Navy Aviator hotshot with "beaucoup" jet hours and carrier landings, helping teach the Air Force. Ego time? No way. Those National Guard pilots were some of the hottest I've ever known. They transitioned to Thunderjets almost overnight. This was not the time to inform my USAF buddies that we aviators on "boats" used pilots to take us to sea.

I had wingmen in my flight who wore senior pilot's wings—stars above their shields—and fellow flight leaders who were command pilots—wreaths around the stars. A great many had combat experience from WW II.

Langley is close to Norfolk, and we had to be careful of overlapping traffic patterns with Navy planes. My favorite recollection is the time I brought my four planes back through Hampton Roads, the entry to the seaport, and spotted an aircraft carrier. Sugar to the flies! We formed echelon right, broke upwind and, with perfect separation, started carrier approaches. No tailhooks, of course, but I figured it's the thought that counts.

My sentiment was not shared. Flags, flares, smoke and I suspect a few impolite transmissions on an unknown channel caused us to leave for the nailed-down runways of Langley.

We crossed the U.S. of A. in railroad trains and were flown to Itazuke AFB, Japan. Thunderjets from an in-theater unit were available to us "on loan." Counting travel time, a period of less than four months was allotted the 136th Wing from first jet flights to combat. But with the talent we had, it proved little problem. We leaped off the Itazuke runway with wingtip tanks, two pylon fuel tanks, two 500-pound bombs and two JATO bottles—with at least 400 feet of runway remaining.

Staggering along, slowly gaining altitude, we flew to North Korea. Once we crossed the 38th Parallel—the established political boundary—we charged our .50 cal. machine guns in anticipation of combat.

The days of wooden swords were over, and those black puffs near us were not greeting cards but messengers of death. When we arrived in Japan with our files and flight gear, relieving a regular Air Force squadron, we repainted their F-84Es with our own colors and insignia. We were a close-knit bunch in the 154th Squadron, with an "every man a tiger" attitude. Only one of our pilots turned in his wings as a result of combat exposure, and believe me, that was well below the average. The bonding of a squadron is almost tribal in nature, and helps the uncertain through the often-difficult transition period while colors and heraldic patches lend the glue of identity.

My father, a WW I pilot and postwar barnstormer, came to visit me at Itazuke. Dad was with 5th Air Force Headquarters in Tokyo, a civil engineer re-establishing bases and airports throughout the Pacific. The guys accepted him immediately, and with many drinks pried flying stories from him that I had never heard. Up until then I had held center-stage, telling the boys how the Navy did things. Imagine being upstaged by your own father...

Allegedly (surely he didn't lie) Dad tried to fly through the Eiffel Tower in a Spad after Armistice Day. At the last moment he "gutted out," thereby simultaneously saving my future by ensuring my existence. But he had other yarns to spin. For instance, Dad never was a second lieutenant; he was commissioned as a first louie. And, standing down at the edge of the bar on the fringe of the crowd, was his son, only recently a bull lieutenant after six years in Uncle Sam's Navy!

Sadly, there are few occasions when a father tells his son the best war stories. I was proud of Dad and later realized that my squadronmates were, too. A number of them diverted to Tokyo during sporadic R&Rs from

Korea to visit my folks, and I took that as a high compliment indeed.

It was a strange environment for fighter-bomber pilots. The base had American families; husbands, wives and children. We flew off to North Korea where we bombed railroads or bridges, jinked to avoid flak, ran low on fuel and landed back at Itazuke on fumes. Every so often a plane and pilot would not return. But we didn't have the fuel to go very far north—nowhere near the Yalu River in MiG country. Those adventures would begin when we moved to Taegu, or K-2 in Korean War parlance.

K-2—a muddy valley on wet days; hot, dry and dusty on sunny days—was a paved strip with pierced-steel planking adding 500 feet to each end of the runway. It had been hastily rebuilt when we returned after the Chinese offensive, so facilities were primitive. The standard takeoff technique with full loads was to taxi onto the downwind matting in pairs. The leader would run up to full power, back off a smidgeon depending upon his personal insurance program, release the brakes and fire his JATO bottles. With smoke from the previous section obscuring forward vision, he followed the yellow line until his nosewheel hit the matting on the far end of the strip and rotate into a climbing attitude. The instrument takeoff switched to VFR when the JATO burned out, and the pair flew out of the swirling smoke.

Somehow, we never lost an aircraft to such an unconventional technique. But we did have one bizarre physical injury. An F-84E engine exploded before brake release, and the plane burned to the ground. The intense fire caused the guns to fire a few rounds, one of which hit the leg of a tall stool upon which a sergeant was sitting. The unfortunate sergeant fell to the ground and injured his back.

Now based nearer to North Korea, we could reach the fabled Yalu. The war zone north of the river was off-limits by political decree. But we could see MiG-15s in the traffic patterns of fields on the other side. And soon they began harassing us. The Russian-built swept-wing fighters flew at contrail level, where their exhaust water vapor traced signatures of each MiG. With our heavy loads, we flew well below contrail level. To put that in perspective, ask any fighter pilot how he likes looking in his rear-view mirror, seeing contrails above and behind, and hearing "Bandits, six o'clock high!" Man, that has to be the number-one bone-chiller of radio calls.

At first when the MiGs started runs on us, we "pickled off" our auxiliary tanks and bombs, getting down to fighting weight. But that merely granted victory to the Reds, who had prevented us from hitting our targets at no expense to themselves.

After a couple of these episodes we decided to keep our loads until the MiGs pressed close enough for a hassle to develop. Then we dropped down toward the rice paddies where our straight-wing 84s had a low-altitude turning advantage over the swept-wing MiGs. I had trained my flight to make carrier approaches and fly the Navy way. As far as I was concerned, we had ourselves a four-plane division that coincidentally resembled an Air Force flight of four. Never mind that we flew Republic Thunderjets with "USAF" painted on the wings.

Consequently, my flight was well-versed in the Thach Weave, perfected by the late Jimmy Thach early in WW II. Our situation was comparable to his ten years before. We were mounted on slower, less maneuverable aircraft than our opponents. But we were smarter. Quick and dirty, the weave worked thusly:

Each two-plane section in the division (or flight) provided mutual support to the other. If one pair were attacked from either side or behind, both sections turned into each other. The attacker had only two choices: break off, or expose himself to return fire from the second section. As long as we kept a good lookout, with our heads constantly on a swivel, we couldn't be surprised. It was simple, it was effective, and it was beautiful. We knew the weave would work in jet combat, and only awaited the opportunity to prove it.

Came the day. Four MiGs closed on my flight from six o'clock high— directly behind us. We broke left and right, one section crossing above the other at the 90-degree point, and continuing through a complete 180 to meet the MiGs head-on. We were lined up almost man-to-man as we climbed toward the descending bandits. A few rounds were exchanged as .50-cal. and 23mm tracers criss-crossed through the air, then the MiGs pulled up.

We maintained the turn back around to our original heading, with the MiGs now well above us and far ahead. They climbed away, obviously in frustration, as they didn't like what we had just showed them. Probably they'd never seen the Thach Weave before and jetted home to ponder the new development.

After completing our mission and debriefing, I was told to take a T-33 with my section leader to the Joint Operations Center in Seoul. I didn't know it, of course, but Zeke was there with Admiral Jocko Clark. I briefed the JOC folks on our use of the Thach Weave, which was accepted as an optimum maneuver for the low-altitude F-84E. The lesson was digested and distributed from 5th Air Force HQ to the two F-84 wings in-country. Yes, the Air Force learned something from the Navy, and I knew one old-timer in particular I wanted to know of the event. So there, Dad!

On another occasion my wingman and I had a lone MiG dead to rights. My Mark One eyeballs had picked him up, and we closed in from his five o'clock, slightly to starboard. I started firing my four .50 cals. at 800 feet or more—too far out. Suddenly my wingman's unmistakable (if high-pitched) voice: "Wally, break right!"

Being brighter than the average jet jockey, I instantly deduced that somebody unfriendly was on my ass. So, obeying the command that has only one response, I grabbed a handful of Gs.

When my wingie and I regrouped, the "lone" MiG was gone and no other remained in sight. Back at K-2, we debriefed and only then did I realize my wingman had called for the break to prevent me from crossing the damn Yalu River! The gun camera film, developed hours later, showed the sparkling hits of .50 calibers moving up the MiG's tail toward the cockpit. And, sure enough, there was the dreaded Yalu visible below his nose. A number of lessons were learned:

One: Use bigger guns—20mm preferred.

Two: Screw the rules of engagement.

Three: Develop air-to-air missiles.

Four: Mark One eyeballs acquire aerial targets very well.

There's another lesson I like to include, which in light of today's headlines I call Lesson Four B: Stealth technology may be great against radar and "smart" weapon systems, but it can't hide from the human eye and it can't deceive a "dumb" bullet. Even after our tremendous success against Iraq, I hope we don't have to absorb that elemental knowledge the hard way.

By summer of 1951 the Korean War had become a fearful battle of attrition, with no clearly-defined aims on the allied side, other than not losing. Two super powers were engaged in a trial of strength and will, with weapons both old and new. Far East Bomber Command had used B-29s continually through the earlier campaigns, but by June 1951, when the 136th Fighter-bomber Wing arrived at Itazuke, the war had stabilized. The Chinese, we now know, were building airfields just across the Yalu in the Antung area of Manchuria. Some 450 MiG-15s were based there. Consequently, allied concern existed that MiGs would be staged into North Korea at Saamcham , Namsi and Taechon.

Daylight B-29 attacks were conducted against these and other fields with limited success. But the MiG-15 was designed specifically as a bomber interceptor, so friendly fighters were essential in escorting the Superfortresses deep into MiG Alley.

At 0900 on 23 October, eight B-29s of the 307th Bombardment Wing rendezvoused with 55 Thunderjets of the 49th and 136th Wings, then set course for Namsi, fifty miles south of the Yalu. The Boeings flew their classic boxes of two four-plane formations. The "cigar-smokers," as we fighter jocks called Generals Rosie O'Donnell and Curtis LeMay's troops, were in for quite a surprise. Hundreds of MiGs were poised across the Yalu, waiting for just such an opportunity.

All the flyable jet fighters under 5th Air Force control, except the elderly F-80s, were launched on this mission in one capacity or another. The F-86s were positioned in squadron formations between the bomber track and the MiG bases, but south of the damned Yalu. The F-84s, also deployed by squadrons (this time without bombs or JATO) provided direct escort to the 29s. An Australian outfit—Number 77 Squadron—was on hand with its twin-engine Gloster Meteors as well. Though the Aussies didn't fly with us that day, they did escort B-29s the next morning, and they tangled with MiGs in their antiquated British twin-engine jets. They'd have agreed when we joked that we were witnessing not merely a "box of cigars," but a bad case of cigars!

A remote island radar station, plus some clandestine forward observers, reported successive "bandit trains" flying into the target area. A train might involve anything from eight MiGs to 100 or more, so we knew we were in for a hellacious fight. The F-86s disappeared in a contrail bowl of spaghetti and suddenly MiGs flashed in from all directions—still more trains! The bombers were under attack, and the fight quickly degenerated into a free-for-all.

I looked down, saw a MiG zooming up from below the port side B-29, and realized the bandit was mine. I dove toward him and almost stuffed my nose up his tailpipe before I pressed the trigger. He spun out of control down toward the paddies. We did not care to follow what looked like a sure kill. My wingman and I stayed with the B-29s, trying to divert other MiGs—

and there were plenty to choose from. But we got no more shooting.

The twenty-minute running battle took a toll of both sides. It still may be the largest jet combat ever, with some 150 MiGs against 89 Sabres and Thunderjets. Three B-29s were hacked down, and four of the five survivors landed with battle damage while one F-84 also was lost. Against that, as many as many as six MiGs may have been destroyed, but everybody knew who had won and who had lost.

Ninety missions went into my logbook much too rapidly, as I wanted more time to work on the pesky MiGs. But my orders arrived for return Stateside, ending my tour with the U.S. Air Force. Friendships annealed in the heat of combat always remain; the respect, "the code" and the humor are facets of wartime life that cannot be developed any other way. The ultimate compliment was an offer of the rank of major in the National Guard squadron, with a lieutenant colonelcy within months if I would leave the Navy. I finally made equivalent rank—Navy commander—almost twelve years later!

I was developed as a weapon system from Day One of Navy flight training, yet my only combat came with the Air Force. A return tour with the Navy to fulfill my self-appointed role as the sea service's best hired killer was not to be. And, frankly, that was a source of lifelong disappointment. I continually wonder why combat-experienced military men of any service— but particularly in the Navy—seem unwelcome at the highest ranks. "No guts, no glory" is a fighter pilot phrase attributed to Major General Boots Blesse, an Air Force double ace in Korea. Yet I wonder how many of our cocktail party, diplomatic-circle admirals and generals have the guts to wage war.

It seems that today we military men have kowtowed to the political way of playing at war rather than waging war. Very few aces, for instance, have achieved four-star rank like the late Jimmy Thach, who was not only a brilliant fighter leader but an innovative anti-submarine practitioner as well. Sadly, the fleet operators—the proven warriors—seldom develop the skills to compete in the Washington arena.

When I look back at my career after Korea, I realize that the naivete' and infinite patriotism of youth no longer was my stimulus. We used to speak of the "platoon" syndrome. A platoon leader tells his men that every other soldier will be killed in the forthcoming action, and half the troops immediately turn to their buddies and say, "Sorry 'bout you, Joe!" Well, now the platoon syndrome was gone for me.

Time trails logic in its wake and, as we mature, we realize that the invulnerability of youth gives way to concern with survival. The human weapon system no longer is honed to perfection. By no means were my flying days over, but the ultimate role as a combat aviator was history. My next tour was not as a test pilot—the job I craved in order to develop an aircraft superior to the MiG-15. Instead, I was ordered to the Naval Air Ordnance Test facility at China Lake, California.

Without realizing it, that was where I belonged.

1953-55

CHINA LAKE
AND THE
MOONSHINERS

I admit that my orders to Naval Ordnance Test Station (NOTS) China Lake, California, disappointed me. I thought I should be on the way to Test Pilot School at NAS Patuxent River, Maryland, but in truth I found the proverbial silver lining behind the outwardly gloomy cloud. For at China Lake, I learned about the weapons that military aircraft are built to carry. And they weren't limited to the puny .50 caliber machine guns of my old F-84E from Korean days.

The Experimental Officer, my immediate superior, was Commander Tom Moorer. He was the first of a series of Toms who made me aware of the new weapons for our Navy. Tom Moorer went on to four stars and CNO. Commander Tom Connolly was his relief and went on to DCNO with three stars. Then Commander Tom Walker relieved Tom Connolly and he retired with three stars. (As an aside: all three Toms maintain that the Tomcat was named after him!)

My assignment was to bring a weapon from the drawing boards to fruition—and what a weapon! It was, well, right out of the space age. They called it "Sidewinder," an air-to-air missile that homed on the heat of its intended victim much like its desert reptilian namesake.

While developing Sidewinder we also mated a radar-ranging capability with the more versatile Mark 16 gyro-stabled gunsight. Despite all the gee-whiz gadgets such as heat-seeking and radar-guided missiles, hardcore fighter pilots still wanted guns in their fighters, and I knew why. The inevitable post-mortems after aerial combats typically tell of getting close in at the opponent's six o'clock position, and opening fire at less than six hundred feet—a reasonable golf shot! But it's surprising how often some young tiger misses an easy setup because his guns aren't boresighted to his sight's pipper, the center dot that serves as his primary aiming point. Usually it subtends one foot at 1,000 feet in front of the aircraft. Even simple weapons like guns can play you wrong. My point is, all the new gizmos need expert attention to work as advertised. And what's the average age of enlisted sailors? All of twenty years!

We fired Sidewinder off a prop-driven AD-4 Skyraider, and later from the twin-jet F3D-1 Skyknight. Our first "kill" was scored by knocking an engine clean off a B-17 drone. But the Flying Fortress wasn't named in jest—that target bird was landed safely by remote control!

But we learned. The magic formula required the attacking pilot to sight his target visually, and slide the boresighted pipper in an expanding circle until an audio tone warbled in his earphones. When the tone decreased to a null he let 'er rip. The missile did all the work, allowing the fighter pilot to claim the glory. Hey, nobody said it was fair.

Actually, the man who deserved the credit for Sidewinder was Dr. Bill McLean, a government scientist who sold his brainchild for the proverbial dollar. He was a wonderful guy to know, innovative, hard-working and fun. He passed away years ago, but would be delighted to know that his baby is still going strong—proof that a simple, well-engineered weapon can last forty years and then some. The guidance package, in modular form, sits in the nose of the 200-pound missile, which is directed by the forward canard wings. The tailfins provide roll stability and enough lift to permit the forward section to guide.

I'm always amazed at how past and present seem to merge as I age. The operative homily, I believe, is "History bears repeating." I attended a reunion of NOTS alumni in the summer of 1990, and I learned a shocking fact. Sidewinder was delayed in its fleet introduction in order to permit the radar-guided Sparrow (an electronically unreliable air-to-air missile) to be introduced first. Sidewinder, highly reliable, would have caused rejection of Sparrow and a loss to Hughes and other contractors. I don't claim to know about the current efficiency of Sparrow versus Sidewinder, but over North Vietnam 1965-73, the heat-seekers proved more than twice as efficient in killing MiGs as the sexy radar missiles.

During the first year of Sidewinder development, I had collateral duty that included escorting senior officers to the test range—about the size of Rhode Island—to observe various weapons under evaluation. One shipborne surface-to-air missile (SAM) was called Terrier, and a test was laid on for the benefit of the brass.

Sure 'nuff, the Terrier launched on schedule as the target plane obediently flew into view. I really admired the missile's flight performance—straight up, peaking out of its climb right overhead, followed by a precise hammerhead turn to descend vertically from whence it came. Admirals' butts were elevated all about us as the bigwigs scratched for cover in the sandy earth. Commander Tom Amen, another Tom, and I watched with amusement, secure in the combat-proven knowledge of the you-can't-fix-it syndrome. Nobody was hurt, but thereafter at China Lake, Terriers were known as "admiral seekers."

A young fighter pilot could have a great time at China Lake and learn a lot in the bargain. Working with other hotshots, dealing with civil servants and PhDs, was an education in itself. But two years to the day after reporting aboard NOTS, I was ordered to Miramar for an obscure organization called "Project Cutlass." I sold my sandblasted Model A Ford to another junior birdman, and the Schirras were off to the Pacific Fleet!

"Project Cutlass" initially involved a small team of pilots and mechs selected to determine whether Vought's futuristic F7U-3 was an appropriate carrier aircraft ready for fleet use. (It wasn't, but that's lowering the tailhook before entering the pattern.) The organization was unusual, to say the least, but then the Cutlass was an unusual flying machine. It was the U.S. Navy's first supersonic aircraft, and the first with afterburning engines; a tail-less bird packing mixed armament of 20mm cannon and (gee whiz!) the much-touted Sparrow radar-guided missile.

The project team initially consisted of a nucleus Cutlass squadron at NAS Miramar. Project Cutlass had a team of seven naval aviators (Do you sense Project Mercury – four naval aviators, three Air Force pilots?) We worked formation, gunnery and rocket flights. Our high point was Project Steam on *Hancock* (CV-19) where we did the first US Navy steam catapult shots. OUr low point was a grounding for a stall called "Post stall gyration". A stall with the hydraucally actuated slats retracted resulted in a non-recoverable event when very low.

Later I became part of a training unit at NAS Moffett Field, California. Thus, the Schirras removed themselves to the Bay Area (there's only one Bay Area in the People's Republic of California, and it be San Francisco), where we purchased a house in nearby Sunnyvale. A United Airlines captain sold it to us at an enormous profit to him—on the order of two percent. At least that's what my wristwatch calculator says when I compute $10,200 from his purchase price of an even ten grand. Ah, youth...

Composite Squadron Three inhabited Moffett Field, previously having provided night-fighter detachments to PacFleet carriers. But now the good folks at VC-3 were concerned with jet transition training: North American's beautiful FJ-3 Fury, Grumman's F9F-6 Cougar, McDonnell's F2H-2 and -3 Banshees, and of course the untried Cutlass.

VC-3 was good duty. No, belay that. It was wonderful duty, with lots of exotic hardware and plenty of flying. San Francisco and environs became overcast with contrails from jets engaged in mock combat, all the way from ego-testing one-on-ones to giant "furballs" pitting squadron against squadron or—better yet—an all-comers free-for-all. A radio call, "Diablo 35," meant someone was inbound over Mount Diablo at about 35,000 feet (plus or minus ten grand—fighter pilots lie a lot.) There were days when, ready for takeoff, you might spot a contrail way above and the mission resolved itself into nailing that particular intruder. Any naval aviator operating today as we did then would surely occupy the prison island of Alcatraz for all the regulations that were violated, broken, abused and otherwise spun, fondled or mutilated.

The CO of VC-3 was Commander "Jig Dog" Ramage who had been CAG for Zeke Cormier earlier. I know now that this small group of fighter jocks bond very well.

Well, as my friend Joe Foss says, the lord giveth and the lord taketh away. In my case, I was taken away from the glorious duty of daytime rat racing with my buddies and demoted to the status of student night-fighter. The all-weather professionals at VC-3 took me on as a new guy in the McDonnell F3H-2N Demon, and I'll never forget the first time I was able to use the radar system. A bright, sunny day and I couldn't see another aircraft. The radar screen showed over thirty targets! Hmmm...maybe the mark one human eyeball wasn't the only way to fighter righteousness.

The Demon was the first all-weather fighter in the so-called supersonic world. Its wings were swept to delay the onset of supersonic drag, as contrasted to most of the older straight-wing jets like the F9F Panthers and F2H "Banjos." The F3H's large fuselage contained a big radar system, one aviator, not much fuel and a voracious afterburning engine. The weapons were 20mm cannon initially, but racks were added for air-to-air missiles.

I knew I had come of age one day after a particularly aggressive hassle with an Air Force F-100 Super Sabre. My wingman, a young ensign, was impressed with how I had outmaneuvered what should have been a superior performer and ended up close astern the Hun's tail. "Gee, Wally, you're pretty good for an old guy," exclaimed my partner. At age thirty-two, I guess I was. Good, I mean, not old!

Despite the avowed night and bad-weather mission of the Moonshiners of VF-124, we found other diversions. Chief among these was a race with a difference: launching four Demons from a carrier in Monterey Bay and pushing the throttle toward Oklahoma City. The results were ambivalent, as two Demons had to land in California. I always contended that I placed second, though Skeeter Carson, the winner of the two-plane finish, insisted that I was last. Semantics get in the way, but I digress.

We conquering heroes descended from our Demons, alit to earth and accepted the adulation of the assembled throng. Ascending the stage, we were met by "Mr. Mac," James S. McDonnell, the president and CEO of the company that provided us with our mounts. He then introduced us to Miss Oklahoma City Airshow, a spectacular blonde whose prime attributes had absolutely nothing to do with her hair color. Mr. Mac presented Miss Jayne Mansfield—"Plain Jayne," he said! Afterward neither Skeeter nor I could recall whatever words we spoke to her.

Eventually the Moonshiners deployed for a Far East cruise in USS *Lexington* (CVA-16) early in 1957. We were trained as a gen-you-wine all-weather squadron, specializing in intercepts in any kind of crud, day or night. I was proud of my craft as a day fighter pilot but realized that the attitude of the night weather jocks did not consider day fighting their venue. As the squadron operations officer I insisted we train for any part of a twenty-four hour day. I felt very proud of encouraging the all-weather concept. The deployment was typically unremarkable for a WestPac in those days. At its close we returned to California and I had new orders to shore duty.

My last trap aboard the old Lex, in my trusty-rusty F3H-2N, would prove to be my last piloted carrier landing ever. Even if I'd known it at the time, I doubt I'd have grieved as much as I do now, because I had The Dream Assignment: Pax River and test-pilot school! I had no way of knowing that my next time aboard ship would be in a Mercury capsule.

In retrospect, I now realize that I was fully prepared for command. a squadron first, an airgroup...a carrier? But firmly implanted was the idea of command. When you take off you are in command of that aircraft. If you command a ship at sea, you are The Boss.

1957-58

PAX RIVER

Navy Test Pilot School was not fun. We were all great pilots, selected by our peers for a higher level of professional attainment. But the academics were tough and the engineering discipline was almost force-fed. The expected result was an aviator who could talk and write flight-test language to engineers; hand signals and sign-language would not suffice.

I'll never forget the humbling experience of a C-minus rewrite on one of my reports as a result of improperly labeling one of my graphs. I contracted a head cold that kept me grounded for two weeks, and I fell behind schedule for test flights. Finally I took out an old piston-slapper AD-4 Skyraider on a low-altitude syllabus flight. I almost blew out my eardrums on descent for landing, and was grounded for another week! That foolish decision to fly could have terminated my career—something I remembered during Apollo Seven.

Aside from the curriculum, the competition was deadly. Jim Lovell was first in our class, TPS Number Twenty, and I tied with Pete Conrad for second. Pete and I probably logged too much time water-skiing while Jim worked harder. But it all worked out when the three of us got together for a mini-reunion at the beginning of Project Gemini in 1962.

It was great to be at the hub of naval aviation; to be involved in aircraft design and configuration changes, but mainly to play with the newest toys before the fleet got them. However, one's mere presence at TPS was no guarantee of being first in line. I wasn't the first, but the thirteenth to fly the first F4H-1 Phantom at Edwards AFB in 1958. That flight was my introduction to Mach two flight, and I planned my future for a return to the fleet as prospective CO of a Phantom squadron, armed with cannons and

Sidewinders. So much for planning: Navy F-4s never got guns and I never got back to sea!

At Patuxent's Naval Air Test Center I was assigned to Service Test, which was my desire, as we evaluated aircraft to fleet standards. I remember being current in fighters plus three cats and dogs simultaneously: one merely changed kneeboard checklists to brush up on procedures. It was not hard to take—the best duty I'd had since Moffett Field.

Suddenly a set of strange orders appeared. I was to report to the Pentagon for three days—an easy trip by automobile. When I arrived, several of my contemporaries showed up in the five-sided palace for a classified briefing. Nobody seemed to know what was going on, least of all we airplane drivers.

Two civilian engineers and a psychologist briefed us on expanding opportunities in the National Aeronautics and Space Administration, NASA. On loan from our parent services, our group of Air Force and Navy or Marine aviators would launch in an Atlas missile, strapped into a "space capsule" to circle the world. We learned that the project was called "Mercury," after the son of the Greek god Jupiter. Our new messenger would show the world that the United States was in the space race to stay. Hell, I figured it was all Greek to me and was ready to head for the "No" desk. I was a tailhook aviator, not a human lab rat!

However, I sought the counsel of older and wiser heads—officers I respected, like Bob Elder and Don Shelton. They said this was my chance to fly higher, farther, faster—what all test pilots strive for. They urged me to go along with the program and see what happened. Stay loose, stay flexible.

So I allowed myself to be subjected to the innumerable indignities perpetrated upon prospective astronauts by the Space Task Force. Jim Lovell, my TPS classmate, washed out at the first stage with a liver ailment detected at the Lovelace Clinic in Albuquerque. Happily, he made the second round by proving he was cured and eventually made four space flights in Gemini and Apollo.

Pete Conrad was another dropped from consideration for Project Mercury. Other than his gap-toothed smile, he was perfect physically. But the shrinks said he had an attitude—and a really bad one at that. I said he was considered one smart ass-tronaut (sorry, Schirras have puns imprinted in their genes). Actually, I thought I had the title until Pete came along—

nobody could compete with him. Of course, he later overcame his "condition" (or at least concealed it convincingly) and made a valuable—and hilarious—addition to the ass-tronaut corps.

The eighteen finalists were narrowed down in late March 1959, but the selection board was unable to agree upon the six originally required. Consequently, Project Mercury chief Bob Gilruth submitted seven names to NASA headquarters, and we were approved by the administrator, Keith Glennan. In mid-April our names were announced to the public.

Charlie Donlan, Bob Gilruth's deputy, had called me in a matter-of-fact way. He said, "We'd like to have you join us in Project Mercury, if you're interested." It was the NASA manner—always low key and studiously casual. I would come to question the approach when flight selections were being made, but at the time I was faced with the most momentous decision of my life. This was my last chance to say, "Hell, no. I'm not going to chuck my Navy career." But I had been conditioned by the winnowing process—the enthusiasm, the competition, my reaction to seeing others fall by the wayside. I decided to join, and put my misgivings aside.

Meanwhile, life went on. Two events stand out in my memory. I was sent back to St. Louis to pick up a new F3H-2M, a missile-armed version of the Demon. I remember climbing out in afterburner to 35,000 feet, coming out of burner and intending to cruise-climb to 40,000. The Demon was so loaded with "improvements" that I cruise-descended to 25,000! What was previously a decent all-weather fighter had become a descending lead sled in less than one year. The early design was "improved upon" by subsequent good ideas to the point it became a marginal fighter.

The second event was coupled with testimony at the Navy Department about the role of the "guy in back" ("GIB") of the Phantom, now clearly successor to the doomed Demon. I felt that the tasks for both seats in the F4H were extremely complex, particularly if one considered head-on radar attacks, vertical yo-yos and countermeasure requirements. I fought to have the GIB a commissioned officer with a career path that could include command. And I won!

I was positioned and experienced enough to project my career as commanding officer of an F-4 squadron and likely would have been busy during the Vietnam War. Instead, I flew over that prolonged conflict frequently, at an altitude of more than 150 miles, safely out of danger in my wingless capsules.

Lieutenant Commander W.M. Schirra and family arrived back at Langley Air Force Base, Virginia, in 1959, eight years after departing there with the 136th Fighter-Bomber Wing for Japan and Korea. So much had happened in those eight years: maturity as a naval aviator, combat with the Air Force, test pilot and now a "space hero" who hadn't even been in space!

1960-62

MERCURY: "GO FOR SIX"

When I joined the space program I remembered my first year as a midshipman at Annapolis, and how I learned that most of my fellow "middies" had been captain of their high-school football teams or president of their senior class. I had told myself that not everyone can be number one, but in a competitive profession that's a reality not always accepted. While making a name for myself as a naval aviator—building a "professional rep"— I forgot it completely. In my first year as an astronaut I was one of seven guys, a member of an elite team, and there was no pecking order. All of a sudden, in 1960, we were faced with flight selection and Things Changed. One of us was going to emerge from the astronaut pack.

The seven of us—two Cs, two Gs and three Ss—went to work in a hurry. We had to evaluate a mockup of our Mercury capsule and make our inputs before hardware entered fabrication. We definitely had to make the capsule pilot-oriented as opposed to chimpanzee-configured, but not everyone shared our views.

We settled into a frantic schedule that called most of us far away from home, reaching out to subcontractors and consultants all over the country. We'd debrief each other every Friday back at Langley, trying to keep current on dozens of subjects, all equally important.

I'd done some very-high altitude test work in the F11F-1F Tiger and the F8U-2 Crusader that required use of the Navy's full pressure suit. I'm sure that was one of my plusses for selection into Project Mercury. Thus, I spent a large amount of my time developing what is now called a "space suit."

The Mercury capsule was pressurized to five PSI (by comparison, sea-level pressure is roughly fifteen PSI) with pure oxygen. The space suit would hold 3.5 PSI with pure oxygen if cabin pressure was lost or for EVA— "extra-vehicular activity" in NASA parlance, referring to "space walks" on Gemini missions. Mobility in the suit was important, but in Mercury, arm mobility and finger tactility were paramount. We were strapped into our couches for the duration of the mission; once unstrapped it would have been impossible to reconnect.

A problem came to sight immediately: we could not use rudder pedals for yaw control. The legs and feet were essentially immobile. What to do?

Fortunately, some bright individual devised a three-axis controller for the same movements as any aircraft: pitch for nose up or down; roll along the horizontal plane; and yaw for slewing the nose right or left. But old habits died hard. I'll never forget Deke Slayton adamantly complaining about giving up his rudder pedals!

We mounted an expedition to Edwards Air Force Base to talk to X-15 pilots who used a two-axis hand controller for pitch and roll. We got the cold shoulder but did check out the system. It was obvious that the working X-15 test pilots weren't impressed by our group, which had arrived in "second-hand" aircraft. What the X-drivers didn't realize was that we would be the first team in space—with no company test pilots flying the hardware before us! All of the X-15 pilots became friends with time, and two, Neil Armstrong and Joe Engle, joined us.

A lot of simulation, a lot of engineering, and numerous compromises went into the design of the three-axis controller. When we settled on the final configuration, we spent hundreds of hours in simulators, developing the technique to get us through the worst thrust offsets of the three retro-rockets on Mercury. I carried a rubber wrist strengthener for months to develop my right forearm and wrist. Many years later, my right wrist still is larger than my left, so the exercise worked. We added the yaw function to the control handle much the same as a motorcycle grip, but in the vertical plane instead of horizontal.

The three-axis controller carried clear through the space program. But in Gemini only one attitude controller was installed—between the two crewmen. Poor Tom Stafford, who flew with me in Gemini, had to learn attitude control with his left hand!

Humor was an essential ingredient of our existence at Cape Canaveral, Florida. It provided relief from extremely long hours of extremely serious work. More important, it eased the frustrations of those early days in Mercury. And we needed some easing when, on 12 April 1961, Major Yuri Gagarin of the Soviet Union made a single-orbit flight around the earth in Vostok One, becoming the first human in space.

Thank God for Bill Dana, who kept us laughing for years—especially for keeping us laughing at ourselves. His real name is Bill Szathmary, a professional comic who had an act featuring a frightened Mexican astronaut named Jose' Jimenez. He would start by saying, in his put-on accent, "My name, Jose' Jimenez," and in reply to a reporter's question about how he would occupy himself in space, he always answered, "I teenk I'm gonna cry a lot." It was a silly, simple sort of comedy—exactly what we needed.

When Al Shepard was launched in *Freedom Seven* three weeks after Gagarin's flight, I was piloting an F-106 chase plane. My purpose was to observe the booster and tell Shepard to abort if there appeared to be a malfunction. But there wasn't, and his mission was flawless. After five minutes and sixteen seconds of weightlessness he was recovered in the Atlantic.

Gus Grissom flew a near-identical mission 21 July aboard *Liberty Bell Seven*. It was not flawless. His hatch, held in place by explosive bolts, blew off shortly after splashdown, and the capsule sank. Gus nearly drowned as water filled his suit through the hole where the life-support system had connected. Gus was grateful to me, he said. A neck dam I had designed probably saved his life.

After three years of sweating out the selection process, we learned who was going to break out of the pack: John Glenn, the lone Marine astronaut. I'd heard that before the Space Task Group began its deliberations, John had been a typical Leatherneck fighter pilot—loud, profane, fun-loving. No more. He was the model boy scout, the very soul of decorum and family values. So, when *Friendship Seven* lifted off 20 February 1962, America took her greatest space hero to her bosom as John made three orbits in just under five hours. It was a technical distinction not only understood by the public and the taxpayers—it was doted upon. The first two NASA manned flights had been suborbital; John had flown in outer space!

But in the long run, I lucked out. Scott Carpenter's carbon-copy of John Glenn's flight, coming three months later, seemingly had deprived me of my turn. But I was ultimately glad of it. I was scheduled to fly Mercury-Atlas Eight—MA-8—and I said I wanted six orbits. Bob Gilruth, our head honcho, and operations director Walt Williams refused to make a commitment. They were worried about the fuel supply. John and Scott had used up the hydrogen peroxide that powers the attitude-control thrusters. My mission would be open-ended, but a recovery force would be deployed in the Pacific. If I did go six orbits, I would land about 275 miles northeast of Midway.

Previous missions had been flown in the "chimp mode," under automatic control, which wasted fuel. I argued that once a man was aboard, it wasn't necessary to maintain the proper attitude for retrofire throughout the flight. The procedure had been to spin the spacecraft around following booster separation—to get the heat shield pointed in the re-entry position and hold it there with the automatic program. I had a better idea and argued for it with Gilruth, Williams and James E. Webb, who had succeeded Glennan as NASA administrator. "I can control attitude by hand," I said. "Let me shut the spacecraft down and drift." I would start up again well before retrofire and return to retro attitude using the manual controls.

I won my case. Once in orbit I walked the capsule around so slowly that I got only a glimpse of the Atlas. I fired my thrusters sparingly, in small bursts. At the end of the flight I had over half my fuel left and had to dump it. That was one of the ways I proved the purpose of putting a man in space, as opposed to a robot.

I proved man's advantage in space in other ways, too. With the photographic experiments, for example, I took the approach of an engineer rather than a sightseer. I sought advice from professional photographers such as Ralph Morse and Carl Mydans of Life, and Dean Conger and Luis Marden of National Geographic. And I decided that a Hasselblad, with its larger film frame, was more suitable than a 35mm camera. I had the Hasselblad adapted. A 100-exposure film container was installed, and an easy-aiming device was mounted. Focusing would not be required from the infinity of space, I figured.

Scientific observations were on my agenda as well. I observed the planet Mercury, not normally seen from earth, because the apparent position of Mercury is too close to the sun. In orbit we're not effected by the diffuse light of the atmosphere, so I would see Mercury as it passed through layers of light. I tracked its passage against a yardstick of time, and I used crayons to color the various bands of light that it passed through to "Mercury set".

Because of my "operational" orientation, I named my spacecraft *Sigma Seven*. Sigma, a Greek symbol for the sum of the elements of an equation, stands for engineering excellence. That was my goal; I would not settle for less.

The Atlas is a volatile missile resembling a stainless-steel sausage. The steel is very thin in order to reduce weight. To maintain rigidity, it is pressurized by its fuel, a combination of kerosene, liquid oxygen and gases. When there is an Atlas mishap, it is spectacular.

As I prepared for my October flight, I was disturbed at the regularity with which Atlases were blowing up—spectacularly. This was the military Atlas, an ICBM launched in a series of tests at Vandenberg Air Force Base, California. It had not been man-rated, or checked minutely for the sake of human life. We had told the Convair folks at San Diego during 1960 that we didn't want the military Atlas—we wanted our own special bird. Nevertheless, that summer we had watched a Mercury Atlas go spastic and blow up during launch.

The Air Force grounded the Atlas, the weapon system, shortly before my scheduled launch. I figured that was one way of quieting reports about the damn thing's tendency to blow up.

The Big Day, 3 October 1962, began at 0140 when I was awakened by Howie Minners, an Air Force flight surgeon. I had the ritual breakfast of steak and eggs with Bob Gilruth, Walt Williams, Deke Slayton and Dr. Minners. We also ate a bluefish I had caught, and since the statute of limitations has elapsed, I can relate the story.

The evening before launch, Slayton and I went fishing. We hooked several bluefish in the five-pound range, but they fought free by severing our leaders with their razor-sharp teeth. I finally managed to land one by slinging it on the beach and pouncing on it before it could wriggle back to the surf.

The Cape is lined with missile gantries, and Deke and I paid little attention as to which was which. We were vaguely aware that a Thor-Delta stood about 100 yards away, since it's a big vehicle—about the size of a Mercury-Atlas—to boost military satellites into orbit. But we were so intent on catching fish that we were oblivious to activity on the pad. It wasn't until we heard a roar that we realized the Thor-Delta was lifting off. We were looking right up the tailpipe of its monster engine, and knew instantly that we stood in the danger zone. Had there been an abort, it would have been a bad day for Mercury, with the chief astronaut and crew of MA-8 incinerated in the surf.

Anyway, the bluefish was delicious that morning.

Howie Minners escorted me to the pad in the transfer van, actually a tractor-trailer rig. I was suited up with the helmet visor closed so I could breathe pure oxygen and purge the nitrogen from my system. Minners was yakking away to keep my spirits up, which wasn't necessary. I wanted to rest and think about my flight. I could have unplugged my radio, but that would have been rude, so I signaled that I wanted him to stop talking by closing my eyes.

Next thing I knew, Minners was tapping my visor and saying by radio, "Wally, we're at the pad." I had dozed off.

We had a near-perfect countdown with only a brief delay due to a radar malfunction at the Canary Islands tracking station. Liftoff was at 0715. At ten seconds into the flight there was a problem that came close to ending my ride. The clockwise roll rate of the Atlas was greater than planned, and it startled the people in Mercury Control who read the instruments. If the missile got badly out of parameters, the range safety officer would have no choice but to abort the mission and I'd get a cheap ride home via the escape tower. But the program straightened itself out, and the Atlas stayed within safe limits. I didn't even learn of the close call until after the flight.

Once in orbit at 176 miles, I began my turnaround with the attitude-control system in the fly-by-wire mode. I was flying the spacecraft. With my eyes fixed on the control panel, studiously ignoring the view, I began a four-degrees-per-second cartwheel. Once in the correct orbital position, I checked my fuel. I had used less than half a pound of hydrogen peroxide. The thrusters worked perfectly. They responded crisply to my touch and shut off without any residual motion. I was able to make tiny, single-pulse spurts to assume an exact attitude.

Glenn and Carpenter had experienced suit overheating, and I was feeling it, too. It was serious. Chuck Berry, our chief flight surgeon, and Frank Samonski, our environmental supervisor, pondered bringing me back after one orbit. But on Berry's advice Chris Kraft, the flight director, gave me an OK for a second orbit, relayed to me by Scott Carpenter in the Guaymas, Mexico tracking station.

By valving water into the cooling system very slowly, I gradually brought the suit temperature down to ninety-some degrees—hot but not unbearable. The problem was solved through no great amount of ingenuity, but my point was that it had been solved by a human. Later I received a plaque reading, "Presented by the undersigned, who sweated more than you did during the first orbit of MA-8..." The signatories were Samonski and his crew, the environmental controllers, and the valve I used to control the water flow was mounted on the plaque.

After drifting awhile to conserve energy, I powered up the capsule over the Indian Ocean and switched to fly-by-wire to check the systems. I had sighted the moon through the window and reported to the station in Muchea, Australia, that I had fixed my attitude using the moon as a reference. I then locked the system in automatic. I knew the tracking stations had been paying close attention to my fuel state, as Mercury Control was deciding how long I'd stay up. I got the word from Gus Grissom at Kauai, Hawaii, "Wally, you have a go for six orbits."

"Hallelujah," I replied. I was to become the American who had flown farthest in space. But by then the Soviets had flown as many as sixty orbits on a mission.

On the fifth circuit Grissom in Hawaii read me a time for retrofire on the next orbit, and in turn I heard Carpenter in Mexico and Glenn in California confirm that communications should be in good shape for re-entry into earth's atmosphere. I was then astonished to hear a voice interrupt from Quito, Ecuador. We had a "minitrack" there, a miniature tracking station, that wasn't supposed to call except in emergencies.

"*Sigma Seven*," the caller interjected. "Do you have a message for the people of South America?"

I was furious. Here I was preparing for the crucial re-entry, and I was expected to utter some hogwash, some glowing statement about how I was proud to be an emissary of the United States, passing over Ecuador. "Roger, Quito," I radioed. "Buenos dias, you-all." Then I was gone.

I knew I would be criticized for being brusque, and sure enough, the telegrams were handed to me on the recovery ship. But there was one I treasured from a U.S. diplomat in Ecuador. He said, in effect, that Schirra had proved his devotion to the people of Latin America by wishing them a good day. And by addressing them as "you-all," Schirra was simply noting that he was soon to become a resident of Texas when NASA moved to Houston.

I had made the point to NASA that my interest in public relations was zero. Nor did I intend to extol the wonders of space or portray the spectacle in vivid language. I was a pilot, an engineer, maybe even a scientist. Sightseeing was low on my list of priorities. If NASA expected poetry, they should have sent a poet.

I armed the rockets on Al Shepard's command. Then I punched a button to initiate the sequence—one, two, three. The retros fired with crisp precision, and *Sigma Seven* was holding steady as a rock. I switched back to fly-by-wire for re-entry, again according to plan. When I jettisoned the retro pack, I felt the capsule wobble and made a quick adjustment. I pitched up to a fourteen-degree attitude and used the automatic controls to damp out the motion. Then I switched on the rate-stabilizing control system as requested by the engineers. The RSCS is a fuel guzzler but I had plenty. The gauge for the automatic system read about fifty-three percent. I allowed as how I was thrilled, in case anyone was able to listen through the ionization communication blackout.

At 40,000 feet I punched a button and felt the drogue parachute pop open. I activated the main chute at 15,000 and watched it blossom at 10,500. I was elated and radioed Shepard, "I think they're going to put me on the number-three elevator." It was a tailhook aviator's reference to an elevator on USS *Kearsarge* (CVS-33), the recovery carrier. Actually, I missed the ship by only four and a half miles. I believe that Captain Gene Rankin was afraid I'd hit him, so he positioned his ship well away! In any case, the crew saw my contrail and heard the sonic booms.

When I was recovered, I remained in my capsule until being hoisted aboard the carrier. I then blew the hatch intentionally, and the recoil of the plunger injured my hand. It actually caused a cut through a glove that was reinforced by metal. Gus Grissom was one of those who flew out to the ship, and I showed him my hand. "How did you cut it?" he asked.

"I blew the hatch," I replied. Gus smiled, immediately vindicated. He'd taken a lot of flak for loss of his capsule, as a lot of second-guessers assumed he'd screwed up by blowing his hatch prematurely. But my cut proved he hadn't blown his own hatch with a hand, foot, knee or whatever—he hadn't suffered so much as a minor bruise.

When I stepped from *Sigma Seven* to the deck of *Kearsarge*, it was ten hours since launch, almost to the second.

There was a big greeting when we landed at Pearl Harbor, and I stayed in Hawaii for a day in Air Force VIP quarters. I was surrounded by VIPs—the governor, a U.S. senator and military brass. But Bill Dana happened to be in Hawaii and he telephoned. "Hi, Wally. How are you?"

"Oh, I've been around," I replied. Then clunk, I hung up. It was too good to resist—one of my better puns, I thought, at the expense of a big-name comedian.

Following my return to Houston everybody drank champagne and patted me on the back, telling me what a swell job I'd done. In fact, I managed to endure the good vibes so long that it was nearly 0400 when the guests and well-wishers left the Schirras' new home in Timber Cove.

I was in my pajamas, ready to climb into bed, when Jo asked sweetly, "Wally, will you please put out the garbage?" What I had done to Bill Dana in Hawaii was nothing compared to what my wife had done to me. The ultimate putdown!

Jo, Marty, Suzy and I went to Washington on 16 October, barely two weeks after my flight. President Kennedy was preoccupied with the Cuban missile crisis, but took time for a private ceremony in the Oval Office. He was especially kind to the children, asking Suzy her age. When she held up five fingers, he took her to see his daughter Caroline's pony, Macaroni. The astronauts were frequently back and forth to Washington, and we developed a rapport with him.

On one occasion the president said to me, "I understand you have no political aspirations." He had heard that news from his brother Robert, the attorney general. Bobby had helped initiate John Glenn's career in the senate. During my postflight White House visit Bobby took me aside, congratulated me and then asked, "By the way, we are quite curious about your political ambitions."

"I'm an engineering test pilot," I replied. "And I'm becoming something of a scientist. That is to say, my decisions are based on facts, and I would find the transition to politics impossible." RFK then escorted me to the Oval Office, and that was that. He may have believed he had paid me a compliment, but I didn't see it that way.

1964-66

GEMINI AND GOTCHAS

Project Gemini was named for Castor and Pollux, the twin sons of Jupiter (I was beginning to speak better Greek!) It was an appropriate name for the next step in manned space flight, as the larger capsule would carry two men. We would fly for periods up to two weeks, walk in space and dock with other vehicles.

The lineup had changed, however. Deke Slayton, grounded medically and unable to fly in Mercury, served as chief astronaut. John Glenn, Al Shepard and Scott Carpenter also were off flight status due to various disabilities. That left Gus Grissom, Gordo Cooper and myself as Gemini crews. In fact, Grissom was concentrating on Gemini even while Cooper and I were flying Mercury. He was hurt and angry at being blamed for the loss of his capsule, and he fought to come back out of the pack. Gus Grissom was a tiger. He wanted the first Gemini flight, and by God, he got it.

It was inevitable that the astronauts received nearly all the publicity and acclaim, but NASA involved thousands of people. And for me, the most important of the folks behind the scenes—managers, engineers, technicians—was an anonymous fellow named Ralph Gendielle (pronounced Gendalee). He was the McDonnell engineer who had babied *Sigma Seven*. We'd become very good friends, and Ralph got himself assigned to my Gemini spacecraft as well. He told me he intended to protect it. Ralph, who died a few years ago, was totally dedicated to the space program. When Gemini ended and McDonnell had not landed an Apollo contract, he quit his job and joined Grumman, manufacturer of the lunar lander.

Gemini was the interim step leading to a landing on the moon. We had learned to crawl in Mercury, now we would walk before making the lunar run. We had to prove that we could operate in space for at least eight days—the minimum time for a moon mission. Some, like Dr. Wehrner von Braun, were already thinking in terms of a permanent space station. But it was cheaper and technically more efficient to send a lunar lander from moon orbit, so the pressure was on. If we failed to accomplish the crucial rendezvous or docking phase, America's manned space program would be ruined.

Navigation was another big concern, for rendezvous in space and re-entry leading to splashdown. An onboard computer was required for that purpose; it controlled the lift vector—the angle of re-entry and the velocity. The vector in turn would determine the landing area, or "footprint."

I was totally resolved to making a spot-on landing, thereby reducing the footprint to absolute minimums. I thought I'd wear out Langley's simulator because I kept missing my "spot" in repeated practice: 3.9 miles, then 4.1, 3.8, and so on. After my Mercury flight I checked the data and concluded that they were in error. The Australian landmass, my last earth fix prior to retrofire, was four miles out of position!

My findings were confirmed in the Gemini missions, and we had to reorient the tracking network—to tell the stations where they were! Chalk up another one for manned spacecraft.

With all the training, study and hard work, there had to be time out for foolishness. I've always felt that humor is the lubricant of adversity, and certainly it was true in Gemini. As I said, Gus Grissom was a fierce competitor. He established his turf. He was first in Gemini, and he was commander of the first Apollo mission when he was killed in the capsule fire. He had planned on being the first on the moon.

But Gus was also a "gotcha" champion, especially where cars were involved. Being fun-loving fighter jocks, we were car crazy—"the need for speed." Gus really nailed Al Shepard once, which was no mean feat. At the Cape in '64, Gus and Al each had new Corvettes. They would drive in formation as if they were doing test flights, comparing data. Al would hold up three fingers for 3,000 RPM, Gus would nod and off they'd go. Or they would stop at a light, side-by-side, and at the green they'd roar off together as if at a dragstrip. Every time Gus just left Al in the dust. Nobody knew why—except Gus and Jim Rathmann, a Cadillac-Chevy dealer in Melbourne, Florida, who had won the 1960 Indy 500. Ol' Gus had Jim's shop increase his gear ratio to produce 4,000 revs instead of the standard three grand. Though more RPM reduces top speed, it increases acceleration. Another Gus Gotcha!

But there were other players. In the back of his parts shop, Rathmann had a wooden box about one foot square by two feet long with heavy-gauge chicken wire on one side, a padlocked door and the stenciled warning: "Danger! Live Indian mongoose—do NOT touch." This was not to be taken idly: Jim stressed that mongooses go for the genitals when they attack humans.

As Shepard watched warily from one side, Grissom and Cooper were beautifully victimized. Rathmann tapped on the box, trying to arouse the mongoose, and Gus peered through the wire. Gordo held up a "pet" baby boa constrictor retrieved from survival exercises in Panama to see if the mongoose would react. Of course, the padlock was for show. The door was held by a hook, and when Rathmann flipped it, a foxtail was released under spring tension. Gordo jumped three feet in the air, flinging the boa at Gus. To keep it from wrapping itself around his neck, Gus threw the snake into the air. The foxtail landed on a table where Shepard was sitting, and Al started mashing the furry thing with a hammer. Rathmann laughed so hard that he fell against a parts bin, knocking it into a domino reaction of crashing shelves.

An all-time great gotcha! There was a twenty-second segment in *The Right Stuff,* showing me pulling the mongoose gotcha, but Rathmann gets credit for it. However, I admit that I've frequently done it since.

Following two unmanned tests in April 1964 and January 1965, the Titan II and Gemini spacecraft were considered worthy. We began manned missions with Gemini Three, when Grissom and John Young launched 24 March 1965. In ten missions during 1965-66 we logged 970 hours in space. Though there were some scary moments, the program was completed without a serious accident.

No Mercury astronauts flew in 1966. The flight commanders were all from the second group, named in 1962, and the pilots came from the "class of '63." Overall, sixteen astronauts filled twenty Gemini slots—Young, Conrad, Stafford and Lovell all flying twice. Of the sixteen, thirteen would fly Apollo.

Three would not. Gus Grissom and Ed White died in a 1967 spacecraft fire on the launch pad. Gordon Cooper was out of favor with the higher-ups. His Mercury mission had been a great success, and nothing that went wrong on Gemini Five could be blamed on him. Yet he was passed over. Gordo's last assignment was as the backup commander of Gemini 12. He was pretty bitter by then.

Though we stopped naming spacecraft in Gemini, I had thought about a patch for Gemini Six, featuring the constellation Orion. Tom Stafford and I planned to do our rendezvous with Orion as a guide. The patch would be six-sided, since six was the number of our mission. Orion also appears in the first six hours of right ascension, a quarter of the way around the celestial sphere.

Our mission, slated for late 1965, was to perform the difficult rendezvous (RV) task. Frankly, we were not sure how to accomplish it. Buzz Aldrin gave us an academic approach. A West Pointer with an advanced degree in science and astronautics from MIT, he was our "doctor of rendezvous." Buzz advocated the Hohmann Transfer, named for the scientist who plotted it in 1925. On paper, it looks great. It's a perfect maneuver in earth orbit, as you traverse the earth once and return to a predicted point. The RV is achieved in half a revolution, 180 degrees. It's the most efficient, quickest and prettiest way to perform a rendezvous, but it is intolerant of error. If you blow the RV, fuel and time constraints won't permit another try.

After much commuting to McDonnell's simulator in St. Louis, and consulting with Houston engineer Dean Grimm, we decided on a rendezvous during 270 degrees of rotation, which offered much more latitude. Stafford and I also spent many hours rehearsing the docking maneuver in the Houston trainer. Housed in a six-story building, it consisted of a full-scale Gemini cockpit and the docking adapter of the Agena. We closed with the target at about one foot per second, an ideal velocity, and tried to make contact with enough impact to secure the latches.

As a rule we practiced alone. There was no need for a copilot, since docking was all eyeball work. But once I was joined in the trainer by Vice President Hubert Humphrey. I knew him slightly from meetings in Washington, where once in awhile he'd take turns playing the bass fiddle with Collins Bird, manager of the Georgetown Inn.

On this particular day, the VP's entourage watched as he climbed the ladder to my trainer while I held it steady. He eased into the copilot's seat and I closed the hatch. When the lights in the complex were dimmed, Mr. Humphrey asked me if his voice could be heard outside the simulator. I clicked off my radio and said, "No, sir." Then he asked, "Do you mind if I go to sleep while you do your deal?" He proceeded to doze for ten minutes, and when he woke he made one more request. "Now explain what you've been doing so I can tell those people down below."

I liked the warm, human Hubert Humphrey a whole lot more than I did Lyndon Johnson.

Reviewing a flying career of twenty-odd years, I can recall a few memorable moments in which I approached the ultimate flying experience. My first carrier landing in the F8F-1 Bearcat was one. Another was the test flights of the F4H-1 Phantom II at Edwards. Test pilots describe their reaction to the performance of an aircraft in terms of the harmony that develops between a man and a machine. If you ever achieve exquisite harmony, you have reached a level of absolute confidence. Man and machine have become one. There is no limit to what they can do together.

Perhaps exquisite harmony is just beyond reach. That's the way it should be, I suppose. But I came closest in December 1965, during Gemini Six. It was when we succeeded in rendezvousing. I was at the controls, bringing her within inches of the target, Gemini Seven. I was cavorting about, literally flying rings around Gemini Seven.

My spacecraft was the equivalent of a fighter plane. It was stripped to the essentials of a twenty-six hour mission. And just as I had a radar observer in the Phantom, I had Tom Stafford in the right seat. We had incredible maneuverability, though in space flight it's called "translation"— changing the spatial coordinates without rotation. I could translate up and down, right and left, forward and backward, just like the cosmic warriors in *Star Wars*. No doubt about it—the Gemini spacecraft was my favorite flying vehicle.

But at first it looked as if we'd never light the fire and get off the ground. Gemini Six's launch was aborted twice—on 25 October (lack of a target, as Agena didn't make orbit) and 12 December (engine shutdown.)

Frank Borman and Jim Lovell already were up in Gemini Seven, and had been orbiting eleven days when Tom and I lifted off 15 December. As we passed overhead Africa, Bormann and Lovell glimpsed our sunlight reflection. Our apogee was 160.5 miles, our perigee was 99.8, while Gemini Seven's circular orbit was a constant 186. At insertion into orbit we trailed her by 1,235 miles, and after one orbit we were behind only 728 miles. The flight plan called for catching the target by the fourth orbit, and we were holding to the schedule.

At five hours and four minutes from launch I dimmed the cabin lights and peered out the window. "My God," I exclaimed, "there's a real bright star out there." But it was Gemini Seven, about sixty miles away, reflecting the sun. I made two midcourse corrections, and at five hours, fifty minutes, we were less than 1,000 yards from the target. I began to brake the spacecraft by firing the forward thrusters. When Gemini Six and Seven were forty yards apart, there was no relative motion between them. Rendezvous!

During the approach—say, from a half-mile out—I maneuvered with tender care. A light touch was critical. If I overthrusted, our orbit might change dramtically. It was tricky, but those simulator sessions paid off. Computer readings based on radar told us our closing velocity, and Tom was doing the computations. "Go right," he'd say. "Go left. Speed up. Slow down." Stafford, whose eyes were accustomed to the light illuminating his plotting board, looked outside just as the RV was secure and shouted, "Holy cow, Schirra! You blew it!" He was looking at John Glenn's famous "fireflies," frozen droplets of water reflecting daylight. He mistook them for a field of stars, and their random movement caused him to sense that the spacecraft was out of control.

"Those are fireflies, Tom," I said, and we both laughed.

I radioed Gemini Seven when we were 200 yards apart. "Having fun?"

"Hello, there," Borman replied.

"There seems to be a lot of traffic up here," I said.

"Call a policeman," Borman commented.

All four of us were overjoyed. We had done something for which we had spent years in preparation. We flew formation for three revolutions of the earth, moving from a range of 100 yards between us to mere inches, window to window and nose to nose. Using my "eyeball ranging system," I did an in-plane flyaround of Gemini Seven, like a crewchief inspecting an aircraft. I could see icicles hanging from one side and sunlight reflected by the gold surface of the mylar heat shield. I was amazed at my ability to maneuver, controlling attitude with my right hand and translating in every direction by igniting the translation thrusters with my left-hand mechanism. Tom and I took turns. We shared the attitude stick between us, and he controlled thrust with his right hand.

Tom and I couldn't switch seats—the capsule was so cramped that we could barely squeeze into our couches. But I'm almost ambidextrous. I write left-handed and can throw and kick a ball from both sides, and I'm more accurate with a pool cue when I shoot left-handed. So controlling translation with my left hand was not difficult. This was the ultimate light touch!

I pulled one of my favorite gotchas during RV, and it was destined for citation in the U.S. Naval Academy history. Three of us were Annapolis grads—Stafford, Lovell and I. Borman went to West Point before becoming an Air Force officer, so you know who was going to get it. With our windows just inches apart, I held up a "Beat Army" sign. But Borman topped me. Before my sign's message could be read to the world, he radioed, "Schirra's got a sign. It says, 'Beat Navy.'"

We had another surprise in store for the folks on Planet Earth. During training at the Cape, I had said, "You know, Tom, it's getting close to Christmas. We might have some fun with that." While overflying the continental U.S. on our next-to-last orbit, Stafford began his message.

"Houston, this is Gemini Six."

"Roger, Gemini Six," Capcom Elliott See responded.

"We have an object, looks like a satellite going from north to south, probably in polar orbit...Looks like he might be going to re-enter soon."

The guys in mission control were beside themselves as Tom continued, "I see a command module and eight smaller modules in front. The pilot of the command module is wearing a red suit." He then started ringing a bunch of little bells, and I took out a tiny four-hole harmonica. I had secured it in my suit by tying it to a pocket zipper with dental floss. I could play eight notes, enough for "Jingle Bells." It may not have been a virtuoso performance, but it earned me a card in the musicians' union of Orlando, Florida. I also received a tiny gold harmonica from the Italian National Union of Mouth Organists.

Gemini Six returned to earth 16 December. We switched off the computer at 80,000 feet, deployed the drogue chute at 45,000 and popped the main at 10,500. Splashdown was eight miles off the "three-wire," in carrier aviator's parlance. We descended within range of live TV cameras aboard the recovery carrier USS *Wasp* (CVS-18), another first. Gemini Seven landed two days later, and Borman won our wager in the "spot landing contest" by just one mile. However, Frank admitted he'd benefited from my briefing on computer procedures.

Most of the lengthy debriefings fell somewhere between tedious and routine, but one was great fun. Jocelyn Gill, a NASA astronomer, was in charge of an experiment in photographing the heavens. Dr. Gill was particularly interested in what scientists called the dim-light phenomenon, and supplied me with very fast film—ASA 4,000—for my Hasselblad. So I decided that there was a chance to settle the question of Glenn's "fireflies" once and for all.

I knew the fireflies were frozen molecules of vapor vented from the spacecraft, and they were with us constantly as a fuzzy cloud. We could distinguish them individually, since they reflected different colors of the spectrum in sunlight. As I said before, their source was water released in the heat exchange process that cooled our space suits. Another source was urine. "We peed all over the world," I'm fond of saying, despite the inevitable groans from any audience.

After the rendezvous, when we had some spare time, Tom and I snapped color photos of the molecular cloud, one every forty-five minutes. We logged each shot with a label—urine drops at sunrise, urine drops at sunset, etc. When the photos were processed at the cape, they were beautiful, and I ordered a set of prints. I had them on the table during an astronomy debriefing, mixed with other celestial photos. Dr. Gill noticed one and asked, "Wally, what constellation is this?"

"Jocelyn," I replied, "that's the Constellation Urion."

It was good to be back.

1966-69

APOLLO

Gus Grissom and I were assigned to command the first two Apollo missions—earth-orbital flights to test the "block one" spacecraft, unequipped with docking equipment or the "lunar excursion module." The LEM wasn't ready for flight testing yet.

We were to launch in the Saturn 1B, scaled down from the humongous Saturn 5. Dr. von Braun once said, "If you make a rocket engine that's very powerful, I will cluster it and make it even bigger." By clustering he meant grouping as many as eight engines together, similar to the V-2 rockets he built during WW II. The joke was that von Braun finally built a booster with so much thrust that at liftoff the earth moved.

My crew was named originally for the second Apollo flight in mid-1966. Cunningham was technically the LEM pilot, and Eisele was the command and service module pilot. We soon became known as Wally, Walt and Whatshisname. People had trouble pronouncing Donn's name, which phonetically is Eyeselee. When Jim Webb introduced us to Lyndon Johnson, the NASA administrator stumbled when he got to Donn, then called him "Isell." From then on, ol' Donn was Whatshisname.

Our flight was to be identical to Grissom, White and Chaffee's—ten to fourteen days in orbit testing a block-one capsule—and I argued against the duplication. Successfully, it turned out. We replaced Jim McDevitt's crew as backup to Grissom.

I admit it was a comedown to be backing up Gus again, a real ego-douser. It was nothing personal, for Gus and I were next-door neighbors, the best of friends. But I'd heard people imply that I'd been selected for Mercury, not Apollo, and it rankled. Of course, if it applied to me it applied to Gus, Al and Deke as well. None of us was ready to admit we were washed up. We just took a cue from Avis: we tried harder.

But for all our patience and effort, the Apollo spacecraft was not checking out; it just didn't have the ring of a pure bell. The electrical system was especially troubling, and one day at North American's plant Downey plant, Gus passed judgment. He hung a lemon on the thing—a big, yellow California lemon.

On 27 January 1967, Cunningham, Eisele and I flew from the Cape to Houston following extensive tests of the Apollo-Saturn system. We landed at Ellington Air Force base and climbed from our T-38s when Joe Algranti, our air operations officer, came running out. "The Apollo crew," he blurted. "They burned to death."

Gus's crew had been winding up a test that lasted all afternoon. The sea level atmosphere in the cabin had been replaced by pure oxygen at 16.7 pounds per square inch—1.7 pounds more than outside. My tests had been conducted using ambient air, which of course was far less conducive to combustion.

I thought of Ed White, the Air Force lieutenant colonel who had made the first spacewalk, and of Roger Chaffee, a new-guy lieutenant commander anticipating his first mission. But mostly I thought about Gus. He was one of our original seven good buddies, my longtime neighbor. I was the executor of his estate. Jo, I learned, had walked over to tell Betty the terrible news, going via a hole in the fence that permitted our wives to visit one another without exposure to the constant reporters.

As test pilots must be, we were accustomed to death. The loss of a colleague is not uncommon. But it doesn't mean we don't mourn our lost friends. When I sail offshore and see the hills surrounding San Diego, I think about Shannon McCrary, my old skipper who is buried at Point Loma. He was killed making an instrument approach and we went to his funeral wearing black armbands. But we don't wear black forever. We mourn the man for a little while, then we live with the loss.

We had lost other astronauts, though not in spacecraft. "Ordinary" airplane crashes had deprived us of Elliot See, Charlie Bassett and Ted Freeman from 1963 to 1966. And C.C. Williams, a Marine aviator, was lost taking off in a T-38 nine months after the tragedy on Pad 34.

There's a film made for test pilots called *You've Got to Expect Losses*. It shows a series of catastrophes, beginning with early attempts to fly. Then you see a Navy fighter going in off the bow of a carrier—kerplunk, into the sea as the ship runs over the plane. And there's an incredible incident showing an F-100 in a full stall at ground level, the famous "tail dance" with flames billowing from both ends of the fuselage before it blows up.

The point is, anybody who's been in aviation—especially flight test—learns to live with losses. That's why so many of us were surprised at the reaction to the space shuttle *Challenger*'s explosion in 1986. It was a combination of ignorance on the part of the media and the public's insulation from flight-test reality. Frankly, NASA shot itself in the foot with the hype and publicity it lavished upon the male-female, ethnically-representative crew. The unfortunate schoolteacher who died with the astronauts only focused more attention on the tragedy and prolonged an unnecessarily lengthy delay in the shuttle program. I think the NASA professionals who perished in *Challenger* would have been unanimous in their recommendation: "Fix the thing and press on!" Instead, we lost two and a half years in hand-wringing and soul-searching.

However, reaction to the Apollo tragedy lingered as well. Lee Atwood, the president of North American, remained concerned about the fire long after he retired. In 1987 he sent me an analysis that expressed his regret. "If the question had been properly put," he wrote, "...that is, did you know that the astronauts were being locked in with all that electrical machinery, and the spacecraft is being inflated to 16.7 pounds per square inch with pure oxygen? I believe a whistle would have been blown."

Remedial action was taken to prevent recurrences. All flammable materials were removed from the capsule, and a hatch was designed to open out as it had on Mercury and Gemini spacecraft. Additionally, the cabin would be pressurized before launch with a sixty-forty mix of oxygen and nitrogen, considered safe and medically acceptable.

On 9 May 1967, Jim Webb announced the team for the first manned Apollo mission: Schirra, Cunningham and Eisele (Jim got the names right this time) as primary crew with Stafford, Young and Cernan as backup. Webb also named a support crew. Jack Swigert, Ron Evans and Bill Pogue would maintain a flight-data file, develop emergency procedures in the simulators, and prepare the cockpit for countdown tests. I asked Swigert to establish procedures in the event of a fuel tank explosion in space—just like the one on Apollo 13 in April 1970. Swigert was aboard, and his checklist helped get the crew home.

At this point the names of mission flights lost much of their significance. The flight that Grissom, White and Chaffee would never make was symbolically named Apollo One, but the second and third (unmanned) missions received no numbers. The next three were named, however—more unmanned missions to test the "all-up" three-stage Saturn Five booster and block one and two improvements.

Apollo Seven, scheduled for late 1968, was going to be my last mission. I intended to retire and would make it official before we flew. There were several reasons. For one, I wanted to quit while I was ahead. I also wanted it clear that I was single-minded about Apollo Seven, that I cared for nothing else.

As the space program had matured, so had I. No longer was there the laughing boy in scarf and goggles, the jolly Wally of spaceage lore. When Gus's crew was lost, I became deeply involved in deciding where we were headed. And when I realized we would try again with me in command, I resolved that the mission would not be jeopardized by the influence of special interests—scientific, political, whatever.

There were those involved in launching us who never got the message—well-intentioned engineers whose enthusiasm for technological achievement ran counter to the well-being of the crew. They and I were on a collision course, and eventually we clashed. My decision to quit made it easier to say I didn't give a damn. I wasn't so susceptible to criticism. I cared not a whit about being in the good graces of the support folks—including the hierarchy.

On 20 September 1968 I announced that I would retire from the Navy and from NASA, effective 1 July 1969.

Meanwhile, the contractor folks had gone to zone-five afterburner on our behalf. The lights probably never dimmed at North American, and I came to respect Lee Atwood's entire organization, especially John Patrick Healey. His mission was to prepare our spacecraft for a successful flight, and in our first meeting he and I were like two bantam roosters in the arena. But instead of engaging in a mutually-destructive competition, we became allies and good buddies. Working with him, I felt I'd attained the ultimate plane of test-pilot karma: communicating with the engineers!

One example illustrates the attitude at North American. In early 1968 I inspected the spacecraft at Downey with company and NASA honchos

Wally's first assignment after winning his Wings of Gold, was to fly the Grumman F8F Bearcat. "It was," he said, "the closest thing to strapping on a pair of angel wings." (USN)

In 1951, during the Korean War, Wally rode into battle in an Air Force Republic F-84 jet fighter as an exchange officer with the 154th Ftr. Bmr. Sq., 136th Ftr. Bmr. Wing. (USAF)

Lt. Wally Schirra, USN, in the cockpit of his USAF Republic F-84E, 154th Ftr. Bmr. Sq., 1951. (USAF)

The future of aerial combat; Flying Douglas F3D Skyknights, Wally tested the Sidewinder air - air missile at Inyokern, CA in 1953. Forty years later the AIM-9 remains one of the most reliable aviation weapons ever developed. (USN)

Vought's old gave way to the new as the F4U-5 Corsair was augmented at Moffett Field by the F7U-3 Cutlass. Developmental squadron VC-3 flew the veteran propeller fighter and the innovative jet simultaneously in 1954-55. (USN)

Landing the under powered F7U on straight deck carriers was a dicey proposition, as Wally learned during trials aboard *Hancock*. The LSO stands behind the windscreen on right. (USN)

Wally's last fleet deployment was with VF-124, flying F3H-2N Demon night fighters from USS Lexington (CVA-16) for 6 months in 1957. (USN)

A youthful astronaut, Wally posed in his shiny new space suit with a model of Sigma 7, his Mercury spacecraft. (NASA)

Easy letdown: Sigma 7 parachuting toward recovery after six orbits of the earth, 3 October 1962. (NASA)

"Closest to the hole" in golfer's terms. Wally's splashdown was only 4.5 miles from target - nearest of any Mercury flight. (NASA)

Project Mercury Astronauts maintained flying proficiency in a variety of high-performance aircraft. Here Wally climbs from a Mach-two F-106B at Langley Air Force Base, 1961. (Schirra)

Fast transportation was afforded astronauts, who frequently commuted between Cape Canaveral and NASA headquarters in Houston. One of Wally's favorites was the T-38 trainer. (NASA)

Project Gemini introduced the team concept to America's manned space flight program. Wally's partner Gemini 6 was Tom Stafford. They rendezvoused in orbit with Gemini 7 crew, Frank Borman and Jim Lovell. (Schirra)

Wally sustained minor damage to his space suit, but safely completed a 26 hour mission on December 15-16, 1965. He remained aboard Gemini 6 with Tom Stafford until hoisted aboard the recovery aircraft carrier, USS Wasp (CVS-18).

justments are made to Wally's suit prior to ering the Apollo 7 capsule for flight simulation uly 1968. The actual mission was flown three nths later. (NASA)

Reinforcing the message that astronauts were pilots, Wally, Walt Cunningham and Don Eisele adopted traditional white scarves for a NASA publicity photo. (NASA)

The Navy used to be enthusiastic about cakes, and the recovery of Apollo 7 after 160 orbits was reason enough to put the bakers to work. Wally practices his slicing style aboard USS Essex (CVS-9) while Cunningham and Eisele offer ample advice. (NASA)

Wally Schirra, astronaut. He remains the only American to have flown in all of NASA's first three manned programs - but admits that he would have been just as happy chasing MiGs over Hanoi. (Schirra)

looking on. Dressed in the required spick-and-span white suit and cap, I was careful upon boarding not to step on anything that might be damaged. But it was a tight fit, and my knee landed on a bunch of wires. Immediately I felt a sharp slap on my face, and heard a woman's voice: "Don't you dare touch those wires! Don't you know we lost three men?"

When she was told who I was, the lady felt embarrassed, but I assured her she needn't be. "Keep it up," I said. "I want people like you working on my spacecraft!"

We've all heard the conventional wisdom about combat flying: hours and hours of dull routine interspersed with moments of stark terror. Well, Apollo Seven was days and days of dull routine interspersed with hours of boredom. We lit the wick of that big candle 11 October 1968, and when we felt the hold-downs release, the excitement was tremendous—on our way at last! But after that, the blahs set in. I've never been as bored in my life as when orbiting those eleven days.

One of our big funs was making the first live television broadcast from space—that's how uninteresting the trip was for me. After the absolute joy of maneuvering Gemini Six, the Apollo spacecraft was a huge letdown. I remember sitting there, strapped uselessly in my couch and thinking, "Well, I'm a bomber pilot now."

We were on Day Four when I realized that 10.8 days can be an eternity. Fascinating as it may seem to anyone who hasn't flown in space, twenty-four hours is still 1,440 minutes, divided by sixteen orbits. And on each orbit you can watch earthrise and earthset, but how many times can you exclaim, "Golly-gee"?

I was wearing a velcro watchband with a small metal calendar for October 1968 affixed to it. As each day passed, I scratched off the date like a prisoner or a man marooned on an island.

Amusements were scarce, as we had no books to read or tapes to play, but we found sport wherever we could. I tried I-don't-know-how-many times to shoot a pen through a "target" Walt Cunningham made of his thumb and forefinger, though I proved more adept at catching cinnamon cubes in my mouth, as one does at happy hour with peanuts or olives. In zero gravity it's difficult to miss!

I also discovered to my delight that spacemen are different, after all. There's the classic line, "He may be president of the United States, but he puts his pants on one leg at a time, just like everyone else." Getting dressed one morning, I snapped on my coveralls, and without thinking I began to pull on my pants. "Hey," I called to Walt and Donn, "we put our pants on two legs at a time!"

But my favorite one on Walt occurred when he was about to urinate into his collection device while floating in his couch near the window. He reflexively turned his back to the window and I asked, "Who's out there, Walt?"

There was a minor medical crisis when all three of us caught severe head colds (mucus doesn't drain in zero gravity, it just stays in the sinuses) and we expended nine of the ten Kleenex dispensers aboard. The cold medication in our kit was a prescription product made by Burroughs Wellcome Co. Years later it would be sold over the counter as Actifed, and I endorsed it for TV commercials. For that reason alone, this mission became best known for our misery. My eleven-year-old daughter, already a genuine Schirra punster, called our spacecraft "the ten-day cold capsule."

At the time I was also on the board of Kimberly-Clark, so I was prone to say, "If Actifed doesn't work, I can get you a deal on Kleenex tissue."

Lest I overstate the ennui we endured, Apollo Seven actually did serve some useful purpose. We accomplished a lot of photography—the Indian government even used our Himalayas shots to locate water sources—and we made some detailed weather observations. And of course we fought with the computers.

Our re-entry was trouble-free. We splashed down in the Atlantic southeast of Bermuda about one mile from the designated impact point—what I call "good enough for government work." We had a moment of concern when the spacecraft nosed down in the water, but she righted herself when the airbags inflated. We were picked up by helo as the capsule was lifted by crane aboard USS *Essex* (CVS-9). The Apollo command module is too heavy for a safe pickup with the crew aboard, but we didn't mind.

Three space flights in five and a half years; 195 times around this old earth, 295 hours in space, and three more carrier "landings."

I achieved my final command with Apollo 7 and was relieved while at sea. My Navy presented me with a deep draft command insignia, but NASA and is flight controllers, never did understand the role of command.

Time for a change. Wally, out.

BOOK III
PHIL

1950
BLACK SHOE SAILOR

My first war began while I was still in basic training. North Korea invaded the South on 25 June 1950, and following boot camp I was assigned to a destroyer being recommissioned at Mare Island Naval Shipyard in Vallejo, California. USS *O'Bannon* (DDE-450) was being rebuilt with state-of-the-art antisubmarine weapons, plus the normal 5 in. 38 cal. guns, 40mm antiaircraft and 3 in. 50 cal. light guns.

From March to May 1951 *O'Bannon* performed sea trials and sailed to her new homeport at Pearl Harbor, Hawaii. In August we entered the Sea of Japan, joining a task force built around the carrier *Essex* (CV-9). *O'Bannon* was to provide planeguard duty for carrier aviators who ditched or crashed into the water. These "irregularities" happened so often in 1951 that Naval Aviation safety took a distant back seat to sortie count and aircraft availability.

Even as an eighteen-year-old "whitehat" in the "blackshoe" surface navy, it was apparent to me that such methods of carrier operations were not normal. Aircraft losses over the side of *Essex* were frequent—either landing accidents or planes loose on slick and rolling decks. It looked like a destruction derby. Clearly, you had to be a daredevil or crazy—or both—to fly underpowered jets off a straight-deck carrier in miserable weather, often returning with battle damage.

It was exactly what I wanted to do.

Among *O'Bannon's* other missions were gunfire support and search and rescue (SAR) inside Wonsan Harbor, North Korea. In December 1951 the battle line was well south of Wonsan, so the communists occupied all the surrounding area. Wonsan has a large harbor with a major rail terminus connecting most of North Korea and China with the south. We shelled the railyards as well as passing trains, waterborne supply craft, boatyards and—most fun of all—the large guns in the hills around Wonsan.

Wonsan was a designated ditching and ejection area for disabled aircraft returning "feet wet" over the harbor. The on-scene rescue ship would pluck the aviators from the always-frigid, sometimes icy waters and shuttle them back to sea for helicopter transfer or highline directly to the carrier. Wonsan had a semi-restricted entrance in that one of the three American-occupied islands in the harbor was in the middle of the entrance. Depending on how secure the area commander felt, Yo-Do Island occasionally had a SAR helicopter stationed ashore. I only remember the two other small islands in Wonsan by their radio callsigns, Icebag and Redlead. They were occupied by Marines who helped South Korean infiltrators get ashore for covert missions in the North.

One December day *O'Bannon* was drifting and sprinting inside Wonsan Harbor with no bombardment mission scheduled. The captain was on the bridge with his shotgun, shooting at ducks that came within range. If he got lucky and hit one of the fast, low-flying birds, he would maneuver the ship to make the pickup by a sailor hanging over the side with a netted pole to haul in the prize.

The carriers off the coast had already launched and recovered their early-morning strikes and the midday strike was over the beach. We heard the "Mayday" distress call from a pilot escorting his wingman's shot-up F4U-4 Corsair back to friendly territory. The decision was made for the wingman to ditch in the harbor where *O'Bannon* would make the rescue since no helos were available.

The Corsair pilot descended from overhead in a circling pattern. I was on deck helping prepare to lower the motor whale boat since I was the boat's designated rifleman, optimistically hoping to shoot any sharks that tried to interfere with the rescue. Since the captain had coordinated the splashdown with the pilot, we were dead in the water. As our boat was lowered into the frigid water, we knew a quick pickup would be crucial. The aviator could be immobilized in less than a minute, even with the primitive "poopy suit" he wore for cold-water immersion. In December the water off North Korea is so cold that the pilot would experience hypothermia after about thirty minutes, leading to serious harm or even death. But the first seconds were crucial, while he could still help us help him.

As we shoved off we saw the stricken F4U descending with a trail of dark burning oil marking his path in the sky. It appeared the rescue would be near-perfect; a source of genuine pride. By Navy tradition the aviator would send us a couple gallons of ice cream from his carrier as a way of saying thanks.

But I learned a lesson that day: something about counting eggs and hatching chickens. The whale boat, the destroyer and the aircraft now were locked into a carefully-planned sequence of events. Any outside stimulus could adversely affect the rescue, though the life of that aviator was our number one priority. I had never been shot at before, and almost hoped it would happen someday. But not at that exact moment. You can't run, you can't take cover, you're exposed with no choice but to grit your teeth and keep moving in a predictable manner. The communist gunners in the hills must have loved the setup.

Our nickname for a particular North Korean gun emplacement was "Mary Lou," though nobody seemed to know why. She was a 105mm long-barrel cannon on rails, deeply entrenched in a cave on the north side of the harbor entrance. She could be rolled out and trained on our ship on her own terms when she found it advantageous to do so. And ours was a situation that definitely gave her favorable odds.

The first shell landed about 100 feet from our "speeding" seven-knot whale boat. The resulting geyser threw water everywhere. "Holy shit," I thought, "that was fired at me and it was meant to do bodily harm!" For some reason, every combat veteran makes that discovery with a sense of wondrous outrage. As if we could expect anything else!

Shells kept landing about every thirty seconds, but fortunately the only injury was to our ears. *O'Bannon* took the gun under fire and, eventually, with the help of the overhead F4U Rescue Combat Air Patrol (ResCAP), "Mary Lou" retired to the depths of her cave.

The pickup was perfect. The plane came skipping to a halt 200 feet from our boat. The pilot exited the cockpit, walked halfway down his port wing, jumped in the water alongside his floating Corsair and we immediately hauled him into our boat. He hardly got wet. When he took off his helmet I was amazed at how young a Naval Aviator could be. He was only an ensign, but grinning from ear to ear while remarking how lucky he was to be rescued by friends in enemy territory.

This event was the turning point in my life. Even today, more than forty years later, I still can remember his face. This single event would become the fuel that kept the fire burning for many years in my own quest to become a carrier pilot.

That was the highlight of the first of my three blackshoe combat tours. I was determined to own a pair of aviator-brown shoes someday. Meanwhile, Lieutenant Commander Zeke Cormier at the Joint Operations Center in Seoul and Lieutenant Wally Schirra flying F-84s out of Taegu as an Air Force exchange pilot were the type of men who would become my role models.

1957-59

DISAPPOINTMENTS
AND
SILVER LININGS

Following my hitch as an enlisted man I returned home to Topeka, Kansas and matriculated at the University of Tulsa in Oklahoma. During my junior year I had a part-time job that afforded just enough money, along with the G.I. Bill and my folks' help, to take flying lessons. My dream of becoming a carrier pilot was still burning a hole in the seat of my pants. Though the civilian job market offered good money due to my high grades and extracurricular activities, I played both options.

The flying school was a small operation run by a retired Navy helo pilot. Just as Zeke's ex-Navy Reserve instructor trained him on a Piper Cub, mine trained me to solo in the J-5 Cub. After gaining my private license I got some free flight time by washing aircraft, sweeping the hangar and performing odd jobs. Perhaps best of all, I got a small stipend flying the Oklahoma gas pipelines looking for oil leaks. But I kept seeing carrier decks down there.

In the summer of 1957, after my junior year, I drove my '54 Ford convertible to Dallas to start the prolonged process of flight training application. The written exams were no sweat, but I failed the near-vision eye exam. With no option, I returned to school very dejected but determined to solve, correct or manipulate the system—whatever was necessary to become a Naval Aviator.

A friend of the family, a retired Air Force flight surgeon, checked me out and confirmed the Navy finding. However, he told me that eyes are like a camera in many ways, and that by practicing how to focus (actually squinting) I could read close-up. Therefore, I built my own instrument and practiced until I could read small print cut from newspapers and pasted on the circular slide. Back to Dallas for a "retake" with the same Navy doctor as before. While I did better, I still flunked and was sent packing with a strong admonishment not to return.

By then I had taken the damn exam so many times that I had memorized the chart. Line A: 2OCOCDC. Line B: RZB8HKFO. My goal meant so much to me that I figured, what the hell. If I couldn't beat them fair and square, I'd cheat.

There was a small, semi-abandoned naval auxiliary air facility at Norman, Oklahoma. On return to Tulsa, with nothing to lose, I swung in and learned the senior doctor, a kindly four-striper, wasn't very busy. Captain Bostick was a real gentleman. He listened to my sad story and agreed to give me a preliminary test to see just how good or bad my eyes really were. Fortunately, he had the corpsman give me the test and I was able to stop the sliding disk at a distance well within parameters, even though the letters were a blur.

"Read Line A," said the corpsman.

"Two, oh, C, oh, C, D, square, C," I rattled off.

"Next line," said the medico.

"R, Z, B, eight, H, K, F, oh." Like a machine gun.

After awhile Captain Bostick looked at the results and said, in effect, that the young flight surgeon in Dallas was incompetent. "Son, you have the eyes of a thirteen-year-old," he pronounced. He gave me an "up" and forwarded my papers to Washington.

In January 1958 I was accepted into the flight training program and reported to Pensacola Fourth of July weekend. It is amazing that the Navy never changed the eye chart for fifteen years, and I was never asked to read lines three or four. I never had the slightest hiccup with my eyes and routinely passed my annual physicals. By the time they changed the charts I was "in bed" with my flight surgeons and—knock on wood—I went 5,000 jet hours without a non-combat accident.

During flight training, because of high academic and flying grades, I was designated for the "CV-jet" pipeline—flying jets off aircraft carriers. Though jets fly higher and faster and force you to think quicker, they are easier to fly than single-engine prop planes. Motor skills in hand-eye coordination and physical strength require less from the jet pilot, not to mention less fatigue from shorter flights.

When I arrived at Corpus Christi, Texas for advanced jet training, little did I know that my ambition to be a fighter pilot would be put on hold for seven years. CV-jet students checking into Corpus were assigned to Chase Field at Beeville or to Kingsville, two outlying fields flying swept-wing F9F-8 Cougars. But in July 1959 the "F9s" had been grounded for awhile because of engine problems which caused a massive student backlog in the jet training pipeline. In most cases the logjam resulted in assignment to other aviation communities—frequently non-carrier communities! The most important goal in my life was about to go up in smoke. What to do?

If I took my assignment that Friday afternoon, that was my fate: antisubmarine props or—ugh!—transports. So I looked up Lieutenant Bell, the student control officer, and asked for one week's leave until the next Friday. I hoped that some jet billets would open up in the next seven days.

But when I checked in again a week later, no jet slots had opened. So I took another week off, hoping for the best, because by now I was out of earned leave.

No luck. The third Friday came and still no break in the logjam. In Naval Aviation, once you're assigned to a non-carrier community the chances of ever strapping a tailhook to your ass is almost nil. So, as repugnant as it seemed at the time, I decided to ask for propeller attack planes.

The AD-6 Skyraider (redesignated A-1H in 1962) was a single-engine World War II design pulled through the air by a sixteen-foot diameter four-bladed propeller. It was popularly known as the Spad, either because it seemed almost as old as the World War I fighter of that name, or because its AD designation lent itself to such a moniker. Anyway, if I won, at least the Skyraider would keep me in carrier aviation. From there I'd rely on wit, charm, subterfuge and luck to get jets.

Lieutenant Bell informed me that my chance of getting a Spad seat also was doubtful because ATU-301, the Skyraider training squadron at Corpus, had taken many of the backlogged students and that a new class hadn't formed in two months. The situation called for extraordinary innovation on my part, because being in the Navy was meaningless unless I could fly from a carrier deck.

Remember, this was Friday afternoon, when all high-spirited aviators celebrate happy hour in the officers' club. I decided to drown my sorrow in booze and see if I could find any Spad instructors at the bar. And did I ever: the whole squadron was there in force, including the skipper, Lieutenant Colonel McDonald, USMC.

It didn't take long to find some young instructors who would let me lose rolling dice and buy them drinks. The three students who most recently soloed the aircraft were chug-a-lugging beer from a single chrome-plated 100-pound bomb canister, taking turns running to the head to barf up the beer so they could make room for more on their next turn. The rules stated that if the three students didn't down the entire three gallons without stopping, they had to buy a round for the entire squadron.

The scene was perfect for me. I told the instructors of my enlisted days in Korea and how I used to watch Skyraiders launch off the carriers and bomb targets around Wonsan Harbor. I told them that my lifetime dream was to fly the "Able Dog" (lying through my teeth), that assignment to ATU-301 seemed impossible, and woe-is-me.

They bought my act, and by this time had drunk enough courage so they escorted me to the skipper and had me tell my lament again. By this time Lieutenant Colonel McDonald was feeling no pain, and in a moment of great emotional giving, most unlike a Marine, he allowed as how he would request a new class of three students on Monday. But he said that my academic and flight grades would have to be high enough to make the cut because he couldn't request me by name.

When I reported again to Lieutenant Bell's office on Monday morning, I prayed to God that the Marine skipper had remembered Friday night. Bell seemed puzzled that I knew there was an opening in ATU-301, and even more amazed that another new class wasn't expected to open for six weeks. That's how it goes. You have to know how to play the game—and make your own breaks.

Professionally, I knew that aircraft carriers exist to launch bombers that put ordnance on target. But being a single-seat prop attack pilot was not my idea of the first team. Looking back on it years later, it was the best thing that ever happened to help shape my Navy career. Humility fighter pilots don't have, and a little humble pie at that time in my life was much needed.

At that time Zeke was leading Air Group 11 off *Shangri-La* (CVA-38), the same command I would have twenty years later aboard *Kitty Hawk* (CV-63) and *America* (CV-66). And Wally had just gone "on loan" to NASA—a letdown, he later admitted, from his prior status as "the Navy's best hired killer."

Like I said, humility is scarce among fighter pilots.

1961

THE YELLOW DEVILS

After twelve months in Advanced Training Command and the AD replacement air group squadron, I checked into Attack Squadron 196 at NAS Moffett Field, on the southern tip of San Francisco Bay. VA-196 was known as "The Yellow Devils," but today flies Grumman A-6E Intruder jets as "The Main Battery." It's a proud name, indicating the attack mission's pre-eminence in carrier aviation.

In June 1961 the squadron deployed with Air Group 19 on board *Bon Homme Richard* (CVA-31). "Bonny Dick" was operating in the East China Sea, preparing to make a port call at Yokosuka, Japan (pronounced yo-KUS-ka) in two days. The carrier had to round the southern tip of Kyushu then make its way north through some heavy seas in the Pacific. Therefore, it was decided at the last minute—as many Navy decisions are, often fraught with disaster—to launch some aircraft prior to the transit. They would fly to Atsugi on Honshu to await the ship's arrival two days hence.

As it developed, the assigned pilots were called to the ready room to "hurry up and wait." The plan was to fly a nuclear profile mission to Atsugi, simulating "World War Last"—a two-hour cakewalk for the jets but an eight-hour ass-buster for we AD prop drivers.

Charts and publications were spread all over the ready room, pilots cutting and pasting routes together, decisions being made to launch, then hold, then cancel, then go. The insanity went on for several hours. The weather along our route was considerable and very unstable. Jets can launch, accelerate and climb above most weather in perhaps two or three minutes.

Not so in props. With the Spad, it was a rare occasion when we climbed above 10,000 feet, requiring oxygen masks. The AD's service ceiling was around 24,000 feet, and only possible after you engaged the turbo-charger by shifting into "high blower," and turned on water injection to increase horsepower at around 16,000. It was not an easy procedure. You had to watch your engine instruments, retard the throttle, pull your propeller pitch to full decrease, slam the high blower home, advance the throttle slowly and increase your prop pitch almost simultaneously. The process was seldom conducted in close formation with a wingman, and virtually impossible flying the wing position with your canopy a few feet from your leader's wingtip in thick clouds. I get sweaty palms just thinking about it, even now.

I was fortunate to be assigned as wingman to the best pilot in VA-196, Lieutenant Commander Hal Gernert, the squadron operations officer. Even though we sometimes carpooled at Moffett and drank together at happy hour, he was still "Mister Gernert" to me. We knew the weather was bad with a frontal passage between the ship and our destination so we decided to rendezvous off the starboard quarter at 500 feet, join up and head north. We'd stay low all the way and hope to get through the front by sneaking underneath. The weather at the ship was light rain, 700 feet overcast with tops estimated at around 15,000. It just was not our day. The weather gods refused to smile on us, and the ship decision-makers didn't help matters by saying "Go."

Right after launch, as we were joining up, one of our senior aviators started screaming "Mayday, mayday!" over the UHF radio. Leading the second section, he stated that he had an impending engine failure and requested permission to land back aboard immediately.

To clear the deck landing area with only a partial air wing launch and no scheduled recovery is a major evolution requiring a pull forward of all those planes parked aft of the island. Just as the ship was reluctantly starting the respot and canceling the remaining launch, our not-so-intrepid aviator's wingman was tucked in close. Lanny Gorman came up on the radio: "You ain't got a engine failure, yer barn doors are hangin' out!"

Lanny's leader had accidentally opened his slablike speed brakes, causing immense drag and slowing the aircraft. The only reply was "Roger. Let's go tactical." Translation: "Get off the primary frequency where everybody in the world is listening to my screwup."

As we headed north the bottom of the ceiling got lower and lower. At 200 knots you can fly very comfortably at 100 feet, but below that altitude, section integrity becomes marginal. Only slight misapplied pressure to the stick can cause the aircraft to climb or—worst-case scenario—dive into the water. Hal turned us around a couple of times, trying to find another path through the weather. Sometimes you'll see light-shaded areas and think they're clear only to find a "sucker hole." Naval Aviators have a mythical flock of birds named for standard exhibits of egregious airmanship, and all are written in blood. This day we were going to follow in the tradition of the "yellow-bellied, pinheaded holeseeker." Hal didn't want to take me through moist thunderstorm weather, though he knew we probably couldn't climb high enough to get on top. But we had no other choice since the last thing we would do was ask the ship to recover us back aboard and admit we couldn't hack the program. As the saying goes, it's better to die than look bad.

We started our slow climb and the clouds were very thick, solid to who-knows-how-high. We were still in radio contact on squadron tactical frequency, and as we approached 15,000 Hal asked me if I could switch to high blower while hanging tucked in under his wing. What the hell—let's go for it, I thought. With Hal calling each movement and very slowly retarding and advancing power as needed, I was able to shift into high blower and still maintain sight of him, just a few feet from his wingtip.

As we approached 22,000 it was obvious we were about maxed-out for altitude with no light penetrating the clouds to indicate we would break into the clear. Hal had to make a decision, and quick. Our wings had iced up, I had lost my airspeed indicator and my engine RPM was fluctuating wildly.

Unknown to me, Hal had decided to land as soon as possible, presumably on something resembling a runway. I had no idea where we were in relation to the Japanese coastline and I couldn't take my eyes off my leader long enough to switch to the frequency he was now using in search of a field. We could communicate by hand signals, which was adequate under the circumstances. We had levelled off and now were in a slight descent to where I hadn't the foggiest notion. I was along for the ride, but if we could stay together I had a chance.

The Skyraider had no ejection seat. Emergency exit was by the old method; open the canopy, unstrap, crawl over the side, fall free and pull the D-ring to open the parachute. As we descended through 10,000 the rain was so thick I almost lost sight of Hal. As we passed through 1,200 feet he gave me the signal to "dirty up": lower the landing gear and flaps. By now my propeller pitch was uncontrollable but I couldn't have cared less about overboosting the engine. I was scared and only knew I didn't want to die.

Still flying wing, we broke into the clear about 200 feet above the ground on short final approach to some runway. Since it was too low and too late to get any nose-to-tail separation with Hal, we would have to make a formation landing; something I'd never done for the very good reason it was prohibited in prop aircraft!

My windscreen was iced over and I couldn't see forward. With the canopy open I could only see to the side peripherally, and as we started our flare for landing I floated above—and what appeared to be on top of—my leader's aircraft. Immediately I added power and, in a nanosecond of time, decided to execute a low-visibility approach to the left, completing a 360-degree turn back to the original runway heading.

The first voice transmission I heard over the emergency guard channel was, "Milestone 407, this is Itazuke tower. The missed approach is to the right, mountains to the left!"

My first thought was, "Where the hell is Itazuke?" My second thought, since I'd automatically broken to port from habit of flying the carrier pattern, was that I was already halfway through my lefthand turn. Only feet above the houses on the hillside surrounding the air base, I had to climb back up into the clouds to avoid the topography. I was on the gauges, flying instruments with no airspeed indicator. If I could complete three-quarters of my turn, a gradual descent could be made back to the runway.

As I reduced power in the descent, my turn radius increased. When I broke out again I had overshot the runway so a series of S-turns was required to get lined up for landing. As the runway passed under my wings I looked from side to side, trying to judge my height when the Spad stalled about twenty feet up. The right wing dropped and I tried unsuccessfully to soften the coming impact by jamming on full power. We were carrying 300-gallon external fuel tanks under each wing, and the starboard tank exploded when it impacted the runway.

As I skidded down the runway, swerving back and forth, the AD was brought under control and I taxied clear. There were no flames from the ruptured tank, but the fire trucks engulfed the wing in foam as the engine was shut down. As I crawled down from the cockpit the Air Force doctor came running up and asked if I was okay. "Hell, no, I'm not okay," I shouted. "I'm scared to death!" I jabbed my finger at the stamped golden wings on my flight jacket, exclaiming, "You can take these things and shove them up your ass. I quit!"

I was so mad that the ship had launched us in such extreme weather with so little regard for our safety that I told Hal to send for someone to pick up my plane after it was repaired. I'd had it. All I wanted was out.

It probably wasn't a wholly unique attitude. Ten years earlier Wally had a "controlled crash" on that same runway. On a flight from Seoul to Itazuki he was unable to extend his T-33's wheels and had to land gear up.

However, after three days of good booze, round-eyed women and an airbase that didn't float, I was ready to charge again. But my personal experience would be remembered when I commanded my own carrier. Always factored into the equation of deciding to launch or not was those young aviators' safety, and never knowingly was anyone launched with the odds of returning stacked against them.

In retrospect, being an attack pilot was a humbling experience but it built character. The early F8U Crusader pilots didn't fly night missions off carriers very often in 1961. Neither they nor their planes were built for the job. They definitely lacked character by not hurling their aircraft and body at that small, often pitching, deck in the dark. Many times as I taxied forward to the catapult for launch on a black, bleak rainy night I envied those day-fighter guys down in their cozy ready rooms, eating popcorn while watching a movie.

From that moment I said to hell with character and humility. I still wanted to be a fighter pilot.

1967

MIG KILLER

The Vietnam War was heating up in 1966 when I left the advanced training command as an instructor with some 1,500 jet hours. Being a fully-qualified LSO also helped me get the type of cockpit and coast I wanted. Though the F-4 Phantom II had been in fleet service for six years, the idea of flying a fighter with a GIB ("guy in back") didn't appeal to me. The trusty old F-8 Crusader was a macho fighter pilot's dream: single-seat, single-engine with a weapon system that made it a true fighter rather than an interceptor.

Each of the Navy's two fighter communities had completely different mentalities about how to engage and shoot down an enemy aircraft. The F-8 pilots were still "turnin' and burnin'," bringing guns to bear along with visual-range heat-seeking missiles as well.

The coast you went to also was important. East coast carriers still were meeting their Mediterranean commitments, whereas all the west coast boats were headed for the Tonkin Gulf. I wanted to get there as soon as possible.

NAS Miramar was called Fightertown USA. It was home of all the NavAirPac fighters including VF-124, the west coast F-8 replacement training squadron. Called the Gunfighters because F-8s had 20mm cannons, VF-124 was led by Commander Merle Gorder who had been on *Bon Homme Richard* (CVA-31) with me. Normally replacement pilots were trained in their aircraft type for five months, then assigned to a fleet squadron just returning from cruise. This allowed the aircrews to train with the squadron throughout the workup schedule for the next deployment. I couldn't wait that long to get to Vietnam. I asked the skipper if he would assign me to the first squadron headed west. Merle obliged me and I joined VF-24 just one week before it sailed in January 1967.

As luck had it, VF-24's home for the next seven months was "Bonnie Dick." It was like an old baseball glove for me. I was right at home with over 300 carrier landings during my two previous cruises. And my roommate was Lieutenant B.C. "Bobbie" Lee. We were the new guys on the block, having just joined the squadron. Though we were senior to all the first-tour "nuggets," we were assigned one of the smallest staterooms on the ship. It was not important—a stateroom was only used for sleeping and writing letters.

Having B.C. as my roomie worked out great. He was a tiger. We kept track of which pilots were getting the good missions, and insisted on our share. We were standing in line, so to speak, for the missions that might allow us to find some MiGs. Unfortunately, my section leader was afraid of his shadow and found any excuse to abort a mission scheduled "over the beach." Rules did not allow me to proceed independently, so we orbited over the water a lot.

As the air war intensified and the North Vietnamese arsenal increased in sophistication and numbers, we started losing more aircraft to MiGs, surface-to-air missiles (SAMs) and "triple A" (anti-aircraft artillery). Many pilots were killed or captured and the volunteers for deep missions became fewer and fewer. My section leader's fear had made him a basket case, and he started drinking a lot in his stateroom. Halfway through the cruise he was shipped off to a staff job in Saigon.

B.C. now became my section leader and we could almost pick and choose our flights over the beach. We already had lost Ken Wood and Stretch Tucker, with no replacement pilots, so most of us now flew two combat missions a day. Every seventh day we stood down so the carrier could replenish fuel, food and ammunition and the air wing could conduct memorial services—lots of them. From March to July we lost twenty-three aircraft and eighteen aviators.

One of the eight squadrons in the wing was VA-212, a light attack unit flying A-4Es. Their Skyhawks were specially configured to carry a new weapon called the Walleye, a glide bomb with a TV camera in the nose. It provided its own guidance to the target—what is called a "launch-and-leave" weapon. After the pilot released the bomb he was free to turn away and exit the target area, thus reducing his exposure to groundfire. Though the Walleye only had a 100-pound shaped-charge warhead, it was deadly accurate. Its seeker head locked onto a shadow contrast—a building window, for instance—and entered the building through that window, exploding inside. The building often collapsed from the extreme overpressure of the blast.

Air Wing 21 systematically started proving Walleye at the start of the deployment so testing actually was conducted in combat. It worked great. We started releasing Walleyes on buildings and bridges in Route Packages I and II in the southern part of North Vietnam. Though we were shot at occasionally, it was a fairly benign environment compared to the nonpermissive atmosphere up around Hanoi and Haiphong in Route Package VI. We worked our way north, dropping the new weapon on progressively more important targets. The "smart bomb" had proven itself.

The Bonnie Dick berthed at Leyte Pier of Cubi Point Naval Air Station in early May 1967 following a forty-day line period. We had only been in port two days, and the air wing was widely dispersed all over the Philippines, recovering from the rigors of war. I had rented a cottage at Bagio, a mountain resort on Luzon, where there was plenty of golf, booze and good food—and, incidentally, a friendly Pan Am stewardess. (What the hell, we were both single.) Five days of R and R usually was enough to rejuvenate body and soul for another month or so in the Gulf.

The knock on the front door came early—too early to be a squadronmate. I opened the door and there stood the biggest, blackest, meanest-looking air policeman you can imagine. All I could think was— what did I do wrong? Then it occurred to me: I had checked in as "Lt. and Mrs. Wood." I was had!

Then the AP asked, "Are you Lieutenant Wood?"

"Yessir, ah, that's correct, sir," I heard myself say. The "sir" wasn't necessary, as he was an enlisted man, but I definitely wanted to be on his good side.

"Sir, you are to report immediately to the airfield for a helo ride back to Cubi. I'll wait until you're packed and ready to go." I didn't ask any questions—just kissed the stew goodby and never saw her again.

As we lifted off from Bagio the helo aircrewman told me the ship was getting underway two days early. Rumor had it that downtown Hanoi no longer was off limits to our bombing. A funny war, I thought to myself. Strategic targets all over the industrial north were selectively eliminated from the list of targets assigned daily by civilians working for Robert Strange McNamara back in the Pentagon.

The frustrations soon became humorous. Some of the targets were a joke. Our favorite was the Cam Loa boatyard southwest of Haiphong. The attack pilots were assigned to thread their A-4s through a maze of AA fire and SAMs to drop their bombs on a derelict, vacant lot that hadn't seen a boat in at least a year. But Naval Aviators are not known for slavish obedience to orders from civilians who don't know their ass from a hole in the ground. We made room for improvisation. During prestrike planning we would find another target in the vicinity worthy of the energy and risk of dropping bombs. If the battle damage assessment (BDA) photos showed no bombs on the assigned target, the aviators just said it was bad aim—they'd do better next time. Thus, we hit a lot of lucrative targets that were not "fragged," even some owned by U.S. companies and therefore "off limits."

We got our sea legs back and started planning in earnest the surgical elimination of military targets in and around Hanoi. Our planning put a lot of emphasis on avoiding civilian casualties adjacent to our targets. But the game was not always played the same by both sides. The North Vietnamese on several occasions placed their AA guns in the yards or on the roofs of hospitals. Even without the big red cross painted on the roof—and it always was—we knew where the hospitals were. We couldn't shoot back to defend ourselves because they knew we wouldn't intentionally bomb a hospital. Late in the war Bach Mai Hospital was damaged and the commies howled their outrage to the world. Nobody seemed to mind that the hospital was adjacent to an enemy fighter field.

Once back on the line, we used the Walleye on a couple of significant, well-defended targets south of Hanoi just to make sure our tactics were sound and that the hardware was functional. The word came down that our primary target was to be the Hanoi thermal power plant—downtown! This would be the first strike ever conducted inside the city.

It made sense for a lot of reasons, but more importantly it was a clear signal to the North Vietnamese government that we would no longer place their strategic assets off limits. At our pay grade level it was a real boost to see some reason for even being there in the first place.

There were plenty of volunteers for this mission. Lots of risk, but it was for something meaningful. VA-212 had the lead on this one, as Commander Homer Smith was the skipper and would lead the strike. Because it would be the first time downtown, we knew it would stir up a bee's nest. MiGs would be launched against us—we hoped. On normal Alfa strikes there would be a bunch of A-4s carrying iron "dumb" bombs and fighter escorts. Support aircraft would include jammers to zap electrons at enemy fire-control radar, and Iron Hands to shoot their Shrike missiles at the SAM guidance radars. The inevitable photo bird and his escort would take bomb damage assessment photography of our hits, and there were various other players. Altogether, usually thirty aircraft comprised this coordinated effort.

However, this strike would be different with the Walleye "smart" bomb. We only needed two Skyhawks as opposed to twelve in a normal raid. But because of the anticipated MiG threat we needed to stack the deck with fighters. Twelve were assigned—six escorts and six flak suppressors. F-8s were terrible in the latter role, but we wanted fighters around while keeping strike composition to a minimum. It was a tradeoff. Crusader pilots weren't highly trained in air-to-ground delivery, and the F-8 lacked an effective bomb sight. Furthermore, it carried five-inch Zuni rockets instead of the preferred weapon—Rockeye cluster bombs with hundreds of bomblets that obliterated a flak site. Actually, sending an F-8 on a flak suppressor mission over Hanoi was akin to opening your canopy and trying to pressurize the world. But that deep in "indian country" you wanted plenty of gunfighters around, and we filled the bill.

Our route to Hanoi would be circuitous, requiring more fuel than normal. As the crow flies, the distance from our launch point in the Gulf would be approximately 150 nautical miles, or 300 round-trip. But a straight-in route would lose the element of surprise. Hanoi lies on the western edge of the Red River Valley delta near the mountain ranges leading to Laos. Because of mountainous terrain masking the radars, and minimal exposure to SAMs inbound, it was decided to head west from the ship, passing south of Thanh Hoa, hit the hills in Laos and head north until we were just southwest of Hanoi. Then our dash from the hills over the delta to the target would only take about six minutes. The A-4s were "slick" without bomb racks and could keep up with the F-8s. Our route out would be every man for himself, striving to reach the water as quickly as possible where airborne tankers waited.

Two diversionary strikes from other carriers were scheduled for the Hanoi area with target times just prior to ours. We had planned it so the enemy gunners would presumably expend most of their ammunition and loaded missiles prior to our arrival. The primary goal was to knock out the capital city's electricity, and we would do almost anything to optimize our chances.

After the details were worked out, the air wing "heavies" assigned the mission pilots. Of course, Homer Smith would lead his two Skyhawks. He picked as his wingman one of the steadiest young pilots in the squadron, Mike Cater. Bobbie Lee, my roommate, and yours truly were chosen to fly the mission. Bobbie would lead a flak suppressor section and I took the escort section with Lieutenant (JG) Bill Metzger as my wingman.

After all the planning was done, B.C. and I went to bed the night of 18 May full of anticipation. We had been in our sacks over an hour, each not knowing that the other was still awake. Not a word was spoken until I muttered, "Bobbie, you awake?"

"Yeah, just thinking." He had a wife and children.

"Bobbie, you scared?"

"Nah, I just hope I don't screw up my switchology over the target." There was that saying again: Better to die than look bad.

We lay there and reviewed together our switch positions for the different weapons we would carry. Little did we know that next day such details would make the difference between getting that coveted MiG kill and being an also-ran.

The launch, rendezvous and refueling overhead the ship were uneventful. The weather en route was beautiful—a requirement for the TV-guided Walleye. As the strike group coasted in south of Thanh Hoa we could see 57 and 85mm flak puffs bursting around us. As we entered Laotian airspace we started hearing the "Big Eye" radar calls, informing us that MiGs were scrambling from their bases around Hanoi. I thought to myself, "I hope those *Kitty Hawk* and *Enterprise* fighters don't shoot them all down—leave some for us!"

Twenty minutes from target we heard the activity around the two diversionary strikes just ahead of us. Someone had really peed off the enemy gunners. Through covert intelligence we later learned that the North Vietnamese had determined that our flight was Air Force F-105s out of Thailand. It was logical. Based on radar information, we were coming at them from the southwest along typical USAF routes. This misinformation would prove costly for the North Vietnam Air Force. They directed their MiGs to engage our F-8s—a very different breed of cat from the "Thud"—to say nothing of the dozen very aggressive fighter pilots flying those Crusaders, each one starving for a MiG kill.

Flying Page Boy 405, I had the lead of the middle section of fighters, trailing the A-4s by about a half mile. The six suppressor F-8Cs were out front. Just as we entered the Hanoi plains area, Bobbie called over the tactical frequency, "Hey roomie, we got a single MiG at our ten o'clock."

I looked left and saw a Grumman Intruder from *Kitty Hawk* heading south, exiting the target area. "Negative, that's an A-6," I replied.

B.C. wouldn't be denied. "I'm telling you Page Boys there's a MiG at nine o'clock." He couldn't chase the MiG because his role was to lead his element into the target area and suppress the anti-aircraft fire. The other two escort sections obviously didn't see the bandit either, as they maintained their position. I looked left again and spotted the MiG-17 closing rapidly on the A-6A's tail. I called "Tally ho" and broke hard left.

The MiG and Intruder were opposite my heading, but when I completed my turn I was at the MiG's eight o'clock, outside gun range. But I was starting to get the Sidewinder missile's "growl," indicating that the seeker head also had a bead on the bandit's tailpipe.

In afterburner, I was closing rapidly. God, was I excited! I squeezed off a missile. Stupid. I had too many Gs on the aircraft, putting the 'winder outside the firing envelope. The missile tracked the MiG initially, but couldn't turn the corner. It went ballistic behind the target but definitely got the MiG driver's attention. Seeing me in pursuit, he broke hard right from the A-6 and dove for the deck while lighting his afterburner. I was now too close to shoot a missile even though I had a steady-state solution. He was heading down a valley, limiting his maneuvering room, and as he appeared in my gunsight I fired two long bursts from my cannons. I detected no hits even though I seemed too close to miss.

All this time I was being led off into the boonies by the lone MiG. My primary mission was to protect the bombers, and this guy no longer was a threat so I broke off the chase and headed downtown, now about five miles behind the strike group. My wingman, Bill Metzger, was nowhere in sight.

I proceeded in burner toward the target, trying to catch the strike. As I arrived over the outskirts of Hanoi all hell had broken loose. The scene reminded me of a cover of an air-action comic book. In living color: the black and gray puffs of AAA explosions, air-to-air missile trails, the white streamers of SA-2 SAMs lifting off their pads, and silver MiGs. The Skyhawks were rolling in on the power plant and I could see two MiGs falling in flames.

Later I learned that my roommate had bagged one of them.

While looking for my wingman I observed and heard cannon shells whizzing by my canopy. Stick hard left, burner on, pull like hell. I could now see a MiG-17 1,000 feet behind me but I didn't feel his rounds hit the fuselage aft of my canopy. I kept pulling, "getting angles" on the guy. He could no longer shoot at me and I was gaining the advantage.

He must have been an inexperienced pilot. He bugged out by reversing course, which allowed me to park behind him at 2,000 feet. He was running for his life. I flicked my stick's armament switch to "heat" and put him in my gunsight. The missile growl was loud. I pulled the trigger and the half-second before my second Sidewinder fired seemed like the proverbial eternity.

As the 'winder left the rail it dropped and appeared to have no guidance on the target. But moments later it started a gentle climb toward the bandit's tailpipe. The missile impact cut his entire tail off. The MiG lazily pitched nose-over and decelerated rapidly.

As I approached from the rear the pilot ejected and his seat took him up and clear of the aircraft. I passed him so close I could tell the color of his skin and see the patches on his flight suit. The pilot got seat separation, but I observed his main chute was a "streamer" and, sadly, knew that he would fall to his death. The only consolation was that he could not be punished by his superiors for losing his aircraft.

By now all the strike aircraft were outbound toward the Gulf. My wingman Bill Metzger, plus Kay Russell from VF-211, had been shot down. We had bagged four MiGs, but that's a terrible exchange rate and the A-4s had inflicted minimal damage on the power plant.

The fun and games were just starting. I still had eighty miles of "indian country" between me and the Tonkin Gulf. Four shells had entered the top of my aircraft and passed through my avionics package before carrying through the engine intake, trashing the engine.

I was now low on fuel and couldn't make it back to Bonnie Dick without a drink from the duty tanker. My radio was out and my engine was only developing ninety-four percent of full rated power. Use of my nonfunctioning afterburner was academic because I didn't have enough fuel for it anyway. Finally, the cockpit air conditioning had been ripped apart and I became extremely hot inside my capsule.

As I egressed toward the water I could see the aircraft ahead of me taking fire from the gunners around Nam Dinh. If the tankers weren't right off the coast there would be some "hurtin' puppies" nearing fuel exhaustion.

Another F-8 was nearby and I joined on his wing. It was Commander Paul Speer, the executive officer of VF-211. As I joined, I passed the visual signal that my radio was out and I was low on fuel. Thank God for small wonders. Paul got on the horn and had the A-3B tanker, driven by John Wunch of VAH-4, meet us as we went "feet wet" over the Gulf. Wunch was a great aviator, widely respected by air wing pilots. He put the Skywarrior right in front of me with the refueling hose already extended. Since there were so many low-state aircraft he could only give me 1,000 pounds of JP-5; just enough to get me out to sea and find any carrier recovering aircraft.

My navigation aids were gone—shot to pieces by the second MiG—and Paul had headed north with the tanker to take his own drink. I had to proceed east.

I was alone, flying into the Tonkin Gulf. I knew that besides Bonnie Dick, *Kitty Hawk* (CVA-63) and *Enterprise* (CVAN-65) also would be recovering strike aircraft. At this point I didn't have the luxury of choosing which one I landed aboard. I was down to 400 pounds of fuel—not much even for a single-engine fighter.

I was starting to get a little smoke in the cockpit when I spotted a big deck below. Traditionally it is a sign of poor airmanship and headwork to land on a carrier other than your own. But in this case, with my battle damage and diminishing fuel, to hell with tradition. I didn't want to get wet!

My descent began from the starboard side of the carrier—the wrong side—but it would draw attention to my arrival. I had to land on the first pass or use my ejection seat. As I entered the groove in the landing pattern I saw A-4s ahead of me, but the interval was too short for both me and the nearest Skyhawk to land. I hoped the LSO would give me enough credit to avoid the wrong ship unless I had a genuine problem.

Apparently the LSO did just that. On short final, the A-4 was waved off and I saw a clear deck. God, it was big compared to *Bon Homme Richard's*. I got the green "cut" lights on the lens to indicate the LSO had me and I was cleared to land.

As I hit the deck and shoved up the throttle to full power, the afterburner section exploded and my Crusader rolled to a stop. I was aboard, but where?

I looked up at the huge white numbers on the island and saw 63. My first-ever landing aboard *Kitty Hawk*! If someone had told this young lieutenant that I would be captain of that big, glamorous carrier seventeen years hence, I'd have concluded they were smoking pot.

My Crusader was a "strike," damaged beyond economical repair. As a yellow tractor towed the F-8 clear of the landing area so other planes could come aboard, local Air Wing 11 maintenance crews began "zapping" Page Boy 405. It was another tradition; any aircraft that lands on the wrong carrier is bedecked with emblems of the resident squadrons before return to its own ship. By chance, the embarked admiral and visiting Governor Love of Colorado observed the ritual and the governor asked about it. He was perplexed that an aircraft that had just returned from Hanoi, shooting down an enemy fighter, would be so treated. My plane was repainted even though it was headed for the "boneyard" at Litchfield Park, Arizona.

Later, through covert intelligence, we learned that the Vietnamese had launched sixteen MiG-17s out of Phuc Yen and Kep Airfields. Four never returned. But though there was elation in Bonnie Dick, the strike had failed to accomplish its mission. Because of scattered clouds over the target, the Walleyes were released low at 3,000 feet in a twenty-degree dive—outside optimum parameters. One bomb did minimal damage to the boiler house of the powerplant and the other hit the administration building.

It got worse. Next day Commander Smith, skipper of VA-212, was shot down on a strike against the Bac Ghiang thermal power plant. He was captured but never appeared among the POWs released in 1973.

However, on 21 May two Walleyes inflicted major damage to the original target. The lights went out all around Hanoi. But the loss of two pilots on the first mission was a poor trade.

Years later our returning POWs told us that the 19 May mission had a residual effect. They related how excited they were; how their hopes were regenerated when they heard and even saw Navy aircraft overhead, with bombs falling on Hanoi. Unfortunately, such positive efforts were an on-again-off-again thing under the Johnson-McNamara regime in Washington.

As each carrier neared the end of its deployment, the custom was for the last strike to be flown against the Thanh Hoa Bridge—the most durable and probably most notorious target in North Vietnam. While we manned aircraft on the flight deck 29 July for our last mission, the champagne was being iced in the ready rooms in anticipation of our return. While the plane captain was strapping me in, I noticed a dark pillar of smoke on the horizon but didn't give it much thought.

At the time to start engines we still hadn't received the signal so we waited. Bonnie Dick turned toward the smoke, no longer steaming into the wind for launch. Still strapped into our cockpits, we pilots made out the silhouette of a large ship as source of the smoke. Shortly thereafter it was discernable as an aircraft carrier. Our cruise was a long way from being over.

Forrestal (CVA-59) was an east coast carrier, only five days into her first combat line period. A deckload strike was ready to launch when a jet starting unit cooked off a Zuni on an F-4B. The rocket fired, impacted a drop tank on an A-4E across the deck, and the resulting explosion sparked a raging, exploding inferno. Forrestal fought the catastrophic fire for hours, and when it was finally controlled 134 men were dead and twenty-one aircraft destroyed.

We escorted *Forrestal* to the Philippines, did a one-eighty and made knots back to Yankee Station in the Tonkin Gulf. Two days later it was business as usual, launching strikes and counting the days until a relief arrived so we could finally go home.

The Navy had a rule that aviators would be "combat limited" after two cruises in order to spread the experience around. Later, pilot attrition was such that the rule had to be rescinded in order to provide enough aircrews. Many of us happily returned for third or even fourth combat deployments, flying 400 missions or more.

As we used to say, Vietnam was a miserable war, but the only one we had. And it beat the hell out of driving a desk. Besides, I had my MiG. My generation of fighter pilots lacked the repeated opportunities of Zeke and his pals in WW II, but what the hell—a kill is a kill.

By that time Zeke had "paid his dues" and was peddling jet aircraft for McDonnell Douglas as a civilian. Wally was preparing to strap Apollo Seven to his ass and launch into space for eleven days. Neither of them missed those night carrier landings, though Wally insisted he was literally "VFR on top, cleared for a straight-in approach"—in Apollo Seven!

1968

"PADDLES"

Landing airplanes on ships is dumb and not conducive to longevity. But early Navy planners figured—correctly—that it was a unique way of extending the fleet's striking range.

So, with the advent of carrier-based aircraft, one of the smartest decisions the U.S. Navy ever made was to put landing signal officers (LSOs) on its very first aircraft carrier, USS *Langley* (CV-1) in the early 1920s. By comparison with today's equipment, the original carrier operations were rudimentary; the difference between a bow and arrow and an AK-47. But even with slow, uncomplicated biplanes and sixty-knot landing speeds, the need for LSOs became evident since the pilot's view of the deck was necessarily limited.

Early LSOs first used hand-held flags, then specially-made gadgets resembling ping-pong paddles to advise pilots on landing. Though the paddles went out of vogue in the mid-1950s with the advent of the mirror landing system, the nickname has remained. Thus, LSOs still are called "Paddles" just as air wing commanders are called "CAG" after the old carrier air group designation. Tradition was a big part of the Navy (until its official banishment in 1992) and simple things like antiquated terminology weave a pattern of continuity into the tapestry of carrier aviation.

Carrier landings in high-performance swept-wing jets have been routine for decades. But if a pilot fails to execute the maneuver precisely, the result can range from a blown tire to a bent airplane to a catastrophic crash and explosion. The velvet in the equation is the LSO. He has saved more lives and aircraft over the years than all other safety procedures and equipment combined. He can detect and anticipate trends in an aircraft's flight path. He can recognize by the sound of the engine if it is underpowered, placing the airplane below the glide slope.

A pilot has very limited depth perception in relation to the carrier deck at night so he must rely strictly on "the gauges" outside two miles from the ship. Inside that distance, he can risk an occasional peek to verify his lineup for final approach. But at three-quarters of a mile from the back end of the ship, his setup must be nearly perfect. At that point he maintains a continuous scan outside the cockpit to check alignment with the landing area's centerline and the "meatball"—the lights on the lens halfway up the deck that show whether a plane is above or below the glideslope. Properly flown, the final approach has the meatball centered with the horizontal datum lights, indicating the pilot is exactly on glideslope so his plane will clear the ramp by twelve to fourteen feet and his tailhook will snag one of the four wires (actually thick cables) across the deck.

During my fledgling years as an LSO in training I was never actually allowed to control a landing aircraft except in the rarest and most benign circumstances. My duties usually were to observe and assist the controlling LSO by writing his verbal grades on each landing. A perfect "trap" goes into the LSO's little green book as an "OK-3" (underlined), meaning the pilot caught the third wire after a flawless approach. Thus, carrier aviation may be the only human endeavor in which perfection merely rates an OK.

On one particular blackass night in the Western Pacific, *Bon Homme Richard* (CVA-31) was recovering aircraft. The last jet in the pattern was an A-3B Skywarrior, more frequently called the "Whale" for its size. It was a big, robust aircraft considered rather difficult to land aboard a carrier since visibility from the cockpit was poor.

As usual, the LSO platform portside aft was crowded with people observing the landings—fourteen in all, which was about eight bodies too many for the limited space. The LSO's position on the flight deck is very exposed since he stands only thirty feet from the touchdown point. If the plane goes low and impacts the ramp, it showers parts and burning fuel over the immediate area. Consequently, the LSOs have a safety net just below the platform so they can jump away from an impending crash. But you have to be quick.

The A-3 pilot, Vince Agnew, had recently transitioned from props to jets; a big jump from land-based transports to carrier-based Whales. His

156

performance had been "colorful"—so much so that he was permitted to fly daytime only. This particular evening he had been launched unknown to the LSOs, and some of his passes were so hairy that the two enlisted phone talkers ducked below to relative safety when Agnew was on the glideslope.

Lieutenant John Huber was the controlling LSO with Lieutenant Commander Ken Wiley as his backup. Ken was the air wing's senior LSO but Wiley, Huber and Lieutenant Joe Ausley took turns "in the barrel." Only the first team for Vince's landings! I was standing immediately behind Huber, acting as his writer. We were the two farthest from the safety net, with twelve bodies between us and survival—a fact of which we were both acutely aware.

At three-quarters of a mile Agnew called the ball. John radioed that he was low, and should add some power. The pilot responded but with too little throttle and continued to settle. At a half-mile John told him emphatically to add power and get back up on the glideslope. Agnew overcorrected and went climbing above the glideslope. Then, to correct the situation he pulled off a whole fistfull of power. The LSO heard the engines winding down and called for a waveoff, telling Agnew to add full power and go around.

It was too late. The Whale was settling rapidly and a crash into the rear of the flight deck—a rampstrike—was imminent. John and I scrambled ten feet to our right to jump into the safety net prior to impact. But there were too many people on the platform. We never made it.

The A-3's cockpit and forward fuselage made it over the threshhold but the main landing wheels took the full impact of the crash. The aircraft exploded and skidded up the deck on its belly. Parts were flying everywhere. Just out of pure rote training, John and I threw ourselves into the net on top of a mass of tangled humanity.

Vince's abused Whale continued skidding up the deck and—miraculously—got airborne off the angle deck. The engines were developing enough thrust to keep the A-3 from settling into the water, and as it slowly lumbered into the sky, spewing sparks and fuel, we opened our eyes to realize we had just cheated death. My flight suit was soaked with jet fuel and a metal part had made a permanent imprint on my forehead.

The stricken aircraft climbed to a reasonable altitude where the three crewmembers could make a controlled bailout. The A-3 had no ejection seats but with the plane on autopilot everybody slid down the chute in the Whale's belly and opened their parachutes. So far, so good.

But now we had an unmanned bomber orbiting the task force. It wouldn't just politely fly away over the horizon and crash into the sea, but droned around overhead for fifteen minutes. Bonnie Dick's skipper, Captain Rip Kline, felt like it was hours. At one point he considered launching a fighter to shoot down the errant A-3 but finally it lost control or exhausted its fuel and conveniently splashed into the ocean.

Eventually there was mutual agreement between the Navy and Vince Agnew. He threw in his wings, much to the delight of our LSOs.

By the time of the Vietnam War many of us had become callous toward carrier landings. We were better at it because we did it twice a day, almost continuously. After being shot at by SAMs and AAA, landing aboard ship in daylight was almost anticlimactic—no big deal. But night landings still were hairier than most of our shootouts over the beach.

One airplane that definitely was not well-suited to carrier landings—particularly night landings on the smaller *Essex*-class ships—was the F-8 Crusader. The "Ensign Eater" was nicknamed for its unforgiving regard for young or inexperienced pilots. Crusaders were assigned almost exclusively to air wings flying off small carriers whereas the bigger, heavier F-4 Phantoms only flew from the big decks such as *Kitty Hawk*. At risk of seeming parochial, I'll state that the balls required to land F-8s routinely on small decks at night were bigger than life. Crusader landing crashes are legendary, and F-8 pilots actually got to the point of boasting about the worst accident rate in naval aviation history.

The pressure of controlling F-8s was immense and it broke some good LSOs. In 1968 I was a lieutenant and the senior LSO in *Hancock* (CVA-19). The responsibilities of the job were awesome since "Paddles" was in large part responsible for the safety of every pilot and aircrewman in the wing. These pressures got to my predecessor during predeployment workups. He became a basket case and was last seen being carried in a Stokes litter down the flight deck to a medical evacuation helicopter.

Though I had inherited the job, in retrospect I wasn't really ready for it. During the 1968-69 Vietnam cruise we had a lot of landing accidents. By way of comparison, Air Wing 21 lost two pilots and four planes to enemy action but four pilots and seven planes to noncombat causes. Some of the latter were caused by pure "dumbass" pilot errors but I'm sure my LSO inexperience was a contributing factor to one or two. Most accidents occur at night, but occasionally you find an aviator who wants to make history in daylight.

Halfway through the aircraft recovery one bright, clear day I was basking, half naked, back on the LSO platform. The air boss called on the sound-powered phone and advised me that we had a returning F-8 with a utility hydraulic failure. A common problem, but the pilot also had lost use of his radio. He was committed to landing aboard because a divert to DaNang was not possible. The pilot—a good one, incidentally—was Lieutenant Denny "Taco" Bell. He had enough fuel for five or six passes at the deck, a luxury not normally enjoyed.

The LSO normally communicates with the pilot by UHF radio. But if the radio is out, an alternate method is available. At the top of the glide slope the green "cut" lights on the lens are flashed to indicate the aircraft is under LSO control. By use of the red waveoff lights the pilot can be ordered to go around and try again. The last signal to help the pilot finesse his approach is blinking the green lights, an order to add more power.

Taco apparently decided that he would land on the first pass—regardless. Out of the turn on final he was signaled to add power by the flashing greens. No response. Again he was told to add power. Too little response. In close, one last futile attempt was made to persuade him to add power or be waved off into the "penalty box." Nothing.

Waveoff, waveoff!

Too late.

The Crusader struck the ramp. As all three landing gear were ripped away and a fireball engulfed the aircraft, even as the LSOs were all in midair en route to the net. Taco's F-8 skidded along the deck and, miraculously, the tailhook caught an arresting wire, bringing Taco and his fighter to a stop.

For a moment I was only concerned why Taco had not answered the mandatory commands—not that he was still alive. When the fire was extinguished and he was extracted from his cockpit, I confronted him along with several others. "Taco, didn't you see the signals to add power?"

Taco just grinned and said, "Yeah, but I forgot what the green lights meant!"

During that same cruise we had another F-8 incident that shows how the odds can build up against an aviator. Lieutenant Commander John Bartocci was a good pilot with lots of carrier experience. He had previously flown F3H Demons and had his fair share of night landings. For some reason, lately John had demonstrated a severe case of "get-aboard-itis," trying to salvage a poor approach for a successful landing. The night before his accident he had allowed his aircraft to go high in close to the ramp and managed to grab a wire by diving for the deck. His F-8 hit so hard from the high sink rate that all three tires were blown.

The skipper of VF-24, Commander Red Isaacs, and I sat down with John in the ready room before he manned up for his next night mission. We talked to him about his ominous trend and counselled him on all aspects of making a good approach and landing. For any landing—ashore or at sea— it is important to get a good start upon entering the pattern. Early mistakes multiply themselves all the way down the glide slope.

The weather in the Tonkin Gulf was hazy below a solid 1,200-foot overcast with no discernable horizon. It meant on the gauges all the way to touchdown. John launched and led his wingman to a Barrier Combat Air Patrol (BarCAP) just off Haiphong. Normally it was a two-hour mission but that night the cards began stacking against Bartocci. Only one of the F-8s scheduled to relieve John's section got airborne. The decision was made to double-cycle John with an in-flight refueling so he could remain on station four and a half hours.

Hancock was the midnight to noon carrier. Our "day" started at 10:30 pm. Rise and shine, eat "breakfast," fly one or two missions, then go to bed at 2:00 in the afternoon. This schedule was a killer. The body just never adapted to the constant "jet lag" and pilots under combat conditions were continually fatigued.

Double-cycling was bad enough, but to return for a landing in bad weather requires every ounce of energy and skill in your bag of tools. All aircraft had been recovered with the exception of the returning fighters. I was standing on the LSO platform, waiting for the last two F-8s. John's recent performance was my main concern. Even though the pilot is flying the airplane and supposedly in control of his ultimate destiny, the LSO often is the difference between life and death. Pilots are trained to follow every LSO command. If one of the two players—the pilot or LSO—fails to respond quickly and correctly, the result can be disastrous.

Hancock's carrier air traffic control center (CATCC) brought John in on a short right-hand circling approach. Really dumb! Here was a pilot who had just double-cycled, who was dog-tired. But to expedite his approach by requiring him to make a nonstandard right-hand approach with a shorter than normal straightaway was just criminal. Carrier aviators always fly left-hand patterns. This sounds trivial to some, but everything associated with carrier aviation requires left-hand patterns. That's the way we train.

The big concern on a fully instrument approach at night is vertigo. Disorientation is caused when the inner ear tells your brain that your aircraft is in one attitude when your airplane is in another. If you react to the false stimulus you easily can lose control of your aircraft. Out of sheer willpower and discipline the pilot must ignore his vertigo.

I made visual contact with the Crusader turning in at four miles— not nearly enough distance to get properly set up. I called on my handset, "CATCC, who set up 205 for a right-hand approach?"

The reply came, "The captain said for us to expedite so he can turn the ship out of the wind." They really were making it hard for this guy, I thought to myself.

John called the ball at one mile, "Two Zero Five, Crusader ball, state two-nine. Paddles, I've got a severe case of vertigo. Get me aboard!"

"Paddles, roger. John, I've got ya. You're looking good. The wind's down the angle at thirty-two knots—we'll get you aboard." The last statement was as much for my own reassurance as John Bartocci's.

Immediately the F-8 started settling below the glide path. "John, you're goin' low. Put the power back on." The Crusader remained low at the middle of the approach. I called again, "John, put the power back on. You've got to pick it up."

A frightened pilot usually will overcorrect, and this was no exception. John started climbing and continued above the glide slope, now in close and too high for a safe landing. I hit the flashing red lights and yelled, "Waveoff, waveoff" just as 205's nose dropped and started down. The F-8 was so high that there was no danger of hitting the ramp. But the Crusader hit the deck nosegear first, so hard that the plane broke its back just behind the cockpit. It snapped in two with the tail section engaging the second arresting wire. The front half continued down the deck, off the angle and crashed into the sea.

No ejection was observed. I'm sure that John was incapacitated on impact with the deck.

What a strange sight: an aircraft's tail section in the landing area with no cockpit attached. Hindsight is always 20-20, but as with many accidents, this one was avoidable. Naval aviation has become safer over the years but unfortunately our lessons learned are written in young warriors' blood. We all enter the profession with our eyes wide open, knowing the risks. We keep charging full steam ahead, knowing for certain it's only going to happen to the other guy.

LSO stories never will be complete without mentioning the best, most colorful and most popular "waver" of them all, Commander John "Bug" Roach. At his prime, he was the most senior LSO in the U.S. Navy. And that meant in the world.

Bug Roach seemingly saved the taxpayers—in dollar costs of Navy and Marine Corps aircraft, not to mention the lives of aviators—something approaching our GNP. He should be good after having "waved" tailhook airplanes for twenty-one years, but he had a special touch that most LSOs never achieve. The reassurance and confidence he gave to carrier pilots, young and old, positively effects their ability to make good landings. Bug was the Great Communicator of carrier aviation. When he talked to you while you flew down the glideslope, it was as if he were actually in control of the stick and throttle. He could train a chimpanzee to make an OK-3— but Bug would eat the banana.

One night off the Southern California coast *Kitty Hawk* was conducting night carrier qualification. I was on the bridge observing the landings while listening to the pilots and LSOs on the UHF receiver over my captain's chair. The A-6E Intruders of VMA(AW)-212 out of El Toro were ricocheting around the deck that dark, low overcast night. It was the exception rather than the rule that Marine aviators flew off carriers at that time, and 212's pilots were attempting their first night traps, ever. One particular young nugget kept going around and around, unable to satisfy the LSO that his aircraft was even close to being set up to land. He had fuel for just one more pass before being ordered to "bingo" to NAS Miramar.

Bug took the radio and thereby took control of the situation. As the Intruder approached the top of the glideslope, Bug keyed his handset and started flying the aircraft for the scared young aviator. A constant patter of "Okay, you're lookin' good, nice and easy, just a little back to the left, give me just a touch of power. Okay, lookin' great, keep it comin'..." Bug was sweet-talking this guy right down to his first-ever night trap.

"Okay, just a little attitude, fly the ball, good, that's it. Now land the aircraft." The Intruder arrested and cheers went up in all ready rooms from other pilots observing the "save" on television.

I picked up the phone and buzzed the LSO platform. "This is the captain. Let me speak to Bug."

"Commander Roach, sir" was the reply, more formal than he knew he had to be.

"Bug, do you think that young Marine realizes that he was just seduced by a sailor?"

With the first trap out of the way, that pilot went on to bag five in a row later that night. Bug Roach had once again earned the lasting respect of an entire squadron. And he demonstrated why all Paddles take such pride and satisfaction in their work. As they say in perverted Latin at the LSO school: "Rectum Non Bustus.

In September 1991, Bug appeared at the annual Tailhook symposium. Returned from Desert Storm, he said that two wars were enough, and from then on he looked forward to training the new guys how to survive and win in the air. A month later he was dead. Flying an A-4F out of Miramar, Bug's engine exploded and he ejected over the water. But his parachute never opened; he died on impact.

1969-77

CHECKMATES SKIPPER

Following my second combat cruise I received orders to Developmental Squadron Four (VX-4), the fighter test and evaluation unit at NAS Point Mugu, California. At the time I was ineligible for additional Tonkin Gulf deployments, and that was all right with me. I was ready for some stateside flying and a little stability in my life.

However, all the stability in the world couldn't have saved my marriage to my college sweetheart. Back-to-back cruises, continual training deployments, ever on the move—these facts of Navy life take a dreadfully high toll of military marriages. While I don't subscribe to the alleged Marine Corps philosophy ("If we wanted you to have a wife, we'd issue you one."), being single certainly focuses one's mind on an occupation very unforgiving of simple lapses of concentration.

After a month of touring Europe, I was informed by the Bureau of Naval Personnel that my orders to VX-4 had been canceled. It was a big disappointment; I really wanted Point Mugu's type of flying. My new orders directed me to VF-124 at NAS Miramar—as head LSO! It was the last job I coveted. Flying F-8s was okay, but waving those beasts aboard at night on a "routine" basis (and it was never routine) guaranteed cold sweats and ulcers. Help!

So I was stuck with the job until Roy Lester, an East Coast LSO, reported aboard. He actually wanted to wave, so my new twofold assignment was that of Director, Navy Fighter Weapons School (NFWS) and F-14 Model Manager for the Tomcat's fleet introduction. A great set of orders that any genuine fighter pilot might covet: lots of flying including air combat maneuvering, plus a bachelor pad atop Mount Soledad in LaJolla.

164

That was the good news.

The bad news was really bad. Our air-to-air kill ratio against North Vietnamese MiGs wasn't very hot in 1969. The Air Force exchange rate was dismal and, except for my beloved F-8s, the Navy's wasn't much better— barely two to one. By comparison, at the end of WW II, Zeke's Hellcat community staked out a nineteen-to-one kill ratio.

Consequently, the two fighter training squadrons at Miramar drafted an advanced syllabus in all aspects of aerial combat. Both VF-121's "Phantom Professors" and VF-124's "Crusader College" obtained combat-experienced instructors who did little else but think up ways to kill MiGs and to impart that skill to the new guys. And we got results. By the time the whistle blew, ending our phase of the Southeast Asian War Games, Navy fighter crews had notched more than twelve MiGs for each loss in the final "quarter" covering 1972-73.

That Topgun succeeded so well was only slightly less surprising to the mucka-mucks of OpNav than to the MiG drivers at Kep and Phuc Yen. Flying safety had become a fetish with the budgeteers and bean-counters in Washington, and let's face it—practicing for war isn't very safe if it's done right. But our bosses were under pressure from on high to perform, and contrary to many predictions, safety did not take the anticipated hit. Even with all that yanking and banking throughout the flight envelope—from supersonic right down to falling out of the sky at zero airspeed—the Navy Fighter Weapon School prospered. Eventually the F-4 and F-8 schools were merged into one institution, today's fabled Topgun program.

Just as I was settling into the best assignment the U.S. Navy had to offer, a forked-tongue detailer called from D.C. to congratulate me on my selection for Naval Postgraduate School—banishment from flying to Monterey, California. I checked my list of "Falcon Codes" and quickly settled on Falcon: Yankee, Golf, Bravo, Sierra, Mike. You gotta be shittin' me! Leave the absolute best flying job on the planet for two more years of college after thirteen years?

I protested in the strongest way possible, with predictable results. Two months later I was dragged, more literally than figuratively, toward Monterey—a doorknob in each hand, leaving heel marks on the deck.

It was tough; not only the academics, but finding time for the minimum 100-hour annual flight time—in a T-28B Trojan, no less. A twenty-year-old propeller-driven trainer! What a comedown for a supersonic speedster like ol' Phillip Ray Wood. After two months of drilling holes in the sky with the "bugsmasher" I fired off a letter seeking clemency from the functional wing commander at Miramar, asking if I could fly Point Mugu's F-4s, F-8s or A-4s. I was current in all three types. I'll probably never know why, but I was allowed to spend weekends for the next year and a half (when I should have been studying!) wringing out the high-performance stuff.

Near the end of my PG School incarceration, the Navy was running out of combat-qualified aviators to man PacFleet squadrons. The attrition was due to a number of reasons, but most important was the combat-limited statute. So the same detailer who had sent me to PG hell called to ask if I would "volunteer" for another combat tour. He explained that he couldn't order me out for a third Tonkin Gulf tour, and the tone of his voice was almost apologetic.

I immediately thought of the Uncle Remus tales, and cast myself as Br'er Rabbit: "Please don' throw me in dat briar patch!"

The detailer took my response as not only yes but hell yes, and I asked what type of aircraft I would draw. His answer was far from what I expected: "You can fly them all. You're going to be operations officer in Air Wing Two aboard the *Ranger*."

Super—a big boat for once! As CVA-61's "CAG ops" I had the proverbial keys to the kingdom. I could fly almost anything I wanted, almost anytime I wanted. After all, the Ops O is the one who makes out the daily air plan. Br'er Rabbit never had it so good.

My third combat cruise was wonderful—and that's not as peculiar as it sounds. We did everything. Carrier Air Wing Two helped end the shooting war and thereby brought our POW buddies home. During the "Ranger Maru" cruise we tested laser-guided bombs (LGBs), mined Haiphong Harbor and bombed Hanoi into submission—at least long enough to get the POWs returned in early 1973. (Congress had other definitions of "ending the war," and few of us in Navy Air thought it was anything to be proud of.) But I was at Clark Air Force Base in the Philippines for three of the homecoming flights, and I cried every damn time. To see my buddies who had been through hell for so long step off that C-141 was the most heart-rending experience I've ever had.

After Vietnam, I kicked around Miramar for a year or so until I was screened for command. The procedure was this: you report to a squadron as executive officer for eighteen months, then "fleet up" to skipper (if you haven't screwed up as XO) for another eighteen months. My first set of orders had me going to VF-151, a Phantom squadron aboard USS *Midway* (CVA-41), permanently homeported in Japan. But while going through F-4 refresher training, BuPers changed my orders to VF-211, at that time deployed in WestPac flying—set your dial for excitement—F-8 Crusaders!

I felt that it took a real rocket scientist to put this scheme together. Go to an F-8 squadron as exec for six months, then take the troops to VF-124 and transition to the new F-14A Tomcat. It didn't take long for more mature judgment to prevail: skip the XO slot and go directly to 211 as skipper flying F-14s.

PacFleet's two newest Tomcat outfits, VF-24 and -211, were part of Air Wing Nine embarked in USS *Constellation* (CVA-64). My counterpart in Fighting 24 was Commander Jack "Stinger" Ready, but two of our contemporaries had run out of work. Carrier Air Wing Nine's two longtime fighter squadrons, VF-92 and -96, were being laid to rest—"disestablished" in Navy parlance. Consequently, two tombstones adorned the entrance to the Miramar Officer's Club for years thereafter.

However, Commanders Ron "Pon" Johnson and Terry "Eagle" Kryway had only been in command of the Silver Kings and Fighting Falcons, respectively, for a few months—far less than the allotted year and a half. Since they would not be competitive for the air wing "bonus command" with their foreshortened CO tenure, they requested to be the "direct input" COs of VF-24 and 211—and rightly so. Stinger and I protested mildly and lost, but in truth, being exec for five months was a blessing in disguise. It amounted to a longer flying tour, and a period to sit back and observe how to be a skipper.

Our two squadrons were the first to receive "nugget" aviators straight from Training Command upon receiving their Wings of Gold. Despite their inexperience, they brought esprit de corps, humor, endearing immaturity (aloft and ashore)—and the ability to perform menial administrative tasks. It takes the knowledge of two middle-grade aviators to match the energy and mischievousness of one nugget, who can find trouble almost anywhere.

Air Wing Nine began an eleven-month Tomcat transition in January 1975. One of our most interesting tasks was selecting who would go to VF-24 and who I would receive in -211. Ready and I had begun our "recruiting" months previously, while stuck in other jobs, but as the squadrons formed, we could see two distinct institutional personalities developing. Both units had good aviators—among the best, in fact—but the VF-24 troops, including the chiefs and whitehats, seemed more representative of the fighter image: raucous, gregarious, and (let's face it) obnoxious. I felt that VF-211 didn't conform as closely to the fighter model, being more introverted and studious—even analytical. But whatever their styles, after completing the RAG syllabus Air Wing Nine's FitRons captured Naval Aviation's top four awards: the CNO Safety Award, the Battle "E" for operational efficiency, the prestigious Clifton Award as the Navy's best fighter outfit, and—of more importance to the JOs—the fabled "Mutha" award as Miramar's all-round best squadron. Regardless of the personalities involved, somebody had strapped a rocket to the new kids on the block, who blasted off to stratospheric heights of achievement.

After five months as XO I relieved "Pon" Johnson on 1 May 1976. The change of command ceremony was held on the parade ground with all hands in full regalia amid hundreds of guests. The band played valiantly, the chaplain prayed earnestly, and the admiral spoke of readiness and why the Navy needed a bigger slice of the defence pie. A four-plane diamond formation of Tomcats flew overhead and our CAG acknowledged the transfer of responsibility between the old skipper and the new.

Now, I'd suffered through my share of change-of-command speeches in my time, and I knew to a mortal certainty that nobody had anything original to say. So, as last speaker, I knew exactly what was on everyone's mind: "Let's get this thing over with and retire to the O'Club." My remarks, including greetings and salutations, lasted all of twenty-eight seconds—undoubtedly a record. Basically, I said, "Thank you for this opportunity; I'll try not to screw things up. Now let's get on with it."

Fifteen years later, people still told me it was the finest bit of oration they ever heard.

Two days later we flew the entire squadron to NAAS Fallon, Nevada for an air wing weapons deployment. Typically, this evolution involved two weeks of day and night intercepts, air-to-ground ordnance practice, flying through electronic warfare ranges and simulated SAM sites. Computers tell you if your evasive maneuvers are effective or if you "died." The last week is devoted to coordinated strikes against "enemy" targets defended by both air and ground forces. Topgun instructors fly the bogies and always engage the strike group inbound to the target area. The dogfights that ensue are chillingly real in terms of defeat or victory without (presumably) the loss of aircraft or crews. You make mistakes but you come back the next day to try again.

In those days, we took Saturday afternoon and all Sunday off for a little R&R, and one weekend I joined a group for some trout fishing. As I rode in a camper and would be gone overnight, I loaned my official sedan, appropriately marked "CO VF-211," to my junior officers to ease Fallon's perennial transportation problem.

That Sunday afternoon, cruising west on Route 50, we passed a very famous whorehouse east of town called "Suzie's." The air wing commander noted that my big, black sedan was parked at the afore-mentioned establishment, which was bad enough (I expected just a bit of discretion from my junior officers.) But not only had the JOs used my car indiscreetly, they waged a psywar campaign as well. Everybody visiting Suzie's signed in as "CDR Phil Wood." Therefore, anyone casually perusing the guest register would conclude that CO VF-211 was the most prolific sex fiend on the North American continent.

I filed the incident in my mental computer, marked "accounts payable."

A typical coordinated air wing strike consisted of about thirty aircraft. To be effective against a heavily-defended target, while minimizing losses, the tactics had to be based upon previous experience while adjusting for our own ever-improving technology.

Today's surface-to-air missiles can fly farther and turn better than ever before; some of them are undetectable by our radar-warning receivers, and some possess a genuine low-altitude capability while we're flying down in the weeds. In Vietnam we employed that tactic, but two things could reach out and grab us while we were low and fast. First, any infantryman can take a potshot at you, and a plain old bullet in the right place can knock down a jet at high speed. Also, it's hard to maneuver at high Mach while only 200 feet off the deck. The SAMs are a lot better today than the SA-2s we dodged over Hanoi; Uncle Ho's Guidelines emitted a solid white contrail you could see for miles. But not today. You only know you're targeted if you have an electronic sensor on the correct frequency to detect the SAM.

Strike tactics are driven by the type of target you're after, and what type of damage you need to inflict. The smart weapons that proved so fascinating to the public—and troublesome to Saddam Hussein—give aircrews a lot more flexibility than ever before. They also improve survivability in the enemy's air-defense network, which naturally enhances aviator morale!

The worldwide threat of enemy aircraft also is vastly improved—in some cases technically superior to our own—with forward-quarter missile engagement, contrary to the good old days of dogfighting for a rear-hemisphere advantage. Soviet- and even Western-designed radars are arrayed against us, permitting a beyond-visual range (BVR) missile shot before we know the bad guy is out there. The major advantage, however, is that our aviators are better trained, and usually more aggressive.

In the strike group the slower aircraft, such as our "airborne eyes"— the E-2C Hawkeye—takes off early and heads for the target area. Support aircraft such as the EA-6B Prowler electronic jammers usually operate independently, suppressing enemy radars and fire-control links. The "zappers" are coordinated into the overall plan, but don't go in harm's way because they cannot defend themselves. If the opposition knows a Prowler is lurking somewhere out on the periphery, believe me that the EA-6 becomes the priority target!

The strike group is composed of bombers and their fighter escorts as well as "Iron Hand" birds that shoot antiradiation missiles at enemy radars. Presumably, if hostile fire-control radars elect not to come on-line, they're limited to firing their SAMs optically, under manual control, and that's seldom effective. Thus, defense suppression is a mixture of blunt, punch-in-the-nose tactics and subtle, sneaky-pete type of "soft kill" options.

Twenty-odd bombers and fighters are divided into "cells" of three or four aircraft within the larger strike package. After launch we join up at a prebriefed point from the carrier at various assigned altitudes, linking up with airborne tankers. Once the group is joined the flight leader, usually the CAG, will "head 'em out" en route to the hostile coastline. The various cells will "hit" the tankers and take on fuel en route to the target area, enabling the strikers to arrive at their coast-in points with near-maximum fuel.

The formation is separated precisely by bearings, distances and altitudes, depending upon the nature of enemy defenses. If you go in low for terrain masking from enemy radars, the fighters will usually be out in front and above, and in trail above the bombers. Obviously, this low-altitude formation will be flown during daylight and clear-weather conditions.

Terrain masking from ground-based radars is very effective but it's not entirely wonderful. It has the potential to ruin your whole day—like flying into the ground. We tried this tactic over North Vietnam, blowing in low and fast in one big gaggle, and we got our asses shot off. We learned that we'd given the SA-2s too much credit and therefore tried to stay below their firing envelope. Later on, we "ingressed" at medium altitudes—15,000 to 20,000 feet—and just dodged the SAMs as they appeared. It was tricky, but it worked if you did it right. It took nerves of steel to sit there, watching that Mach-two telephone pole burning up at you, while you resisted the screaming urge to maneuver too soon. Timing was crucial, or it was the end of the hunt!

Usually we launched, rendezvoused, tanked and approached the target "zip lip," in complete silence. Radio transmissions are detectable by the enemy and alert him not only to the fact that you're inbound, but from what direction. So we used hand signals, cockpit to cockpit, for everything. Radio calls were reserved for rare circumstances—like "I'm ejecting. Please send help!"

Approaching the enemy coast, you start trading altitude for speed. The old saying is true: speed is life in combat. The bombers are slower than usual because they're heavy with all that ordnance hanging from their wings and fuselage. So once we went "feet dry" overland, we started mild jinking within the formation, maneuvering laterally to deny obnoxious flak gunners a steady tracking solution on us. When SAMs or AAA start coming up, the jinking becomes more violent, depending upon where your aircraft is in relation to the incoming missiles or bullets.

You also know that enemy fighters are being vectored in for a shot at you. Their first order of business is to shoot down the bombers, or at least make them jettison their ordnance. The enemy doesn't want to engage our fighters because he knows he'll probably lose. So the name of the game is to figure out where the "bandits" will appear and position yourself so you can see them on your radar as soon as possible. Frequently, just being in position to engage them will discourage poorly-motivated enemy fighter pilots.

In Air Wing Nine's training missions flown on the Nellis Air Force target complexes, our most capable opponents were the Topgun instructors and USAF aggressor squadron pilots in the role of enemy fighters. The guys flying red-starred F-5s, F-16s or A-4s are all experienced and skilled. If you can get to the target, drop your bombs and " get out of Dodge" unscathed, you have learned to do it right. Most of the cards are stacked in the aggressor's favor: he knows where you're coming from and where you're headed. He picks his point where he'll attack you, and on what terms. But if he makes a mistake and commits too early, I'll own his ass.

Flying an F-14 as fighter escort, my air-to-air radar, augmented by that from the E-2 or Air Force AWACS bird, will be looking for him long before we enter the target area. If we see him on radar, we light the afterburners, accelerate toward him and leave the strike group. It's a doctrinal matter of lasting controversy in the business. In daylight, bomber guys like to see lots of fighters stacked up around them—makes 'em feel good. But we fighter jocks know better. Our best chance of breaking up inbound bandits is to hit them early, as far from the strike group as possible.

A good enemy command and control net, despite our radio silence, will see our fighters depart the formation and begin to intercept the opposing fighters. Our biggest concern, however, is not radar or jet aircraft nor even missiles—it's politics. The service and civilian politicians who determine our rules of engagement (ROE) live in deadly fear of what we call "Blue on Blue" kills. The public learned of it as "friendly fire" casualties during the war against Iraq, and it does happen—no denying it. But concern about such things can impose unduly restrictive handicaps on the fighter crews attempting to shoot down the bandits.

In the air-to-air business, ROE seldom allow us to fire beyond visual range, which negates the long arm of our most capable missiles like Sparrow and Phoenix. Usually our opponent operates under no such stricture, and you can bet your sweet empennage he's not going to wait if he has us locked up on his radar with a firing solution!

On training missions we always engaged the adversaries in close-in dogfights, even though our long-range missiles presumably could have shot them down if the hassles were for real. But it was always a thrill to enter a dogfight head-on, closing at speeds of twice the speed of sound. You pass canopy to canopy with the enemy pilot, sometimes less than 100 feet apart. Then it's time for the headwork that makes or breaks a fighter pilot—outthinking the opposition. What's he likely to do? Turn right or left, climb or extend? If he commits early or makes the wrong move, I'm going to exploit his mistake. The name of the game is to bring my missiles or gun to bear—to kill him quickly so I can turn my attention to the three or more miles of airspace around me.

The "enemy" over Nellis likely flew the F-5 Tiger II or F-15 Eagle, both highly-dangerous opponents if flown according to their relative merits. The opposing pilot is probably as good at dog fighting as I am, so the match turns into a prolonged fight, sparring for position. Continually pulling high Gs; now losing, now gaining an advantage, constantly watching for an opening. All the time monitoring my remaining fuel so I can get home after zapping this guy.

In days of yore, it was conventional wisdom that the first one back to the ready room won the fight. I've seen some of those long-ago debriefs degenerate into little more than a military version of the kid's game: "I killed you on the first pass."

"Did not."

"Did too."

"Did not!"

"Did too!" And so on and so on; et cetera et cetera; ditto ditto.

Today, multi-plane hassles covering hundreds of square miles and tens of thousands of feet in altitude are minutely monitored by electronically-instrumented ranges. The sensors record, document and analyze every conceivable aspect of an air-to-air engagement. For instance, if you squeeze the trigger too early, firing a Sidewinder outside its effective envelope, the computers invalidate the shot. The same function applies to almost every type of aviation ordnance.

After landing, you're safely seated in a comfortably-padded chair in the auditorium or in your ready room. There, in electronic real time or on a TV screen, every teeny-tiny mistake is evident for the world to see. As the old saying goes, you learn more from failure than from success, and the lessons are shown for your benefit. The object of such exercises as Red Flag is to get our aircrews up to the equivalent of ten real-life combat missions before they ever launch in earnest. Knowledge is not only power in aerial combat—like speed, it is life. So when you launch off the carrier deck in the Persian Gulf on your first genuine combat mission over Kuwait or downtown Baghdad, you'll remember all the mistakes you made in that other desert arena just outside the chinsy glitter of Las Vegas.

The record indicates that Red Flag works extremely well. The air-to-air score during Desert Storm was pegged at forty-five to one, including Iraqi helicopters. And those kind of odds are hard to beat, even on The Strip!

During our air wing workups with *Constellation*, prior to deployment, the air wing was scheduled for a three-week "mini-cruise" to Hawaii for a major fleet exercise. As a result of a tennis injury, my left knee required surgery, and the rehabilitation period was pegged at six weeks. Unsat! But the flight surgeon automatically gave me a "down chit" which prevented me from flying during the fun and games, so an alternate plan was devised.

My rehab would take only two weeks, assuming I could demonstrate competence. In this instance, I had to show the flight surgeon that I could walk without crutches and climb into and out of a cockpit without assistance. Worth a try, right?

The two weeks following surgery were painful—lifting ankle weights, walking short distances, whirlpool baths with the knee taped. But the demonstration took place on "Connie's" flight deck and Dr. Carl Trussler, our beloved "fighter doc," observed as I hobbled to an F-14's ladder. He didn't notice that my thirty-five pounds of flight gear were missing, or maybe he ignored that fact. However, all my practice sessions in scaling the boarding ladder had been conducted with helpers. This time the crippled skipper's adrenalin was pumping overtime, and I had to bite off a couple of painful oaths—but I made it, easing into the Tomcat's front seat. Doc Trussler was gracious in defeat, calling up to me that he would sign my "up chit." He then invited me to accompany him to sick bay to fill out the papers.

Breathing hard, trying to ignore the pain in my knee, I blandly replied that I wanted to sit in the cockpit awhile to refresh my switchology.

As soon as the doc was out of sight, the maintenance crew lifted me from the cockpit and gently lowered me to the deck—the same procedure they followed during the next three weeks. Maybe not one of my smarter moves, but it kept me flying during an important fleet exercise.

Literally at the last minute before sailing for the RimPac exercise, I learned I'd screened for the coveted CAG slot—air wing commander. This meant rolling early out of one flying job, preparing for another. The squadron XO/CO tour is supposed to cover three years, but mine lasted only sixteen months, including eleven as skipper. Ordinarily I'd have felt cheated, but leaving VF-211 early to assume command of Air Wing Eleven cheered me up—CAG is the best flying job in the Navy.

However, there still remained the matter of RimPac—the annual exercise with Pacific Rim allies—not to mention that lingering "accounts receivable" bill to my JOs after their gotcha on me at Suzie's in Fallon.

At the end of the exercise, all participating units—the Blue good guys and evil Orange guys—entered Pearl Harbor for the debrief and some liberty. The first afternoon in port my executive officer and I rented a small Japanese car and headed for Waikiki Beach and some sun. My XO was Commander Gary "Slats" Hakanson, a very fine gent who was going places in Uncle Sam's Navy. We drank too much wine and got too many rays, but we discussed matters of pressing importance.

When a carrier enters port away from home, the embarked squadrons always set up an "admin," a hotel suite to be used as headquarters ashore. It's a place to relax, change clothes, sleep and party. Usually we send a junior officer ashore before the ship docks, to rent the room, buy all manner of liquid refreshment, and hand out invitations to the local lovelies at embassies, hospitals, airlines, etc., for the customary arrival party. The revelry that night was well provided with feminine companionship—my JO had done good.

The tone of such events will always be established by the skipper and XO. Things can get out of hand and become an animal act if the two leaders don't make it clear that any JO who oversteps the unwritten limits will be harshly dealt with. That's not to say these parties are tea dances, but throwing waitresses from the third-floor balcony into the swimming pool is a little too much. Somewhere in between is standard behavior.

At some point in the festivities it is appropriate that the CO address the gathering, welcoming the guests and letting the aircrews know that they did a good job at sea. "This clambake is your reward for doing good, guys. Have fun." That sort of thing.

During my remarks that evening, the Checkmates XO appeared to have consumed a bit too much, and took verbal exception to my speech. As the skipper, I told Slats that he should drink less, keep his comments to himself, and comport himself as an Officer and a Gentleman. To no avail. He persisted in baiting me.

Now things had gone too far. Slats' vocalization had degenerated to the point that it couldn't be ignored and had to be dealt with. He was challenging my authority before the entire wardroom, to say nothing of our lady guests. Next thing I knew, Slats and I were face to face, shouting and jabbing fingers in one another's chests. The tension in the suite was palpable, with sideways glances and saucer-size eyeballs from the JOs. I could read their minds. "What's the skipper gonna do?"

Now, understand that the CO and exec have no peers in the squadron. They are usually much older and certainly more senior than any other officers; all authority rests with these two. Therefore, anybody else would be extremely reluctant to butt in on something as untoward as a CO/XO altercation—especially in public. To do so would be risky business, with the prospects of future reprisals from one or both combatants. The attitude was, "Leave it alone and hope for the best."

Slats and I were now beyond shouting and poking—we'd progressed to shoving, which in turn led to wrestling. We both went down in a tangle on the floor, punching and kicking, grunting and groaning. A real OK Corral. The JOs didn't know what to do. Aghast, none of them stepped in. If nothing else, I know they resented such boorish behavior from their leaders and the embarrassment it caused among the ladies present.

At some point in the fisticuffs—I don't recall just when—I gave a subtle signal. Gary and I abruptly stopped fighting, pulled each other up off the floor and hugged. Then we erupted into laughter, facing the startled ringside guests.

We had pulled off the biggest gotcha in Checkmates history. My "accounts receivable" file was paid in full!

I turned over VF-211 in March 1977, and Gary took the squadron to even greater heights. But sadly, he ran afoul of a petty, publicity-seeking Democratic congressman named Jim Bates. Gary and two other senior officers at NAS Miramar were wrongly, unjustly relieved of duty for problems that predated their tenure by as much as three years.Secretary of the Navy John Boy Lehman refused to stand up for his guiltless troops, thereby losing a good deal of trust among the less politically inclined. But there was ultimate justice in 1990 when "Bugler" Bates lost his congressional seat to a Republican challenger with impeccable fighter credentials—Vietnam War ace Randy "Duke" Cunningham.

Meanwhile, I looked forward to playing CAG—a long, long way from that miserable whaleboat in Wonsan Harbor twenty-five years before.

1977-79

LUCKY ELEVEN: PART TWO

With my departure from VF-211, I would have only eight months to complete my prospective CAG training to relieve Captain (Select) Sam Leeds in December 1977. To do it right, a new air group commander should check out in every aircraft type assigned to him, visit each air station where his squadrons are based, and attend five or six schools.

In the late Seventies the typical carrier air wing had eleven squadrons or detachments assigned, with six or more aircraft types including helicopters. Not only does the CAG lead on the deck—he is expected to lead in the air as well. To set the example, he should demonstrate an ability to fly them all and understand their capabilities. However, this was back in the good old days, before the "Super CAG" billet was established which limited the air wing commander's flight time and put tactical leadership upon his deputy—what I call the "real CAG."

To qualify aboard ship in all types would be impossible owing to training time constraints, but in my case it was reasonable to car-qual in the F-14A Tomcat, A-6E Intruder and A-7E Corsair II, day and night. If it sounds like fun, it was! Being CAG is absolutely the best flying job in the Navy, limited only by the extent of leadership and administrative duties on the ground. The CAG can pick his missions, but he should always share the responsibility with the squadron COs who work for him. You shouldn't be a flight-time hog, but you should take your share of hard missions.

My three Vietnam cruises had shown me the extremes. There were CAGs who flew the most demanding combat missions in all sorts of weather. Others didn't like to be shot at, and consequently never carried their load over the beach by leading from up front. The best were always there when needed, but still allowed the squadron skippers to lead some of the major strikes. You don't find many timid CAGs because the screening process is very competitive; selection is based upon your past service reputation.

Following seven months of training, I headed for WestPac where USS *Kitty Hawk* and Air Wing Eleven were operating—almost twenty years after Zeke Cormier led "CAG-11" from *Shangri-La*. I caught up with the "Kitty-Eleven" team in Japan so there could be a sea period and observing the ship/air wing operations before taking over.

We got underway from Yokosuka and steamed south around Kyushu into the Sea of Japan. Once off the coast of South Korea, far enough north for the Soviets to come play, I observed a finely-honed air wing. The December weather was terrible: rain, low ceilings, and tops so high you couldn't refuel in flight. Soviet Naval Aviation flew south out of Vladivostok to simulate strikes against the carrier and her escorts, almost as if they were saying, "Welcome, CAG Wood."

I was impressed with CVW-11, and wondered how I could improve on such a well-orchestrated team. Rear Admiral Gene Tissot was the carrier group commander, with CV-63 under Captain Ned Hogan, a former fighter pilot himself. The outgoing CAG, Sam Leeds, would be relieved in Pusan, our next port of call. These leaders had put together a winning team, and I was grateful to inherit the benefits of their hard work.

During the change-of-command ceremony in Pusan, the air wing JOs put on a series of skits poking fun at outgoing CAG Leeds. Though done with humor, the squadrons' productions could best be described as cruel and unusual punishment—the roast of all roasts. Reading between the lines, I made mental notes of the points so outlandishly made. I would have to establish leadership in the sky by flying at night, in rotten weather, to lead the strikes and to remain a practitioner as well as a theorist.

My first test would be a war-at-sea exercise against USS *Midway* and Air Wing Five, permanently forward-deployed in Japan. They were "the best in the west," the PacFleet experts who were pitted against newly-arriving carriers, and they always kicked ass. Being closest to the potential action, CVW-5 was always "on cruise" and as ready as they come.

But that challenge lay in the dim future. Following the reception, life looked exceeding sweet since my staff had produced a very fine bottle of French *chateanuef de pape*, a great red wine that goes straight to the brain. Thereafter I met my date for the evening, an American teacher stationed in Pusan who had theater tickets.

The lady had parked her car in front of the officer's club, where many of my guys had gathered to see me off and remind me that we would get underway next morning. As I walked around the back of the car to get in the passenger's side, I felt myself suspended in midair. It was dark and I was falling in space. It seemed an eternity before hitting bottom.

I hadn't seen the ditch. My date had parked right up against a *benjo* ditch—an open latrine. After stepping into space, and my resultant crash in flames, I was knocked unconscious.

The next thing I remember, I was being hauled to the surface. The port side of my face had taken major battle damage and, bleeding and groggy, I was driven by the nice lady to the dispensary for medical attention. My dress blues were a strike—damaged beyond economical repair.

The next morning, after Kitty was underway, I went on closed-circuit TV to address the air wing in the ready rooms. Here's a brand-new CAG nobody could recognize through the tape and bandages, explaining his grand strategy against the dreaded *Midway*. Talk about laughter—those aviators were having a hard time controlling themselves. Later I heard that one of the junior birdmen commented, "Now this is a CAG I can relate to."

The captain and the admiral were less favorably impressed.

As The Hawk's battle group headed south out of the Sea of Japan into the Pacific east of Okinawa, *Midway* would get underway from Subic Bay in the Philippines for her transit north to Japan. The object of the war-at-sea game was relatively simple: to strike the other carrier with your air wing, any way you could—within certain guidelines. As mentioned earlier, *Midway* had competed in this exercise many times, and reputedly had never lost. They had learned their lessons well, and didn't repeat a mistake. All their tactics and technology would come to play: intelligence, deception, concealment, circuitous routes, new wrinkles—and they'd cheat like hell.

Kitty Hawk would be constrained to a box-shaped operating area 200 miles southeast of Okinawa. The OpArea's four sides were well-defined, and the carrier was prohibited from leaving that box. However, our opponent could approach by a number of routes: from the Philippine Sea to the east, from the Bashi Channel between Luzon and Taiwan, or she could loop north beyond Taiwan and Okinawa. She selected the latter route, opting for a highspeed transit to deny us early positioning data. Even if we had located her, we couldn't overfly Taiwan at all, and only Okinawa on rare occasions.

BOOK III – PHIL

We had low-confidence intel that *Midway's* battle group was heading north from Subic. Therefore, we sent some long-range S-3A Vikings southwest to search the Bashi Channel—but no joy. Based on those early reports, we did a dead-reckoning plot based on a predicted course and speed, and next day sent S-3s west to scout between Taiwan and Okinawa. Our Vikings contacted some gray "navy" ships just southwest of Okinawa at dusk, heading north at high speed. The aircrews thought the contact might be an amphibious group, but because of reduced visibility in rainsqualls, and the ships were in a restricted area off-limits to aircraft, the ID was spotty.

The last report would have placed *Midway* a little north of our estimated position, but we had no information on any amphibious surface action group in the area. The situation weighed heavily on my mind all night. Soon *Midway*, if it were she, would be protected by the Okinawa landmass, and we couldn't fly all the way around the northern tip with enough fuel to return to The Hawk. The report just seemed like too much of a coincidence; it had to be "Midway Maru."

I made a decision. If *Midway* could cheat by operating inside the ADIZ—the air-defense identification zone which planes only can penetrate by permission—we could play that game, too. But if my plan failed, the new CAG-11 would be in Big Trouble—along with the ship's captain and the battle group admiral.

I called in my trusted agent: Lieutenant Commander Doug Connell, an A-7 pilot on my staff. He was one of our air wing LSOs, and smarter than hell. We had to locate *Midway* before she got too far north and out of range. The only way was to overfly Okinawa and illegally penetrate the ADIZ. I gave Doug the option, strictly voluntary, that if we got caught, the buck would stop with me. He not only agreed, he was a warhorse chompin' at the bit. He picked his wingman with care, briefed him, then manned up and launched.

In broad daylight, Doug's section flew away from The Hawk, eastbound—the wrong direction. After twenty miles the two A-7s turned off their IFF transponders so they couldn't be illuminated on any interrogating radars. Doug then turned back, heading northwest toward Okinawa, flying as low as possible to avoid radar detection. The two Corsairs picked their coast-in point and routed themselves across the island to avoid airfields and densely-populated areas. They flew down the lush, green valleys undetected by radar or, apparently, human eyeballs. After twenty minutes of terrain-hugging flight, they popped out into the East China Sea.

Because our quarry's position was estimated only on an assumption, and was moving at about twenty-five knots, finding her would be like a nautical version of needle-in-the-haystack. Doug's problem was compounded by the need to remain low; he couldn't take the luxury of popping up for a look-see because he might be detected by *Midway*'s radar, or—worse yet—Okinawa ADIZ.

Searching the open ocean is extremely difficult; most ships are indistinguishable from afar so you have to get close to classify the type, its course and speed. Doug and his wingman separated laterally to extend their search area. The A-7E had various electronic warning receivers that could detect and classify an emitter, while showing a strobe to indicate its bearing. But if *Midway* was out there, she certainly wasn't emitting. The searchers had to continue the old-fashioned way: by eyeball.

Then Doug's wingman spotted a smallboy—probably a destroyer. He rocked his wings to indicate a visual contact, as radio transmissions would reveal their presence. Doug saw the signal and closed up. Sure enough, dead ahead was a U.S. Navy destroyer headed north at high speed, its wake churning up much white water. *Midway* had to be nearby. The section turned north to avoid visual ID by the destroyer screen, but that direction was only a hunch on Doug's part. The carrier could just as easily have been to the south or west.

About three minutes later, as blind luck would have it, there was *Midway* on the horizon, heading 030. Doug and his wingie stayed low. They planned to fly over the deck at one hundred feet. If the carrier was at flight quarters, and did not give permission, the overflight would be a serious safety violation. But the Corsairs pressed on.

USS *Midway* was caught completely by surprise. The carrier was in total emission shut down. When the two A-7s screeched over the flight deck, simulating dropping bombs, Doug could see the two alert F-4N Phantoms on the catapults as their crews lay on the wings, soaking up rays. They had no time to react.

As Doug's section headed back the way it had come, the mission was completely successful. *Midway* now knew that her position was known to *Kitty Hawk*, following a predictable course and speed. She also knew that we would be generating restrikes while Air Wing Five still had to locate us inside a 40,000-square-mile box. The war had begun.

We found our victim again that night with A-6 Intruders. In turn, we observed one *Midway* strike approach as close as ninety miles but turn away without finding us.

As dawn arrived, most of two air wings were passing each other en route to the opposition's carrier. At this point the outcome was pretty well determined in favor of The Hawk, but training for all hands was important, so we flew for most of that second day.

The wing was really pleased with the outcome, even though we had admittedly stretched the rules to achieve our victory. It was obvious when we debriefed the admiral on our search procedure that we had violated the Okinawa ADIZ. I told him of my decision, stating that I would accept full responsibility for any flight violations that may ensue. But Admiral Tissot decided that if the U.S. Air Force didn't realize that its airspace had been penetrated, he certainly wouldn't tell them! And since no objections were raised by *Midway* (they broke the rules all the time), the matter was closed. Whew!

We had our win over the Scourge of WestPac, and the rest of the cruise was good flying, plenty of great liberty, and we returned to San Diego on time in May 1978.

Shortly after arrival in ConUS, I was advised that the East Coast was short one air wing to deploy in *America* (CV-66) to the Mediterranean in March 1979. Air Wing Eleven would do a quick turnaround, proceed to Norfolk, Virginia on 2 January to begin workups with the ship over a six-week period.

We faced a major challenge. To return from cruise, stand down for thirty days, then regroup, go to Fallon for coordinated air wing training, car-qual off the West Coast, take a little time off for Christmas, then move the entire wing cross-country is no small task. The logistics alone require a herculean effort. But we did it.

After arrival at Norfolk, we got underway for the Caribbean Operating Area off Puerto Rico. We steamed around for five weeks, checking all the boxes on the list that normally require three months of training. AirLant operates differently from AirPac, and though it's not to say one is better, there are problems. The East Coast procedures, the facilities, target areas, the weather—even little things like radio frequencies you've memorized over the years—are different. The visiting aircrews don't exactly start from scratch, but their "data base" requires more inputs to complete the training requirements. In short, it was not easy melding the ship and air wing into a strong team.

Like people, aircraft carriers have personalties and reputations, both good and bad, that shift back and forth over the years. These reps can be in terms of a "real operator," or the opposite; clean or dirty, good or poor chow. Some ships have more fires or accidents while others have engineering plants that are always "up" or too often "down." In nearly every case, such foibles are the direct result of the commanding officer. The skipper of a ship forms its personality, varying from a can-do attitude to a cover-your-ass attitude, or anywhere in between. But a good CO can take over a loser ship and usually has enough time to turn it around.

Air Wing Eleven's arrival on the East Coast generally—and in *America* particularly—was not a pleasant one. The Hawk and CVW-11 had been married approximately forever, including six combat cruises to the Tonkin Gulf dating from 1966. However, my air wing arrived onboard *America* as a bastard child. The ship didn't want us, and we were struggling to get up to speed, adapt to the ship and the East Coast community—and, by the way, to fly safely without losing any aircrew or planes while remaining combat-ready.

We found that several of the carrier's spaces normally reserved for the squadrons had been occupied by ship's company. When the air wing is ashore, it's natural that some of those vacant spaces will be used by the ship's crew with the caveat that the precious space will be relinquished when the squadrons fly aboard. Not so on United States Ship *America*, even though I raised hell with the ship's exec and finally with the captain.

The ship was dirty by comparison to The Hawk. The food left a lot to be desired, and there were unreasonable restrictions on aircrews being authorized to eat meals in their own wardroom while wearing flight suits. The ship's XO insisted that aviators change between flights and eat below in the more formal wardroom.

We also had financial problems. Our monthly mess bills were higher than we expected, and each officer was assessed an extra $400. It turned out that a junior supply officer in charge of the wardroom had not been paying the food suppliers. Instead, he pocketed the cash and walked off the ship with a bundle of money.

Because of the many perceived inequalities I felt about our treatment, I became a constant pain in the ass to the captain and executive officer. It was my job as CAG to try to resolve such problems, but I made very little headway. Therefore, I reported the situation up the chain of command and got a special team to fly out to the ship to investigate the allegations. ComNavAirLant eventually agreed with my report. Things changed, but the ship/air wing harmony improved very little. As I escorted the senior team member to his departing airplane he said to me, "CAG, you're getting screwed."

My old friend from Miramar and VF-211 days arrived to relieve me in April. Commander Jack "Stinger" Ready was a welcome sight to behold. He is one of the best aviators I know, and possesses a positive leadership style. A real warrior. After a few days at sea, *America* pulled into Naples where Stinger and I moved into a tennis resort to complete the turnover.

Upon my departure the ship's captain was obliged to give me, in person, my final fitness report on my performance under his command. It was actually better than I had anticipated. Under the block titled "working relations" he had graded me with a D—not too good on a scale from A to F. I told him that I wished he had marked it F so future selection boards would recall how bad things were on his ship. He kicked me out of his cabin.

Stinger and all the squadron skippers put me on a rented bus to escort me to the airport for my flight to Washington. The champagne flowed freely and I told Jack, "For the first time in my career I'm actually ready to leave a flying billet." Stinger, to nobody's surprise, went on to three well-deserved stars and a career that ended too soon for the good of naval aviation.

Meanwhile, I'd have a chance at doing things right—with my own ship.

1981-1986

DRIVING SHIPS

If carrier aviators survive the promotion boards, command selections, night landings and the woo of airline salaries (not to mention combat missions), we transition from flying airplanes to driving boats. It sounds unglamorous and closely akin to the blackshoe Navy, but about the time our ages pass the big four-oh, we are ordered to jobs requiring slower reflexes, where eye glasses are permitted. Carrier aviation is for the young.

As aviators growing up, we are taught to look with disdain upon naval officers who drive ships. We go to great lengths in avoiding ship's company assignments in non-flying status. We know that only carrier aviators are eligible to command aircraft carriers, but the rewards were too far in the future to consider surviving to reach that plateau. But in retrospect, I could not imagine that commanding ships was a far greater challenge than flying fighters from carriers. In comparison, flying high-performance jets makes conning a ship seem like animated slow motion. However, unlike the maneuverable jet, once a large ship is put in motion, its direction is difficult to alter. Decisions, once executed, tend to be irrevocable.

The turn diameter of an aircraft carrier at thirty-two knots is six miles. And the distance covered from the time a "backing bell" orders the ship's screws to reverse rotation, bringing the ship to a stop, requires five minutes to halt all forward progress. Obviously, driving a large ship is vastly different from driving a jet fighter.

But a junior aviator deploying on his first carrier cruise can be exposed to professional training in the boat business. In addition to his flying duty, he can volunteer to learn the intricacies of shipboard management, standing bridge team watches, or even engineering watches. Thus, by the time he takes command of his own "deep draft"—usually an oiler or supply ship—an aviator has been exposed to the discipline for twenty years and has taken nine months of continuous schooling. We aviators have been accused by our blackshoe counterparts of walking aboard our first ship as the commanding officer and asking the officer of the deck (OOD), "How the hell do you get this thing underway?"

An aviator's trump card—particularly if he has combat experience—is the ability and willingness to make quick decisions, and an acute awareness of relative motion. The rest is a lot of on-the-job training—and luck.

My first command was USS *Wabash* (AOR-5), a new combat replenishment ship out of San Francisco. It carried some two million gallons of fuel oil, dry goods, fresh, frozen and dry foods, and ammunition. These ships are the life support line for a carrier battle group. The carrier and its escorts operate on an almost daily dependency on such replenishment ships. Theirs is a long and honorable tradition; at the end of WW II the Japanese identified our ability to supply task forces at sea for months on end as a main reason for victory in the Pacific.

The new captain must cut his teeth on one of these supply ships before commanding an aircraft carrier. Although the "Wabash Cannonball" was 700 feet long and displaced some 42,000 tons, it was considered small compared to a super carrier. But size has less bearing on the stepladder to command at sea than experience and competence. The latitude for error in command of a ship is enormous: collisions at sea, running aground, oil spills or allowing race riots, just to name a few. Obviously, it was preferable for a prospective carrier skipper to deal with such pitfalls aboard a noncombat vessel rather than with one of fifteen flattops then in the United States Navy.

I arrived on "Gonzo Station" in the North Arabian Sea in July 1981 to relieve the Cannonball's departing skipper. *Wabash* was part of the carrier battle group operating off Iran. Normally the two captains take a week to turn over command of a ship but it took us twenty-four hours. The ship was a mess; the material condition was in a sad state, the ship was dirty and, most importantly, the crew's morale was at its lowest depth. I figured that advice from the departing CO wouldn't be terribly valuable, and a quick change had to take place.

Most new skippers enjoy a "honeymoon" period while the crew sizes up the new captain, but we needed some winners to turn things around. Having been an enlisted man helped, but the crew needed some warm strokes and consistent guidance. We soon got our chance.

On my first day as captain of *Wabash*, the rear admiral commanding the battle group ordered me to make a twenty-knot transit to Diego Garcia, an Indian Ocean atoll that had only recently been put to use as a fleet logistics base. We were to pick up some sorely-needed aircraft engine parts and return to Gonzo Station as soon as possible.

Diego's lagoon was small, shallow and not completely charted. Additionally, the entrance was narrow with strong cross-currents. Ships only entered and departed during daylight. We arrived at night and I sent the admiral a message that I intended to enter port at first light. Minutes later he replied, directing me to enter port immediately. Rear Admiral Huntington Hardisty wanted those engine parts pretty damn bad!

My reply was "Aye, aye, sir." But I included an oh-by-the-way, are you aware of the restriction on entering Diego Garcia at night? That message didn't get answered. This was history in the making—a "winner" if we could pull it off to become the first ship to enter Diego at night.

I called the port control officer on bridge-to-bridge radio. "D-Gar Port, this is *Wabash*. We are standing off your entrance, requesting permission to enter port. We'll need a pilot and two tugs. Over."

The delayed response carried overtones of "Who are you kidding?" and "Not at night, dummy!" Actually, they said, "Negative, *Wabash*. Your pilot and tugs will meet you off the harbor entrance at 0600 tomorrow. No entries at night are authorized. Over."

"D-Gar, this is the captain speaking. Advise your base commander that the restriction is waived. I'll bring her in tonight. My H-46 helo will pick up the pilot at base ops in one hour. (I hoped he wasn't already belly-up at the bar.) Request two tugs meet me just outside the entrance, over."

Long pause. "Roger, *Wabash*. Be advised that half the channel buoy marker lights are out of service, and your visibility will be reduced in rain showers, over."

My reply—"Roger, out." There was nothing more to say. God, I'd only had command three days and the remainder of my career was dancing before my eyes—with visions of early retirement. I never aspired to be CNO, or even to make flag rank. I just wanted my airplanes and a carrier command. But what the hell—like Korean War ace Boots Blesse said, "No guts, no glory."

The helo returned with the unhappy harbor pilot. He didn't get paid enough to do this kind of stuff. He allowed as how he had never piloted a ship in at night before. I said, "Well good, we can both do it for the first time together." I didn't have the heart to tell the poor SOB how little experience I had.

Because of the strong cross currents you could either crab the ship a lot or come in faster than normal. I elected the latter. Since the channel boundaries were narrow and marked by mostly inoperable lights, I put one tug on each side of the bow, had them turn on their spotlights to illuminate the buoys. If this didn't work, another record would be set—the shortest command tenure of any Navy captain, ever!

The rain showers didn't help much, but my navigation radar was breaking out the buoys well enough to steer inside the channel and keep from running aground. Once we reached the turning basin, safely inside the lagoon, everyone on the bridge relaxed a little. We tied up at the new fuel pier and started our loadout of supplies immediately. I would let the crew off the following day in two sections for three hours each so they could see the island, get their Diego Garcia T-shirts and drink a couple of beers. Lord knows they needed a break; they had been at sea continuously for seventy-five days.

Other than the Master Pilot of Western Australia trying to ram my ship head-on into a pier, and too-numerous-to-count merchant captains playing "chicken of the sea," my remaining time on the old Cannonball was relatively uneventful. I mention the *Wabash* tour to give some insight into command of an aircraft carrier, when almost everything is multiplied times ten. The deep-draft tour pales in comparison. It's a benign existence alongside life in the fast lane.

Carrier command is humbling and can put a strong man on his knees immediately. I had the good fortune when I took over *Kitty Hawk* to be relieving a CO who had the ship in great shape in every respect. Captain Dave Rogers presented me with a jewel of a ship in August 1984. It would be hard to improve upon his act.

To put a *Kitty Hawk* class carrier in perspective, one should start with its size. It is more than 1,000 feet long and, with a full complement of aircraft aboard, displaces the equivalent of 100,000 tons. Plug in the $F=MV2$ equation and you have a finer sense of mass in motion, and how painfully evident it becomes if you make a wrong turn.

The flight deck is the size of four football fields, and the distance from keel to top of the mast is as tall as a twenty-story building. The crew complement of 5,300 men includes young "whitehats" whose average age is only nineteen. That crew can consume 1,000 dozen eggs and 15,000 cups of coffee or soft drinks per day. There are six dining halls, a hospital and dental clinic, and enough electrical generating capacity to serve a city of 50,000 people.

In fact, *Kitty Hawk* actually was a floating city, dynamic in every sense of the word. Imagine yourself as captain, being the father of some 3,000 teenagers. The three chaplains assigned helped a lot in that area.

After I assumed command of The Hawk, we were "welded" to the pier at NAS North Island for two months. The ship had just returned from a Western Pacific deployment where it became famous for virtually running over a new Soviet Victor III class nuclear submarine that had been shadowing the carrier task force in the East China Sea. The Russian skipper couldn't believe what was happening. While at periscope depth, eyeballing the carrier, he saw *Kitty Hawk* abruptly reverse course and head for him at full speed. He couldn't get out of the way in time, even with the carrier's wide turning circle.

According to photographs taken the next day with the Victor surfaced, we estimated the nuke boat was diving stern high, going away, when The Hawk's bow impacted the sub portside aft. The collision rolled the submarine over, "flaming out" his nuclear reactor. The Victor was observed by Captain Rogers tumbling down the starboard side of CV-63 as the big carrier passed over. I can only imagine that the Russian skipper had a healthy respect for carriers in future shadowing operations—if he isn't chipping holes in the hard Siberian earth. You can almost hear him telling his comrades at the Socialist Submarine Drivers' convention: "Those American carrier captains are crazy!"

If nothing else, Dave had showed the opposition who had right of way.

By October I was really chomping at the bit. Anything to put my ship to sea, to turn that big beautiful hummer into the wind and start launching aircraft. It's hard to imagine the orchestration required to bring it all together; to launch and recover aircraft with a supply ship alongside, connected by wire cables and rubber fueling hoses, taking on fuel and provisions. The coordination, communication and endless training involved defies comparison to any landbound operation I know of.

A carrier skipper's first and foremost mission in life is to protect his crew and ship from harm. Safety comes first, while presumably doing everything possible to bring the ship and air wing's combat readiness to a peak just before sailing. It's a ticklish balancing act, complicated by the inherent contradiction between operational safety and realistic preparation for war. Our thermometer in judging a carrier skipper's performance usually will be one question: how many lives did you lose and how many aircraft were damaged or lost? Everything you do okay after that is icing on the cake, but it's fairly rare for a carrier to return from even a peacetime deployment without one or more deaths.

A typical two or three-week operating period with an air wing embarked off the California coast consists of three primary elements: train, train, train. We flew around the clock with very dedicated people working in extremely harsh circumstances. They didn't bitch or complain unless the mail plane with letters from home didn't arrive on time.

Arriving on time also applied to returning to port and our families. But just as we say in aviation, "The flight ain't over until the bird's in the barn," neither did merely reaching the harbor entrance conclude an at-sea period.

The battle group was scheduled to arrive at San Diego's outer buoy at 1400 with the carrier leading the way and the escorting "small boys" in column. The night before I had started positioning the ship toward San Diego. The only thing left to do next morning would be launching the remaining thirty aircraft for the beach, then enter port. A sailor's delight!

One of the twenty or thirty telephone calls I received that night was from the OOD. He informed me of the decreasing dewpoint/temperature spread, forecasting heavy fog at sunrise. "Okay," I replied. "Just review your low-visibility procedures and keep me informed."

The next morning as I entered the bridge I observed heavy fog. Visibility was too low to measure. We call it WOXOF—indefinite ceiling, obscured, zero visibility in fog. Prior to kicking the air wing birds off for their respective roosts, we confirmed that North Island, at the harbor entrance, was clear with twenty-plus miles visibility. It was only twenty miles away so we could launch aircraft and proceed to port.

Pilots are trained to launch in zero visibility. On the catapult stroke they are only along for the ride, as nothing they can do will change anything. There have been aviators who locked their brakes just before the cat

190

shot, but it didn't reduce their endspeed one knot as their aircraft were hurled into the air.

The launch commenced and the planes were out of sight before they reached the bow. All the aircraft flew away and we headed for port.

By now the fog was within two miles of the harbor entrance. There was no time to spare if I was to get these kids home to their loved ones tonight. All the helos were launched with one designated to stay just ahead of the ship, on top of the fog bank to report when the ship should break into the clear. The chopper could only see the top of The Hawk's mast—that's how thick the fog was.

It was a race. The fog was forming closer and closer to the beach. The helo pilot, talking directly to me on the bridge radio, kept providing encouraging words: "Lookin' good, Captain. Keep it coming."

Well, I'd been down that road before and I knew better than to rely on just one source of information. Fortunately, my two navigation radars were working perfectly. On the scope I could break out Point Loma, the North Island quay wall and jetty, the two entrance buoys and the admiral's headquarters. That last point gave me some food for thought. As commander of one of the fifteen most prestigious targets afloat, you are always subject to close scrutiny from above. The tendency is to play it safe, to avoid even the appearance of rashness. But then I thought, "Hell, I've been here so many times before...go for it."

There is a point of no return with a vessel that size. You can't turn around, and backing the ship down to avoid running aground is an inexact science, to say the least. I slowed to all ahead one-third—about five knots. Once you've put your bow into that first set of buoys you are committed. Obviously, running aground is serious business. The Navy takes a very dim view of such things, particularly if it's one of their capital ships. Exceptionally good captains, men with stars awaiting them, have been relieved of command after running aground—sometimes to the Navy's lasting detriment. But hardly anyone gets a second chance.

Only until I noticed that my navigator was visibly concerned did I realize how much we were in harm's way. Jim Haley was perhaps the finest navigator in the world—certainly he knew more about seamanship than I did—and he recommended turning the ship around. My air wing commander, Jay Finney, had the conn on the bridge, giving the orders to the helmsman. I asked the helo for an update. He said it would be close, as the fog was forming ahead of us.

"On the bridge, this is the captain. I have the conn." I relieved the CAG, since it was not his responsibility.

The navigator was working the radar and advised that the currents were setting the ship to the right of the channel. We were too slow. "All ahead two-thirds, left ten degrees rudder, come to new heading three-five-zero." The last time I experienced that cotton taste in my mouth was in a tight situation over North Vietnam, nearly getting my tail shot off. Now it was too late to reverse course.

"Port lookout reports a buoy," came a shouted report from the phone talker.

Simultaneously Jim Haley and I yelled in unison, "What color?" It if was a red buoy, the ship would be hard aground within the minute. Rules of the road said, "Red right returning." Then came the reply, "A black buoy, sir."

"Thank you, God! We're in the channel. Now if we can just stay there."

The helicopter pilot reported, with a rising tone to his voice, "Captain, you're breaking into the clear." Seconds later I could see Point Loma and the buoys.

It was too close for comfort. The ships in trail didn't make it in until the next day. One can speculate that those captains exercised a little more caution than I did, but my crew made it home to their friends and families that night. I felt about as good as a skipper can feel.

One of the many obstacles that a captain and crew must handle during predeployment workups is evaluation of the ship's engineering plant, and the ability to effectively fight fires or flooding. This inspection is called an Operational Propulsion Plant Examination, OPPE for short. It's a big deal because you can't "pass Go" until you have successfully completed the OPPE at sea. Everything scheduled beyond that has to slide, including the six-month deployment.

A lot of industrial machinery repair or replacement is done by civilian shipyard workers. During the at-sea portion of OPPE it was discovered that five of the eight new main feed pumps had been incorrectly installed. The show would not go on. The time required to remedy the problem would take about eight hours dockside. I hurried into San Diego to effect repairs

(Right) Remember when you were this young? Phil Wood after his first solo flight at NAAS Saufley Field, 1958. (USN)

(*Below*) Phil's first fleet squadron was VA-196, flying Douglas AD-6 Skyraiders. The last prop-driven attack aircraft in the U.S. Navy was affectionately called the "Spad" after the famous WW I fighter. (Wood)

Now a jet pilot himself, Phil examines an ATM-9 Sidewinder missile on his F-8C Crusader during "Bo[n] Dick's" 1967 cruise to the Tonkin Gulf. This was the same air-to-air weapon that Wally Schirra had hel[ped] develop at China Lake in 1953. (USN)

Phil Wood in his VF-24 F-8 Crusader on Barrier CAP in the Northern Gulf of Tonkin off Haiphong, 19[ ] (Wood)

one that got away. Phil's F-8 (center, near bottom of photo) dodges an SA-2 missile exploding over
phong harbor following an attack on ships unloading ordnance. This dramatic photo was taken by an
8A reconnaissance jet. (USN)

Crusader drivers at the "Red River Valley Fighter Pilots Association" meeting in San Antonio, TX in 19
All had been north in Route Package 6, indicated by the pointer. L-R: Lt. Cdrs. Jerry Houston, Dave Me
and John Nichols; Cdr. Bill Parrish, Lt. Wood and Lt. Cdr. Ted Schwartz. "Pirate" Nichols, "Rat" Wood a
TR Schwartz already were MiG killers; "Devil" Houston got one in 1972. Dave Metzler was killed a wh
later. (USN)

his is what carrier aviators call "the blunt end." Seconds from touchdown on USS Constellations's ngled flight deck, the landing pilot is well lined up but just a tad high, according to the "meatball" the mirror landing system to port. (Wood)

r an F-8 pilot, the F-14 represented a professional change of life. Switching from single-seat Crusaders two-seat Tomcats posed a challenge for Phil, here (front cockpit, nearest) ready to "buy" a new fighter om Grumman Aircraft at Calverton, Long Island. (Wood)

Phil's dream assignment: command of USS Kitty Hawk (CV-63) with her "main battery" on deck, 1985. V
are 49 of Air Wing Nine's 70 plus aircraft: fifteen A-7A Corsair IIs, twelve A-6E Intruders, three EA-6B Pr
ers, two S-3A Vikings, two E-2C Hawkeyes and fifteen F-14A Tomcats. (USN)

As CAG-11 on board Kitt
Hawk, Phil had two
fighter squadrons aboard
with Air Wing 11. This F-
14A of the VF-213 Black
Lions launches off one of
the "waist" catapults.
(Wood)

...3 being "attacked" by A-6 Intruders during a firepower demonstration. The bombs exploded farther to ... than may be evident in this dramatic shot.

...derful Christmas present was "the Hawk's" return to San Diego in 1985 following her six-month Pacific ... deployment with Captain Wood at the helm. The crew earned the Battle "E" and Admiral J.H. Flatley ... for this cruise.

(Left) Phil Wood, Captain USN, at the time of his retirement in 1986. (Wood)

(Below) L to R.: Wally and Schirra, Zeke and Kitty Cormier, and Nellie and Phil Wood at Rancho Santa Fe, CA, 1995. (Schirra)

so the ship could continue the examination as soon as possible.

We arrived pierside at 0700 with the parts and workers standing pierside, ready to come aboard and begin repairs. As the day proceeded it became evident that eight hours was an overly optimistic assessment. I had not granted liberty because we expected to get underway late that afternoon.

Aircraft carriers don't get underway from North Island at night, though it's not physically difficult or unsafe. It just isn't done. Of course, I wanted to get underway as soon as the repairs were complete to get on with the program, day or night. The tug crews were reluctantly available and the docking pilot had to be pried away from his TV. Now all I needed was permission from on high. I called Vice Admiral Pete Easterling, ComNavAirPac.

"Admiral, this is Captain Wood. I'm requesting permission to get underway at 2200, sir."

His first remark after some delay was, "Skipper, it's dark out there. What's the hurry?"

I finally convinced the admiral that it was a good idea and was in everyone's best interest. Why not? Easterling gave me official permission with a subtle warning. "You screw this up, captain, and your ass is grass." It doesn't take a PhD or brain surgeon to figure out that kind of message.

My wife Nellie was sitting in our car on the pier, waiting to see if we would really leave. I may have needed a ride home. As the tugs were making up alongside and the line handlers were singling up the lines, I called my senior chaplain, Don DenDulk, to the bridge. He had once told me he had a "direct line" to the Big Guy up above, and we needed as much going for us as we could muster. I told Don to give special attention to this night sortie. The evening prayer always is given at 2200. What the hell—if it worked for General Patton maybe it could work for us!

Just as the boatswainmate of the watch struck four bells, the ship was easing away from the pier. Hundreds of friends and wives huddled on the pier, watching *Kitty Hawk* leave again. They also heard the 1MC speaker as Chaplain DenDulk broadcast his evening prayer. "Oh Lord, please watch over this ship, crew and captain. Let our journey to sea and back be a safe one. Watch over our loved ones. Especially, dear Lord, let this night transit be successful, for we like our captain and want him to be our skipper for at least a few more months. Amen."

What can I say? Don DenDulk proved that he did in fact have a direct line upstairs.

Following a year of workups with Air Wing Nine and our escorting ships, The Hawk sailed from San Diego 24 July 1985, en route to the Persian Gulf. Leaving families and modest stateside luxuries for six months is not everyone's first choice, but as for me, I couldn't wait to get out of town. Admirals—especially former carrier skippers—tend to micromanage, sometimes because they're bored and feel obliged to provide "rudder" in running a ship. Additionally, Representative Jim Bates, Democrat of San Diego, had been an irritant for the previous six months; ever since a psychopathic sailor deserted the Navy. He got religion, claiming he was saved from sin and walked off the ship to report the evils of *Kitty Hawk*'s supply department to the congressman. Bates and Seaman Jackson, who had been "saved" again, made great bedfellows.

As we got underway, slipping into the channel, we were escorted by many boatloads of *Kitty Hawk* friends and well-wishers. Among them were Schirra, Cormier and Ernie King on Wally's sailboat. The large banner they displayed read, "Go for it, Hawk. Make us proud." We'd certainly try.

Putting to sea and operating with the fleet is where the carrier and its crew belong. After a few years of Navy life we develop gypsy blood in our veins and become nomadic, and we learn to live by the deployment cycles of our ships.

After a brief encounter with our eastbound sister ship, *Constellation* (CV-64), near Hawaii, we proceeded across the Pacific through the Bashi Channel between Taiwan and Luzon, conducting day and night flight ops. Off Poro Point on the west coast of the Philippines, *Kitty Hawk* came very close to losing several aircraft during lousy weather. Making a decision to launch is a complex evolution. You consider the availability of a divert field in case of an emergency, and how far away it is; you consider the pilots' currency, how long since they last flew at night; the status of operating radars and air control equipment; how many aerial tanker aircraft are available; and you look very carefully at present and forecast weather. The last consideration, miscalculated, almost certainly is the one that will bite you on the ass.

With the permission of the battle group admiral, we decided to launch sixteen planes on daylight missions. The existing weather had scattered rain showers in the vicinity, with no large thunderstorm cells showing on the radar. One KA-6D tanker would be airborne with a ready tanker on deck.

After all aircraft were launched, I turned the ship out of the wind and beat feet for Subic Bay, where we were scheduled to arrive the following day. About an hour after launch, twenty miles south of our launch position, the weather was becoming overcast with flashes of lightning in the area, indicating thunderstorm activity. The wind was increasing and the sea state was becoming heavier. I decided to recover the aircraft early and had a recall signal broadcast.

Normally it takes at least fifteen minutes to get all aircraft back overhead in the "marshal" pattern to begin the recovery. The carrier must turn into the wind to recover aircraft, meaning the direction of the prevailing wind dictates the ship's course, which should be perfectly down the angled deck from bow to stern. The wind velocity over the deck should be around thirty knots, and normally that is no problem. But the weather was deteriorating rapidly, and in order to land aircraft we would be headed directly into the coming storm.

We had only a limited distance and time before the ship would enter the middle of the thunderstorm. I launched my ready tanker to get additional fuel in the air just in case, but that meant one more airplane would have to be recovered as a result.

All planes were marshalled in the holding pattern and we started them down single-file with two miles separation between aircraft. The visibility was decreasing to one mile in rain showers, the deck was wet and slippery, and the sea troughs were making the deck pitch about twenty feet. It is very difficult to land on a heavy, pitching deck, for a number of reasons. But primarily if the deck is rising as the aircraft arrives at the ramp, the plane has no clearance and must climb, resulting in the tailhook missing all the wires. The pilot must go around, burning valuable fuel as a result.

The first three aircraft broke out of the gloom at one mile and successfully "trapped" aboard. The LSOs were making a valiant effort to "catch" the planes, but if the deck was out of cycle, there was no chance. Two F-14A Tomcats were waved off because they broke out too close and were not aligned. Rain had reduced visibility to three-quarters of a mile. Two bombers, an A-6E and A-7E, still had enough fuel to make it to Cubi Point, the divert field, and they headed out. By now the weather had deteriorated to a point where the aircrews could not find a clear area to join on the airborne tankers.

I decided to put the remaining planes in a low holding pattern while I started driving The Hawk, dodging rain cells, to find a clear area for recovery. The ship had increased speed to thirty knots, traveling as far as possible in the least amount of time. The planes were getting critically low on fuel and the only choice they had, other than ejecting, was to land on my "bird farm." As a former LSO, I knew the airborne pilots now would be extremely nervous, with exceedingly limited time remaining.

I was driving the ship towards a light spot on the horizon, praying that it was not just another "sucker hole." My airborne helicopter was six miles ahead, reporting that we would be entering a clear area. It would take twelve minutes to get there. But now the airborne planes' fuel state was critically low, not allowing me the luxury of proceeding to that area, confirming improved weather and calling them down. I had to make the decision—go now or lose some airplanes and probably some aviators. I directed all aircraft to begin their approach.

The timing was beautiful. Though I had sixty knots of wind over the deck, the planes started landing. The last one brought to an arrested stop on the slippery deck—after hook-skipping the first three wires—was an F-14 flown by Lieutenant Jim "Gusto" Usbeck, our air wing LSO. He had 700 pounds of fuel remaining—not enough for even one more pass.

I sat back in my captain's chair and thanked that Big Guy in the sky again, wondering why anybody would want to command an aircraft carrier. If you win, it's the most rewarding job in the world. If you fail and lose someone, it will haunt you for the rest of your life. But at the same time I reflected upon the satisfaction as well as the risks of that occupation, thanking God that I was born an American.

Five days later, as we departed Subic Bay heading west across the South China Sea en route to the Indian Ocean, my thoughts were of the Soviets flying out of Cam Ranh Bay, Vietnam. There was no doubt in my mind they would reconnoiter our transit.

About a year earlier the Russians had deployed surveillance, strike and fighter aircraft to the large airbase we had built two decades before on the Vietnam coast. Our route would take the battle group right through the opposition's back yard, and I knew they would come out to look us over.

Our staff had devised a plan in which the carrier would be defensive, establishing a combat air patrol (CAP). The CAP stations would be well clear of Vietnam boundaries in international waters.

At that time the MiG-23 was one of the Evil Empire's newer fighters, and our aircrews had never been eyeball to eyeball with the Flogger. But the American fighter pilot is the most aggressive in the world, and my concern was to avoid an international incident involving a border violation by my aviators or—worse yet—a midair collision with a Russian. Boys will be boys, and it's difficult to temper their enthusiasm. After all, if they were wholly cautious and docile they'd be useless in combat.

But our "trolling" tactics worked and the Soviets' curiosity as to what was orbiting just outside their airspace set the hook.

A lone "fast mover" was picked up by our E-2C Hawkeye's radar as the bogey went "feet wet" right after launch from Cam Ranh Bay. The two VF-24 Tomcats were advised of the bogey's outbound heading, closing their position. I was monitoring the fighter radio frequency as I sat in my chair on the bridge. The radio transmissions were increasing in octave as the "bandit" closed on their position. You would have thought it fifteen years earlier when a genuine engagement was about to occur—resulting in an actual shootdown.

The lead Tomcat pilot got the first visual on the MiG-23. The "tallyho" and "padlocked" calls sounded like he was about to wet his pants. The F-14 and Flogger were closing on a collision course at 1,200 miles per hour. Both fighters carried air-to-air missiles with live warheads. I tried to imagine myself twenty years earlier, as a lieutenant in that cockpit. Would it become so real that the Tomcat pilot would forget he had no clearance to fire? That's when you hope the professional training pays off.

The two fighters passed head-on. The F-14 pilot pulled into a vertical climb while the MiG driver put his aircraft into a hard lateral turn; the wrong maneuver. The Tomcat started down, heading for a one-mile astern position behind the MiG. After about two turns the MiG driver realized the Fourteen was in the saddle behind him. The Tomcat's camera recorded the MiG's two afterburners igniting, diving like hell for his home base.

The internationally-recognized border is twelve miles, but there's no big, bold line on the ocean to mark the spot. Consequently, with the VF-24 plane in hot pursuit, the E-2 started calling warnings to the F-14 crew that they were closing the border. "Break it off, Renegade, you're warning yellow and about to go red."

No response. The wingman finally got the attention of his section leader. "Animal, you asshole, you've scared that poor Russian out of his jock. Knock it off."

The lead Tomcat broke away just outside Vietnamese waters and headed back. In the debrief after they landed, my suspicions were confirmed. The F-14 pilot had become so carried away that he had armed a Sidewinder missile and had firing tones in his headset. He had forgotten for a moment where he was.

But it was understandable. The training our aircrews receive is so intense that they can get carried away. Our motto is, "Train like you fight and fight like you train." Words to live by in the warrior business.

After transiting the Singapore Straits and the Strait of Malacca we entered the Indian Ocean, headed for Gonzo Station in the Northern Arabian Sea. Following a brief turnover with *Midway* near Diego Garcia, the long, monotonous "station keeping" for three months would begin.

One of the highlights of an Indian Ocean tour is the day the crew receives a ration of beer. Each sailor receives two cans of Miller High Life after forty-five days have elapsed since the last liberty port. Most carriers make a big deal of this event. We called it our "steel beach barbecue." The flight deck was transformed into a "tropical paradise" with green indoor/outdoor carpeting, fake palm trees, portable swimming pools, lawn chairs, and the BBQ cookers. The troops play football or volleyball, hit golf balls into the ocean and generally take a respite from the day-in, day-out IO routine.

The beer ration is the lubricant that makes the day special. Some young sailors can get knee-walking drunk on two cans. Though it's against the rules, those who don't drink can sell their beers for as much as fifty dollars a can. One hundred dollars is nothing to a crewman whose only expenses for two or three months has been cokes and toothpaste.

Every ship has its crazies; kids who demonstrate aberrant behavior. It's manifested in many ways, but we had our "Mad Fodder." FOD stands for foreign object damage. Any small particle—a bolt, screw or cotter pin, for instance—that can be sucked down the intake of a jet aircraft will cause severe damage or catastrophic failure for a turning engine. Extreme measures are taken to avoid such events. Two or three times a day, prior to launch or during breaks in flight operations, over one hundred crewmen will gather forward on the flight deck, form a line abreast, and slowly walk aft. They pick up any form of FOD that may be lying in wait for a jet engine to ingest into its intake. The flight deck has to be immaculately clear, and usually is.

When parked, jet engines have covers in place. Prior to any startup, the plane captain will crawl into the intake with a flashlight to insure no FOD has accidentally been left behind by a maintenance man or intentionally by a "sickie" who places a coin or small metal object in the intake.

Our Mad Fodder used small BBs. Surreptitiously he would place the balls down an intake while a plane was parked. The BBs always were found, but now we knew that someone aboard was attempting to cause damage to the planes or endanger the lives of the aircrew. He was determined in his demented condition to accomplish his goal, and his covert actions were getting bolder and bolder. One night during launch, an A-7 Corsair was being fired off the number one catapult when the pilot reported severe engine vibration as he cleared the bow. There immediately followed an engine fire warning light.

The A-7, being single-engine, was in serious trouble. We stopped the launch and started an immediate "pull forward" of the planes spotted aft for launch in order to clear the deck for landing.

From my position on the bridge I had observed the A-7's launch and the sparks emitting from its tailpipe even before the pilot made his distress call. Usually the sparks are the first sign of a fodded engine, so I called the air boss to prepare the deck for recovery. I also had him isolate the catapult area to see if we could find the cause of the incident.

Only minutes later the air boss called me, relaying a report from the cat crew that an individual had been seen in the starboard catwalk forward, near the catapult. He had been in a kneeling position seconds before the Corsair was fired down the track, and as the A-7 approached his position, he was observed in a throwing motion. Then he disappeared from the catwalk.

Our suspicions were confirmed moments later. BBs were found on the flight deck near the catapult. The Mad Fodder had struck again! It was imperative that this sickie be apprehended. I immediately got on the 1MC announcing system throughout the ship, telling the crew what had just happened, ordering a report on any suspicious characters who may have been observed near cat two.

The crew had been kept abreast of the situation since it started. I was close to my crew and, as a former whitehat myself, we related well to one another. Therefore, my final comment during the announcement was that if any sailors caught the SOB, they had my permission to "cut his balls off."

The Corsair pilot got back safely, but with nothing to spare. When the engine was inspected, it was in shreds. How it continued to develop enough thrust to get around the pattern, only that Big Guy in the Sky will ever know.

Kitty Hawk's men realized this was serious business—we were after a potential murderer. But apparently the Mad Fodder knew it, too. For whatever reason, he went underground and we never heard from him again.

The remainder of the cruise was relatively uneventful. Ninety-five days in the Indian Ocean with five-day liberty calls in Mombasa, Kenya and Colombo, Sri Lanka is not really a sailor's delight. We were all happy just to return home in time for Christmas.

As my beautiful ship nestled alongside the pier at North Island, her final stop under my command, I was overcome with relief. My right-hand man, navigator Jim Haley, looked at me and we spontaneously grabbed each other and embraced. With a lot of luck and help, we had gone eighteen months without putting a scratch on The Hawk. No lives had been lost, and CAG still had all his airplanes.

The ending of my naval career could not have been sweeter. I had made the decision to leave the Navy for the "private sector." After thirty years, six combat cruises and having the best job in the Navy, it was time to grow some roots. The Navy had provided me the best of everything: the thrill of flying, the challenge of combat, the satisfaction of command. When I hung up my helmet, I just hoped I had served the Navy well in turn.

EPILOGUE

What more can we say, we three ancient warriors, but to reiterate that the common thread of our naval lives was that we enjoyed being there? Each of us would do it again, though perhaps only Wally would opt for "Plan B" by taking that Phantom squadron hunting MiGs over North Vietnam rather than becoming the only triple-threat entrant in America's manned space program.

Naval aviation—particularly carrier aviation—has changed drastically during our collective careers of nearly a half-century: bigger ships, better equipment, more sophisticated airplanes, smarter weapons and better-trained aircrews. When aspiring heroes entered flight training in the early 1940s, the U.S. Navy possessed seven oil-fired carriers, the largest of which grossed 33,000 tons. Its fastest aircraft was barely capable of 300 knots in level flight.

Forty-five years later, Phil's *Kitty Hawk* also was fuel-oil powered. But she grossed 80,000 tons, and five of her fourteen sisters were propelled by the most elemental power in the universe. Her fighters were capable of more than twice the speed of sound; the only propellers on the flight deck belonged to the E-2s' turboprops, and helicopters featured prominently.

But one aspect that hasn't changed in two generations is the motivation of naval aviators. Today's tailhookers are much like those of Zeke's era. Young fighter pilots are motivated by the same impulse: knowing that you belong to an elite—if you make it—is extremely compelling. The challenge, the danger, the pride, the sense of camaraderie all draw young aviators to the sea.

Yet each of us has seen a maturity in carrier aviation as well. During WW II, and later in the difficult jet transition era, flying safety was held a distant second to accomplishing the mission. Training attitudes frequently were cavalier: "Kick the tires and light the fire." We recognize that such an attitude wouldn't work with today's ultra-expensive airplanes.

However, it's natural for vintage comrades to sit sipping adult beverages and to reflect over the way the current generation has gone astray. Therefore, we three wonder what makes this honored, exciting profession so unattractive to the young tailhooker that he prefers to drive commercial transports rather than fighters. Phil recalls, "I have talked—no, listened—to dozens of young aviators who were leaving the Navy. Their specific reasons for getting out were varied, but one common thread ran throughout the interviews. 'Captain, with minimum flight time and cruises devoid of liberty ports, it just isn't fun or rewarding anymore.'"

Some taxpayers are bound to ask, why the emphasis on enjoyment? What obligation is there to keep our military professionals entertained? The answer, of course, is that fun is not the operative word. Perhaps the answer we seek is found in the late John Gillespie Magee's epic poem, High Flight:

Oh, I have slipped the surly bonds of earth and danced the skies on laughter-silvered wings.

Sunward I've climbed and joined the tumbling mirth of sun-split cloud...Now, that is what flying an airplane is all about!

There is no question. Flight time is the answer, and lots of it. It's why men become pilots. And women, too.

However, Zeke feels that the full-court press to put ladies in combat cockpits is not so much a matter of political correctness as it is a dangerous double standard. Female pilots in flight training and fleet squadrons are evaluated to different performance standards than their male counterparts. It's not merely unfair—it's dangerous.

One wonders what impact this will ultimately have on combat readiness on the crucial intangible called morale. Knowing that some criteria have been lowered to fill some seats, resentment is inevitable. There has to be one standard for all, or no standards will matter.

As former naval officers, each of us has known exceptional leaders—skippers who inspired, educated and motivated their people to heights of accomplishment. And, unfortunately, we have known the other kind.

The privilege of command, and subsequent leadership, is granted to one who has earned the role. The feeling of accomplishment in that role, while at high risk, without loss of your subordinates and equipment is the reward. Too many who have not had the opportunity will not understand.

Over the years, the service chiefs have not been completely blameless. Before the Tailhook scandal, the Navy was most poorly served during the Zumwalt era, when the command structure broke down and the authority of commanding officers and senior noncommissioned ranks was severely undercut. The Navy took more than a decade to recover its sense of priorities. Wally says, "NASA never did."

But things did get better. During Desert Shield/Desert Storm the Navy came early and stayed late. When things popped in Kuwait in early August 1991, the thirty-year-old *Independence* (CV-62) was on station to help stay Saddam's greedy hand. For the first several days of the crisis, her Air Wing Fourteen constituted the major opposition to an invasion of Saudi Arabia.

After Tailhook '91, young aviators voiced a recurrent question: "Where are the leaders?" They saw politicians in and out of uniform scrambling for cover, without uttering a syllable in defense of thousands of guiltless officers whose lives and careers were upended without due process. They see too many officers selected for flag rank without one day of combat to their credit—aloft or afloat.

Aviator morale took a beating in the four years after "Tailhook," and unnecessarily so. In fact, young aviators began saying that "naval leadership" has replaced "naval intelligence" as an oxymoron. Certainly part of the problem was the dominance of submariners for fifteen years, resulting in a succession of chiefs of naval operations (CNOs) with no combat experience. After all, the submarine's primary mission is deterrence; as a warfighting tool it has been irrelevant since 1945. No less a sub booster than Tom Clancy has noted that the nuclear-power community is far more concerned with engineering than leadership, and the result was the Tailhook scandal. The "leaders" forgot or ignored their responsibility to their subordinates. At risk of seeming parochial, we think the Navy needs combat-experienced admirals at the helm—and that means aviators.

This is not to say that naval aviation is immune from the virus of political correctness. It is possible for a carrier skipper to run his ship aground (ordinarily enough to ruin a career) yet go on to make three or four stars! Such admirals have earned an endearing nickname: "Windsock." They blow with the political winds.

As for the annual Tailhook symposium, that event matured from a purely social gathering in the mid-1950s into a professional forum—at Navy request—in the 1970s. The association never at any time had responsibility for (and therefore control over) active-duty personnel. Not even the illegal methods of the Naval Investigative Service or Department of Defense could find any wrongdoing by the association—and believe us, they tried.

Now, after all the foregoing malevolence, some people may wonder what's right with the Navy. Among many things, there's something deliciously indefinable about the sense of community, the sense of belonging to tailhook aviation. Walking into the ready room after a hairy flight—a memorable combat mission or just a "routine" landing on a choppy, moonless night—is a reward in itself. Everyone there knows exactly how you feel, and nobody needs to say a word in order to express it. The effect is atmospheric; you can perceive it like a change in the weather. It's one of the best feelings this life has to offer.

Zeke retired from the Navy in 1963 and entered a second career as a McDonnell Douglas representative in Europe. With his lovely wife Kitty he opted for the quiet life in Rancho Santa Fe, California, which many of his Navy contemporaries consider "the place with the right stuff." Cormier keeps in touch with current Navy activities via his close contacts with active-duty folks at NAS Miramar and his continuing participation in the functions of the Aerospace Museum in San Diego where he is a member of the advisory board.

After leaving NASA, Wally assisted Walter Cronkite on the remaining Apollo Mission broadcasts. He served as president, chairman, vice president and director of various Fortune 500 companies. Most recently he retired as a director of Kimberly-Clark. Now he is devoting more time to travel, sailing, hunting—and gotchas. He and Jo also settled in Rancho Santa Fe, and a Navy blue Ferrari may be seen exceeding redlines (and the posted limit) on the sportscar driver's dream roads along Via de la Valle.

Phil lives in nearby Del Mar with his favorite redhead, Nellie. Upon retirement in 1986 he accepted a position with Northrop Aircraft working with numerous military programs. Remaining part of the fighter community lends not only continuity, but enthusiasm to his own second career.

Meanwhile, we three amigos of Rancho Santa Fe still have time to contemplate what we want to do when we grow up. But we are in full agreement on one thing: that light at the end of the tunnel is not a freight train coming the other way. It's a gleam from the rainbow containing the pot o' gold—wings of gold, to be precise.

Naval aviation cannot continue to shoot itself in the foot and keep quality aviators on active duty. Money and bonuses are not the answer; that's not why people work so godawful hard to wear Navy wings. Instead, young warriors need a different tonic: Show them some leadership; let them fly; and keep it fun!

ABOUT THE AUTHORS

	TOTAL FLIGHT TIME	CV LANDINGS	COMBAT MISSIONS
ZEKE	4,972	603	166
WALLY[1]	4,577[2]	267	91
PHIL	5,042	964	272

1. Second naval aviator to achieve 1000 jet hours. Bud Sickel was first.
2. Includes 295.2 hours space flight.

MILITARY DECORATIONS

Zeke: Silver Star, Distinguished Flying Cross with two Oak Leaf Clusters, Air Medal with five Oak Leaf Clusters, Presidential Unit Citation, Navy Commendation Medal with Combat V.

Wally: Navy Distinguished Service Medal, Distinguished Flying Cross and two Oak Leaf Clusters, Air Medal and two Oak Leaf Clusters, NASA Distinguished Service Medal with one Oak Leaf Cluster, NASA Exceptional Service Medal with one Oak Leaf Cluster, Philippines Legion of Honor (Commander).

Phil: Silver Star, Distinguished Flying Cross, Legion of Merit, Air Medal with twelve Oak Leaf Clusters, Meritorious Service Medal, Presidential Unit Citation.